TECHNIQUES

OF MODERN

ORCHESTRAL

CONDUCTING

TECHNIQUES OF MODERN ORCHESTRAL CONDUCTING

Benjamin Grosbayne

Harvard University Press
Cambridge
Massachusetts
1956

Distributed in Great Britain by
Geoffrey Cumberlege,
Oxford University Press, London

Library of Congress Catalog Card Number 53–6030
Printed in the United States of America

This book, composed on the Intertype Fotosetter by Graphic Services, Inc., York, Pennsylvania, was printed by the Murray Printing Company of Wakefield, Massachusetts, on a special paper produced by P. H. Glatfelter Paper Company, Spring Grove, Pennsylvania, and bound by the Colonial Press of Clinton, Massachusetts. The binding fabric was manufactured by the Holliston Mills, Norwood, Massachusetts. Type images composed on film combined with photographic films of the illustrations have been used in the making of the photo-lithographic printing plates of every page. No conventional metal types or engravings were employed at any stage of manufacture. The work represents the use of the most modern developments in the graphic arts field. It was planned by and produced under the direction of Burton L. Stratton assisted by John Hawkes and Howard H. Bezanson of the Harvard University Press production staff.

To my sister

EVELYN

ACKNOWLEDGMENTS

Each writer in a technical field leans heavily upon the labors of his predecessors. The most recent book in a field serves merely as the temporary top of a pyramid created by the efforts of those who have preceded him. The present writer, therefore, wishes to pay tribute to the authors of many articles and books written in the past which he has consulted with pleasure and profit.

Few readers realize the debt writers owe to the patience and generous aid of librarians. Again, my indebtedness to workers in many music libraries here and abroad is great. I acknowledge with gratitude the hours of time and drudgery saved by their aid amid unfamiliar routines, which often vary confusingly from country to country.

An author's friends are always fair game for intellectual piracy. The roll call includes Miss Marcel Roy, Miss Edna Yost, Dr. Joseph Braunstein, Mr. Raymond Hall, and Mr. Harry Parker, whose sharp eyes ferreted out many a typographical slip. Thanks are due to Mr. Josef Alexander for composing an excerpt to illustrate a technical problem, to Mr. Heinrich Gebhard for delightful discussions and consequent clarification of issues, and to Mr. Peter Herman Adler for stimulating wrangling over eternal questions of tempo.

Appreciation is due to Mr. Vincent Lagano for drawing the patterns which depict the motions of the baton, to Dr. Carl A. Rosenthal for the musical autographs and helpful suggestions, and to the publishers who permitted quotations from copyrighted compositions.

My special thanks to Professor Siegmund Levarie, Chairman of the Music Department of Brooklyn College, who waded through page proof despite a very crowded schedule.

In a very large sense, then, those cited above have been colleagues, and I am happy to acknowledge my debt.

B. G.

Gloucester, Massachusetts
August 31, 1954

CONTENTS

Part II: Style and Interpretation

CONTENTS

Everyone concerned with the art of musical interpretation comes to the realization that its study must be approached from two points of view: that of purely physical techniques and that of the creator's message, which is to be conveyed to the auditors. During various epochs in the history of music, interpreters have gone through periods of stressing one of these points of view, often at the expense of the other. To illustrate tendencies toward such one-sidedness and exaggeration, we need go no further than to recall certain styles of coloratura singing, schools of so-called "virtuoso" conducting, or over-romanticized and highly subjective instrumental performances. To point out these tendencies, however, is not to deny technical brilliance its proper place in music.

Every interpreter, whether student-apprentice or mature artist, is faced with an endless search for the true meaning of the music, which he seeks to convey to his hearers by means of technical competence on the one hand and his understanding of music on the other. A text dealing with conducting techniques must attempt, then, to present in codified and sequential form what has evolved to meet both these aspects of every interpreter's problem.

The present text has been divided into two main sections, with this dualism in mind. Part I deals principally, though not exclusively, with the physical skills involved in such basic techniques as beating in single and combined pulses and giving attacks, releases, and holds, and with such stylistic characterizations as *legato* and *staccato*, all achieved with the two hands completely independent of each other. It deals, in short, with the skills involved in fashioning physical patterns so appropriate and suggestive that a group of instrumentalists may easily, comfortably, confidently, and without hesitation or doubt of the conductor's intention, be brought into obedience to one unifying concept, the conductor's.

The other, and indeed the major, side of the conductor's art—interpretation—cannot be wholly ignored, however, even in the earliest study of basic techniques. To ignore it would transform what is certainly an art into a science. Psychological command of a body of fellow interpreters is a major part of the conductor's total assets, and it is always present as he transmits his concept of the music by means of physical skills. Every technical point studied, every exercise practiced, every motion executed, every attitude held—all must be learned with the thought of their double purpose: to help lead a group of players, and to do justice to the music being interpreted.

There is still another goal, at which some virtuoso conductors have been known to aim with almost total disregard of the two main purposes. This third goal, the histrionic effect of physical techniques upon an audience, is, if kept within its proper part of the whole frame, an integral aspect of the interpreter's appeal. Only when it becomes the too predominant aim of the conductor to impress an audience by such means does this tendency degrade the music.

We cannot, then, consider the purely manual, physical, or kinetic bases of the art of conducting in complete separation from the interpretative demands and connotation of the music, or from the effect these skills will eventually have on the audience. We can, however, simplify the approach to the conductor's problems by stressing the technical side of his art first, while temporarily minimizing the interpretative aspects of the music being studied. Such is our aim in Part I. But the student should never lose sight of the final goal: making his physical techniques *per se* so automatic that they eventually become spontaneous and subservient to his interpretation.

In Part II of the text the stress is placed principally upon style and interpretation, through actual application of the techniques learned in Part I. Here the student meets more advanced aspects of a conductor's techniques, such as tempo, rests, silent or empty beats, rubato, cadenzas, and recitative. In order to impart to the student a feeling for context, I have presented analyses from several points of view of large sections of some works which represent various categories, and have made a study of certain aspects of Beethoven's Seventh Symphony. The final chapters discuss marking and correcting scores and some of the problems met by the conductor at rehearsals.

Since it would be neither desirable nor possible to exclude technique *per se* when considering the interpretative aspect of the conductor's art,

Part II does not attempt this exclusion. Many a technical problem which does not appear in the sort of geometric paradigms with which we treat isolated musical snippets in the early study of skills, crops up in high and bold relief only when one considers the actual phrases, passages, and context essential to the study of interpretation.

Hopefully, I anticipate that this book will be used by two types of readers: teachers and students who meet for regular classes, and conductors and apprentice conductors who must work and study far from musical centers.

To facilitate classroom use, the text has been planned to provide material for two full semesters' study by classes meeting for three hourly periods a week. Since classes vary from term to term in size, capabilities, background, and potentialities, the teacher should adjust his use of the text to the needs of each class. It is a good plan to make, for each class, an outline based on the text but adapted to the needs of the specific group. It is well to share this outline with the class.

In making his adjustments, the teacher may decide to follow the main order of the text, or to omit certain portions and return to them later. He should stress the points each particular class needs, and also choose the examples for illustration and practice according to student need. The text provides sufficient material in enough detail to give the teacher a liberal degree of choice.

In classroom work, it is of great importance that the theory of technical principles be translated at the earliest possible moment into practice. The student conductor must learn to think on his feet. As soon as he has begun to acquire some ability in securing good attacks, balance among the various choirs, reasonably good intonation, and the elements of style, he should practice upon a singing group made up of members of the class or upon a similarly composed instrumental ensemble, no matter how small or how heterogeneous. When pianists are in preponderance in a class, some may play "second" instruments or those instruments most easily learned in their initial stages. Pianists may also double on percussion; while string, wind, and brass players may perform on other instruments in the same family as their major instrument. Clarinetists may become saxophonists; violinists may become violists or even contrabass players, and so on.

In all this practice, the teacher should insist that the student conductor sing out whenever performers falter or stray from pitch. The conductor should be able to solfège instantly any part, with some degree of imitative facility, in order to show the singers or players what he wants them to do. Furthermore, the teacher may well have his students make their own vocal and instrumental arrangements for any combinations which are possible and technically suitable for the class involved. This exercise will give the student opportunity to prepare for conditions likely to confront him later.

The conductor or apprentice conductor who must work and study away from musical centers will find in this book an exposition of the theory of the conductor's art. But the problem of obtaining a good working technique presents a challenge more difficult of solution for him than it does for students in musical centers. He will, however, have broadcast and recorded music available in enough profusion to enable him to progress from acquaintance to intimate friendship with a large repertory of standard works. He should also develop every possibility his community offers. He should practice with local pianists and organists, take advantage of special musical programs in local churches, form small groups of singers and instrumentalists, and make his own arrangements for varying combinations of performers. In all of these ventures, this book should guide him.

As indicated in its title, this book deals literally with the techniques of orchestral conducting and it is limited to that terrain. Certain facets of rehearsal procedure, such as the routining of amateur orchestras, phrasings, bowings, balance of different instruments and choirs of instruments, unsatisfactory and weak notes produced by some members of the orchestral ensemble, and the idiosyncrasies of various instruments, have been omitted. They have been omitted premeditatively, because some of them, like the routining of amateur orchestras, do not lend themselves to written exposition but must be learned in actual practice; and because others, like subtleties in tone balance and the technical knowledge of orchestral instruments, have been presented with extreme clarity and great detail in easily available books, e.g., Forsyth's *Orchestration* and Scherchen's *Handbook of Conducting*.

This book offers but one of a number of possible approaches to the art of conducting. Behind it lie two decades of testing in the author's own classes, under the most varying conditions.

INTERPRETATION OF PATTERNS

The student must not forget that, while motions made during actual conducting move in three directions, line drawings can be made to represent only two of these directions. The student must therefore mentally supply the missing dimension of depth as he studies the patterns.

Strong beats, which usually fall on down strokes although sometimes also on other strokes or parts of strokes, are shown in the diagrams by dark lines; weak beats, by lighter lines.

Arrows and numbers show the general direction of strokes; letters show subdivisions of main strokes.

Dotted lines represent preparatory motions, and, by extension, combined cessation-preparatory motions.

Apostrophes stand for breath pauses.

The small half moon with a dot in its center is used in its usual sense, to signify a hold, the length of which depends upon the context.

ABBREVIATIONS USED IN MUSICAL QUOTATIONS

Alto Flute	A.F.	Full Orchestra	F.O.
Bass Clarinet	B.Cl.	Oboe	Ob.
Bass Drum	B.D.	Piccolo	Pic.
Bass Trombone	B.Tbn.	Snare Drum	S.Dr.
Bassoon	Bsn.	Strings	Strgs.
Chorus	Cho.	Timpani	Timp.
Clarinet	Cl.	Trombone	Tbn.
Contrabass	B.	Trumpet	Tpt.
Contra Bassoon	C.Bsn.	Viola	Vla.
English Horn	Eng. Hn.	Violin	Vln.
Flute	Fl.	Violoncello	Vcl.
French Horn	Hn.	Wood Wind	Ww.

Part One

THE PHYSICAL BASES

OF CONDUCTING

Chapter One

GENERAL CONSIDERATIONS

The art of conducting, poetic and rewarding as it appears from a seat in the audience, presents an altogether different aspect to the aspirant who is preparing to practice it. He will soon discover that it is the most diffi-cult, the most profound art in the whole realm of musical interpretation, and the one demanding the greatest versatility. So difficult will he find its demands, in fact, that he is often likely to question whether or not he possesses the innate qualifications for success in this most inclusive and exacting of arts.

If, in the midst of his early misgivings, he is subjected to certain ideas sometimes expressed about conducting, he may find himself wondering whether it is worth while to hope that study will help him master the art. A half-truth has long been current and often stated that conductors are born, not trained, and that the art of conducting cannot be taught. Anton Seidl, in his essay, "On Conducting," takes the point of view that only the specially anointed may hope to become conductors and that training is neither necessary nor helpful.

"The ability to conduct," he writes, "is a gift of God with which few have been endowed in full measure. Those who possess it in abundance do not wish to write about it, for to them the talent seems so natural a thing that they cannot see the need of discussing it. This is the kernel of the whole matter. If you have the divine gift within you, you can con-duct; if you have not, you will never be able to acquire it. Those who have been endowed with the gift are conductors; the others are time-beaters."

If Herr Seidl means that inspiration, as apart from mere technique, is a divine gift, no one will dispute his thesis. But that the man with in-born ability to become a successful conductor must also learn from study is acknowledged in Herr Seidl's statement elsewhere that he himself learned to conduct recitative from Hermann Levi. The whole truth is that conductors are prepared by heredity to be trained; and that while many of the qualities which go into the personality of a conductor, especially those relating to suggestive and hypnotic powers, evade and defy analysis, other phases of the art do admit of both analysis and training and can be studied either in class room groups or alone.

Three main tasks confront the conductor: mastering a score, rehearsing a group of performers, and interpreting this score before an audience. Each of these tasks presupposes natural gifts, but gifts upon which must be superimposed highly specialized training. Yet because conducting is an art and not a science, a man may have most of the gifts that are subject to definition or description, plus the specialized training, and still fail to reveal that indefinable capacity to project lifeless musical symbols into sounds which convey an emotional message to an audience. Facets of every art can be taught; mastery of its physical techniques is possible to many. But the final spark which, in the case of a conductor, lifts orchestral music from the realm of acoustically acceptable sound into the realm of living art cannot be generated unless it constantly lives within the man whose task it is to elicit this phenomenon from the instruments of the players he conducts.

Certain definable gifts must be possessed by the man who would succeed as a conductor. To master a score he must be endowed with the ability to hear inwardly each part of that score. He must be able to memorize, though inability to *conduct* by memory does not disqualify a conductor. To rehearse an orchestra, a man must have not only inborn qualifications for leadership but also the capacity to beat time, a capacity, incidentally, which is not nearly so common as the aspirant may suppose. "The power of beating time," Hector Berlioz has written, "is difficult to secure and very few people really possess it."

A critical faculty is also essential for success in the conductor's task of rehearsing his group, as is understanding of the nature and compass of each instrument in his orchestra. It is not necessary that he be a master of any particular instrument—successful conductors have risen from the ranks of those playing almost every instrument, including the timpani— though ability to play one or more of them satisfactorily is an asset. But it is essential for him to have control of his vocal cords well enough to sing out or hum any part of a score, to show his men what he wants when it is not forthcoming from the instruments.

Yet all these, and other qualifications as well, are not to be confused with the art of conducting. They are of paramount importance in a conductor's equipment, but in the final analysis they are only preparation for his art. Possession of them does not necessarily make one a conductor. The ability to hear inwardly an orchestral score is one possessed by a fairly large body of musicians. Many auditors and orchestral players know by memory a fair number of orchestral words in the standard concert repertory, but this feat does not make them conductors. The critical faculty is possessed in varying degrees by most listeners and students. Many a professional critic knows what a conductor should be able to project, and can write both entertainingly and instructively on the matter. Many a pedagogue or pedagogically talented time-beater can rehearse an orchestra efficiently and effectively. A conductor must have all these abilities in some degree of competence, but they are only preparation for his main task: that of interpreting a musical work before an audience.

So, while it is undoubtedly true that some men are born with innate gifts for translating musical pulses, phrases, dynamics, and tone balance into clearly understood and poetic motions, coupled with the gift of mobility of countenance which makes inspiring facial expressions possible, it cannot be repeated too often that such natural gifts must be carefully trained and supplemented with musical theory.

To stress the need for study is not to deny the fact that a self-taught conductor does occasionally emerge, who has overcome his faults through years of practical experience. Self-taught conductors, nevertheless, are usually just as effective as self-taught instrumentalists or singers, barring the rare cases of genius. And usually, even in such a rare case, a tremendous amount of time and labor might have been saved under competent teachers.

Certain principles of time-beating have evolved over the years and have been generally accepted throughout the musical world. Conductors who understand these principles may travel from orchestra to orchestra and, with a few rehearsals, show their collaborators what they want, despite partial or even complete linguistic barriers. Knowledge of these principles and respect for them do not preclude individuality. On the contrary, they permit and encourage it, if the principles are not followed too literally.

It is natural for those studying conducting, whether under teachers or alone, to watch and try to imitate well-known conductors. At any stage of the learning process, this experience may prove very valuable, but it is much more likely to be so if the student has already undergone study which has developed his discrimination. After such study he will see and hear prominent conductors with sharpened eyes and ears and with new understanding. To be able to recognize how much of a conductor's success is due to excellent nontechnical abilities, such as emotional drive, skill in organizing and program building, scholarship, overpowering personality, and so on, is essential, if the student is to be able to distinguish clearly those technical features of the great conductors which are worth imitating. By all means copy the good facets, but do not assume a conductor's performances to be canonical simply because he is famous.

The student who watches several well-known conductors of recognized excellence should not expect to find unanimity of technique. The conscientious conductor makes signs to show his interpretation of a musical work with the same infinite care and exactness as a string virtuoso fingers and bows. Just as no two players necessarily finger or bow in the same way, so do no two conductors necessarily beat alike in all details. Just as there are idiomatic ways of fingering and bowing, so there are idiomatic ways of beating. These vary with the proficiency of the players and singers of each group, with the conductor's familiarity with his group, and, above all, with his mood. These facts show another reason why formal study is a good forerunner of or accompaniment to the student's independent, personal study of successful conductors. It can bring clarity where, otherwise, the main end result might be confusion.

The student will soon discover that the technique of the baton is just as difficult as that of an instrument and will take just as long to master. Indeed, the student will probably later recall this assertion as an understatement. When he reads that an aristocrat of the baton like Felix Weingartner states that it took him years to achieve complete harmony between heart and hand, the student need not despair. It must never be forgotten that the conductor is playing upon living human beings and not, as is the instrumentalist, upon an inanimate collection of materials. The harmony between his own heart and hand, so difficult even for the most highly gifted, must be the tool, also, for harmony between himself and the living human beings from whom he must evoke his interpretation of the music.

At no time in history has there been more demand for capable young conductors. Motion pictures, broadcasting studios, theater orchestras, wind instrument bands, church choirs and ensembles, educational institutions, and community orchestras founded away from great musical centers—all offer opportunities to the trained organizer and conductor. High and ever-rising technical standards make it imperative that he secure as careful training as does the instrumentalist. Conducting, it cannot be repeated too often, is an art, not a science, and nothing less than the most serious and concentrated preparation should be contemplated for this most difficult of the interpretative arts.

Chapter Two

REQUIREMENTS

AND EXPERIENCE

The first query which naturally concerns the student is what theoretical knowledge is desirable or necessary for him to acquire before he proceeds to the study of baton technique. The usual reply presents a long and formidable list of studies which practicing conductors have mastered toward the height of their careers. The student is here advised to do what most of these conductors have done: acquire all such knowledge gradually, while gaining practical experience.

The conductor, when all is said and done, is an interpreter. He is not primarily a pedagogue, theorist, composer, or critic; although his art certainly calls upon each of these branches of musical activity to no little degree, their chief function should be to furnish him with an understanding of the musical compositions he must re-create before an audience. Over-stressing theory, criticism, or composition, however important they may be to other musicians, sometimes results in a style of conducting, easily seen in certain conductors, which exaggerates studies that should be a less conspicuous means to an end.

It is an open secret that more than one successful conductor has been distinguished by his comparative lack rather than by his knowledge of music theory. Some of these men began as pianists, organists, or opera coaches. But they have usually been able to acquire two formidable weapons in the conductor's arsenal: an intimate knowledge of many items in the standard repertory, and a workable baton technique. Such men, having been knocked about in the rather rough and ready school of experience, have usually managed to obtain a pretty good understanding of what voices and instruments can do.

To speak of the success of these men is not an attempt to decry, even by implication, the importance of sound theoretical training. Without underestimating its supreme value in other fields of musical endeavor, however, we must consider it merely as background in a conductor's equipment—a means to an end. It is quite surprising to discover how relatively little theory serves for practical purposes, if that modicum is thoroughly mastered through the eye and ear and not on the printed page.

At the other extreme, however, one occasionally encounters pedantic conductors who, although very gifted, are overburdened with peripheral knowledge. Such men have been known to lecture their players on musical philosophy, aesthetics, and history for long periods, and embarrassing episodes have occurred in protest, as in the case of Willem Mengelberg. The matter may be summed up by pointing out that it is possible to strike a balance, as did Sir Donald Tovey and Felix Weingartner, who juggled their profound learning very gracefully indeed.

Let us turn now to consider what theoretical equipment is practical for the conductor. Although it may seem redundant to insist on a thorough knowledge of rhythm, musical notation, solfège, musical architecture, harmony, and counterpoint at this time, a careful review often reveals that students have surprising gaps in early training, which may prove disconcerting later. Such gaps should be remedied at the earliest possible moment, or they will come back to plague one. The student should be able to read easily not only the usual bass and treble clefs, but also—and this is extremely important—the C clef on all five lines. Such clef-reading will be useful not only in reading old manuscripts but also as a means of transposing instruments. The student is urged to practice clef transposition at the piano and, more important, with his voice, so that he will be able to sing any passages suddenly to his players. At his fingers' tips as well as at his tongue's end, he should also have a working knowledge of the usual instrumental transpositions, ranges, registers, and tone colors, singly and in various combinations; and he should be familiar with the technical possibilities of instruments and voices, bowings, fingerings, special effects, and breathings; traditional orchestral parlance; foreign terminology; phrasing; and the mood and style of various epochs, schools, and composers. But such collateral study should be taken slowly and diluted with much study of baton technique.

In addition to studying all this theory, the student conductor must continue to develop ceaselessly certain specific abilities. The first is a sense of just intonation, which means *relative* pitch: the ability to distinguish even slight deviations of one note in relation to another. *Absolute* pitch, the ability to name or to sing a note without previous reference to another, is an interesting faculty as often possessed by mediocre musicians as lacked by good ones. To detect a slight variation in a solo instrument is one thing; to do this in an inner part amid many tone colors is quite another, especially when more than one instrument share the same note in *forte* passages. The student will soon learn that it seems to be far easier, ironically, to detect such variations from a seat in the auditorium than from the conductor's podium. This paradox may be explained partly by the fact that while the hearer is unhampered by the actual details of the rehearsal and receives an over-all acoustical and aural impression by being at a distance from the stage, the conductor, assailed and harried by innumerable varied sounds at close range, is sometimes likely to become disconcerted. At first, differing nuances and combinations of sounds, tone colors, and degrees of loudness tend to muddle up the conductor; but practice, experience, and concentration will gradually develop his perception in these matters. Much of the initial difficulty is undoubtedly psychological, and only time will bring self-assurance.

Detecting a wrong note or deviation may be termed a positive aural ability; singling out the missing note of a chord in a mass of sound, a negative aural ability. Neither comes easily, and conductors differ amazingly in this regard. A thorough training in solfège, chordal structure, and intervals is the best preparation for these abilities. Experience will aid the process. Have a friendly pianist play series of chords, each with a wrong or missing note, and then try to identify the errors, as part of the training process. Pay special attention to very low notes, which many musicians find difficult to take apart aurally.

A practical understanding of the possibilities of orchestral instruments is indispensable to the conductor. Perhaps the simplest way to acquire this knowledge is to study one instrument from each representative family, i.e., one string, one wood wind, one brass, and one percussion. For the string section, the viola or contrabass is recommended as being easier than the violin or violoncello; for the single reed, the clarinet, which, though not so easy in some ways as the flute, oboe, or saxophone, presents certain acoustical quirks with which the conductor should be familiar; for the brass, the tuba or cornet, which will teach the conductor what he wants to know without forcing him to submit to the appalling task of trying to play the French horn; for the percussion, the timpani, both manual and pedal, of course. The ability to play the piano or organ will help, not only in playing scores but also in training the mind to think polyphonically. Inability to play one of these instruments may prove a handicap which only intense work can overcome. There is no doubt of the fact that keyboard players have some initial advantages, although they also have disadvantages. A list of successful conductors, who have played all sorts of instruments, proves that it is the man and not his instrumental background which determines his success.

It is recommended that the student take a few lessons on each of these instruments from a teacher who is aware that not technical velocity or ferocity is the aim, but an understanding of the instrument's possibilities. The student should also read mentally various beginners' methods for each instrument and peruse the latest catalogues of manufacturers, a process which will bring much practical knowledge in a short time. All this training definitely improves the student's beat, which he will often have to vary according to the section he conducts.

It is well to remember that, although score-reading is a necessary skill, some famous score-readers have been undistinguished as conductors. Opportunities to hear musical works repeated over the air, on phonographs, and in the concert hall are numerous nowadays, so that a student has many chances to practice score-reading. If he plays in an orchestra, so much the better, for then he can learn scores being rehearsed at first hand, not forgetting that music sounds different in various parts of the orchestra pit and unlike its effect at the conductor's podium. The student should read scores away from the piano as much as possible.

The problem of obtaining actual experience in conducting has never been an easy one to solve. For this is not simply a matter of getting an instrument to practice upon; one must practice upon a body of men, and quite naturally, no body of men likes to be practiced upon. One traditional method is to play in the orchestra and to act as the assistant conductor, another is to coach an opera choir and then start with backstage bits and operettas. These methods have obvious advantages: one goes gradually to more and more difficult tasks, and one may consult with the chief conductor on knotty problems.

The student should enlist the aid of a pianist who can play from score, preferably section by section, and whom he can "conduct." Four-hand piano arrangements are even better for this purpose. He should also follow performances, either at the concert hall or over the air, by beating time. If he is at a concert hall, he can do this unobtrusively on his knee. At the concert he should try to get a seat in front and to the side, where he can watch the conductor's facial expressions and left hand. Even if the composition being played is wholly unfamiliar to him, beating time simply up and down and backward and forward will prove of immense value in establishing a feeling for the translation of tempo and phrases into visible patterns. Incidentally, it is far better for this purpose to hear one program many times than a half-dozen programs once each.

Finding an orchestra to practice with is largely a matter of ingenuity, circumstances, and luck. Municipal, educational, and church organizations frequently offer opportunities. If your orchestra or band is small, lead with a violin, piano, or band instrument. Make everything count.

Whenever you see a puzzled look on the faces of your men or whenever they become unsteady, assume it to be your fault. It often will be. At any rate, such an attitude will make you strive constantly for greater clarity in giving your indications. Even when you know your men were at fault, consider that you yourself might have been so clear that they could not possibly have gone wrong.

Explain your wishes and manner of beating to your men when any confusion arises. Very often some of the more experienced players can make helpful suggestions in procedure. If accepting their advice seems to the apprentice conductor to be gratuitously revealing his inexperience, he may be assured that in any event the routined men will recognize his qualifications for what they are worth after he has conducted only a very few measures. Do not forget that some of them have played under many conductors—good, bad, and indifferent. So unless you are pretty sure of yourself, and few conductors are unless they hold the economic whip hand or have had many years of experience, do not be diffident about placing your case frankly before older players. You can do this without losing your authority. No less a musician than Richard Wagner did this on occasion.

Chapter Three

THE TOOLS

Not many tools are required to pursue our conducting studies. Access to a good library of orchestral full scores is of particular consequence. A piano or organ should be available, although scores are learned in one's head and not in one's fingers. A friendly colleague alternating at the piano helps to make study more interesting, and each student may thus derive the benefit of someone else's reactions. A radio-phonograph may be most helpful to those living away from musical centers, in hearing how professional conductors interpret items in the standard repertory. Attentive study of broadcast and reproduced performances may prepare the student for the time when he can perform the works himself. A metronome should be part of the student's equipment. Since metronomes are usually made now to ring only at the beginning of two, three, four, and six beats to a measure, an ingenious student might rig up an attachment which would also ring on every five or seven beats. A mirror, tall enough to reach from the student's waistline to a foot above his head and wide enough to show the sweep of his arms wholly outstretched, should adorn the studio. He should practice within easy reach of the score-stand, the piano, and the radio-phonograph.

In choosing a baton, avoid the sort often presented by admiring choral groups to their directors. These batons may possess definite artistic distinction and give evidence of genuine affection, but they are rarely practical conducting tools. A good stick may vary in size from that of a pencil to about fifteen or twenty inches long. Length, weight, and thickness are entirely a matter of personal preference, and the final choice may take a long time. Some conductors keep changing styles; others hit upon what they want almost immediately. There is no hard and fast rule. It is recommended that the student try a fairly long and lightweight stick

at first, one long enough to make a wide sweep with the slightest movement of the wrist, and light enough to be used for three hours without
discomfort. The color should be light enough to be visible to the watchers, but the baton should not be glaringly enameled. It should taper
from the grasping point to the wrist. Some conductors like a swelling
knob at the grasping point; others, whose hands perspire, use a cork
handle. The wood should be free from knots and not brittle, or a slight
sharp tap on the stand may cause it to split. Occasional sandpapering
may improve its aesthetic appearance. As time brings naturalness, ease,
and facility, the student's tastes in this matter may change until he hits
upon one or two styles which seem best to fit his personal requirements.
It is no easy matter to find suitable batons.

There are conductors, good, bad, and indifferent, who do not use a
baton but conduct with empty hands. Much might be said about this
practice. It is more difficult to give exact directions without a baton
than with one. A large body of instrumentalists requires more precise
signals than a small group; and a group of instrumentalists requires more
precise signals than a group of singers, because (among other reasons) instrumental music is almost invariably more ornate and complicated than
vocal music. Theater, ballet, and opera orchestras need more precise
signals than does a concert orchestra, not only because theater pits are
more dimly lighted than the average concert hall, but also because dramatic music usually changes tempo more often than absolute music.
A newly formed orchestra needs more precise signals than a body of
players which has functioned as a unit for a long time. A guest conductor with limited rehearsals must give more precise signals than a resident
conductor who rehearses his forces day in and day out.

Many student conductors, not accustomed to handling a baton with
ease, *think* they can fashion patterns in the air better with their empty
hands than with a baton. With negligible exceptions, this assumption
simply is not true; it just *seems* so to the beginner, especially to one who
has never learned how to handle a bow and play a stringed instrument.
Certainly, from the point of view of the player, it requires much more
attention and strain to follow empty hands than a baton; and one frequent result of batonless conducting is that the conductor is gradually
forced to make wider and wider sweeps, which are liable to be ungrace-
ful and exaggerated.

The student should remember that under ideal circumstances, a conductor of authority and experience (not necessarily synonymous) may
dispense with a baton and achieve enviable results. If a student witnes-
ses such a performance, he should try to analyze whether the lack of a

baton or the presence of other qualities is responsible for the good results. An apprentice conductor, lacking in experience and routine and with a limited number of rehearsals, is simply adding to his own problems and to those of his players when he conducts without a baton. In very broad passages without frequent changes in tempo, where the musical outline suggests vocal writing, one may sometimes lay aside the baton for hand delineations; but in general, it is recommended that the student use a baton. If, despite all that has been said, any student feels that *his* message to the world of music imperatively demands that he free himself from the shackles of the baton, that is his own affair and he may decide as he wishes. It is suggested, none the less, that he learn first to conduct with a baton before experimenting without one. After he has acquired a good baton technique, he will be ready to permit himself on occasion to direct a bit of expressive *legato* without a baton. Fashions in this matter do change. Spohr met astonishment from London audiences in 1820 when he first introduced the baton to that city; Sofanoff encountered a similar reaction there when he conducted without one, early in 1900.

One more matter related to the baton should be considered, that is, the tendency of some conductors to drop their batons in the midst of a performance. This problem is psychological and usually results from one of two situtations: the conductor's hand becomes so tense that he loses control of his hand muscles and the baton flies off, or he becomes so absorbed in his task that his hand muscles loosen naturally and the baton falls away. In either case, over- or under-attention will bring about the same results: loss of the baton and consequent embarrassment. The cure is to pretend always that the baton is an elongation of the index finger and thumb, and to think through to the tip of the baton at all times as if it were living tissue. This will also forestall the picture presented by some conductors, who hold a baton lifelessly and inertly in their hands and really conduct with their wrists and cuffs, held rigidly.

The question of whether or not to conduct with a baton brings up a related question, whether or not to conduct with a score. The reply to the latter is simple. Other things being equal, conducting without a score does not make the slightest difference in a performance from a musical point of view, though it often makes a tremendous difference in an audience's reactions. The spectacle of a conductor guiding a large group of singers or players through a concert without a score (and often also without a baton) appeals strongly to the imagination of many untutored auditors, to whom such an exhibition seems nothing short of conjuring. From the musical point of view, however, a poor performance with or without a baton or score is still poor; a good performance gains nothing from the absence of either.

There is an old saw to the effect that some conductors have their heads in the score and others have their scores in their heads. Good orchestral players look closely at the conductor and glance at their music occasionally through the corners of their eyes. A good conductor has such a command of his score that it is not a fetter but an aid; such a conductor keeps his eyes upon the players and glances occasionally at the score through the corners of his eyes. The sight of a conductor whose countenance is buried in his music is hardly inspiring, either to the players or to the auditors. Such conductors are not really conducting an orchestra; they are conducting a score, merely by beating time, and in extreme cases, they are so wrapped up in their task that they are gazing inward instead of outward and consequently are conducting no one but themselves. To conduct players, one must meet their eyes.

If memorizing comes easily, conduct without a score; but remember that unless you have an established reputation for doing so with ease, there is liable to be tension in the orchestra and audience. Every conductor, even with limited experience, realizes that he must know his score very well indeed before he ever goes to the first rehearsal. With such command of the score, he uses it merely as a safeguard and as a reassurance to his players. The contemporary trend toward batonless and scoreless conducting has been forced upon conductors by what they think is the pressure of public opinion. Once again, other things being equal, it does not make the slightest difference musically whether one conducts with or without a baton or score. All that matters is the musical result, that is, the justice done to the composer.

Chapter Four

PREPARATORY EXERCISES

It is intriguing to inspect diagrams for beating time contrived by early writers in the field. While admittedly it is almost impossible to get down on paper in two dimensions what the conductor actually outlines in three, a comparison of these early diagrams with the attempts by beginners to delineate musical speech through gestures will reveal a striking similarity between them. It looks as if inexperienced conductors of today have to go through preliminary stages which resemble the mature work of by-gone practitioners, before they can develop ease, naturalness, and fluidity. The stark geometric rigidity of the patterns and models found in the writings of theorists up to about 1900 shows how long a time it has taken to evolve simple, precise, and yet artistic motions in the art of time-beating. One practical use which the study of these early attempts suggests would be adapting some of them as setting-up exercises.

At the start of our studies, most of us find that our wrists are a bit stiff and that they tend to become tense after prolonged use. The reason, of course, is that our muscles are not sufficiently relaxed. At first our joints lack pliancy, resilience, and flexibility, and they require some sort of calisthenic preparation before responding automatically to our wills as they should.

It is wise to postpone for a bit the actual handling of the baton, in order to loosen up the muscles and joints of our hands and wrists by means of a few simple exercises, which are to be practiced daily even after a good working technique has been acquired. These exercises are to be done first with each hand alone and then with both hands in similar and contrary motion, with variations in rhythm, pattern, style, and tempo, in the same way that an instrumentalist studies five-finger exercises for limbering up. Do not overdo at the outset; watch carefully for signs of fatigue and stop when they occur. Increase speed and length of practice time very gradually.

Keep in mind the concept of the baton as a lengthened index finger, intended as a focus for the attention of the players and singers. It becomes a lever for your hand to work through. In your warming-up exercises, arrange your fingers (first those of your right, then those of your left hand, and then both together) somewhat like a printer's index sign. Consider the forefinger the baton. Practice the exercises as follows: first with the forefinger, then with the part of the hand below the wrist, then with the arm below the elbow, finally, with the whole arm from the shoulder down. Reserve the upper joints for broad effects and dynamic contrasts. It is important to avoid exaggeration of movement at the very start. The smaller the group of performers, the softer the music to be interpreted, and the more delicate the nuance, the more the hand is used.

At first, to insure that only the wrist and hand move, rest the arm on a table letting the hand project over the edge so that the wrist is allowed full play. When you are able to perform these exercises easily in this position with practically no motion of the wrist, discard the table and continue practicing before a mirror. Practice slowly and guard against fatigue by resting frequently. Later on, when you adapt these exercises for the left hand, reverse the directions left and right.

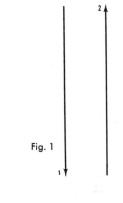

Fig. 1

Exercise One

Keep the palm facing the floor and in a straight line from the shoulder to the tip of the forefinger. Move the wrist up and down until the hand is as nearly possible at right angles to the arm, in both extreme positions. Do not force the muscles (Fig. 1).

Fig. 2

Exercise Two

Turn the hand so that the thumbnail is uppermost and let the hand assume the position of a printer's index sign. Move the hand alternately toward the left and right. Try to raise the hand at right angles to the rest of the arm in both extreme positions without forcing (Fig. 2).

Fig. 3

Exercise Three

Turn the hand away from you as far as possible without straining, so that the palm faces almost to the right. Work the wrist back and forth toward the right and the left. Again try to make the wrist approach a right angle in the extreme positions (Fig. 3).

Exercise Four

Turn the palm upward and turn the wrist alternately upward and downward, following the suggestions of the previous exercises (Fig. 4).

Fig. 4

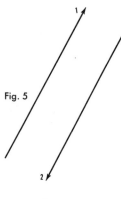

Fig. 5

Exercise Five

As a supplement to the previous exercise, practice similarly upward and downward with the palm facing both up and down, first from southwest to northeast, and then from southeast to northwest (Figs. 5 and 6).

Exercise Six

Roll the hand around, first from right to left and then from left to right, with the palm facing both upward and downward. Keep the wrist as the pivotal point and the arm motionless (Figs. 7 and 8).

Exercise Seven

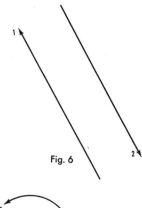

Fig. 6

For further variety, describe simple geometric figures like squares and triangles with the tip of the forefinger extended as an imaginary pencil. At the start, try to execute the figures as exactly and with as sweeping a motion as possible without moving any part of the arm above the wrist. Make the angles clean-cut. In the early stages of this exercise, stop for a moment at the end of each direction to give the wrist and palm time to turn and to adjust before proceeding in the next direction. As facility and litheness gradually increase, the movements will tend to coalesce (Figs. 9, 10, 11, and 12).

Fig. 7

After some degree of ease in the execution of these exercises has been reached with each hand, practice them with the arm to the elbow. The arm from the elbow to the shoulder is now to remain motionless, in line with the side of the body and in front of it. At the start, rest the elbow on a table to insure this position. Now practice in two ways: first with the wrist turned toward each successive position without bending, and then with the wrist bending toward each new direction. Finally, use the whole arm from the shoulder down, first with no bending at the joints but simply the wrist and palm turning toward each direction; then with bending at both wrist and elbow.

Fig. 8

These preliminary exercises have been described in some detail with a purpose. They are not so simple as they appear at first sight, and their effect in making for grace, ease, and sustained power, after faithful practice, will later become more apparent than seemed at first credible.

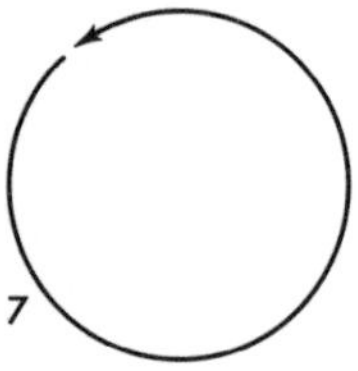

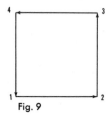

Fig. 9

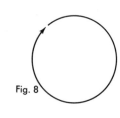

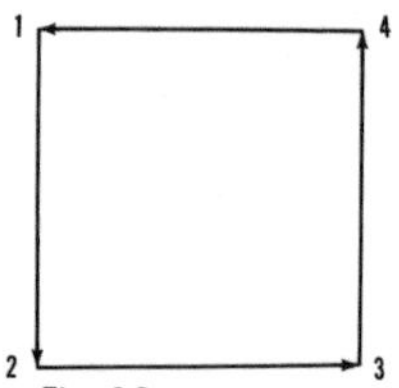

Fig. 10

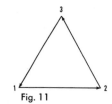

Fig. 11

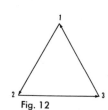

Fig. 12

Exercise Eight

Set the metronome at a very slow tempo and do all the foregoing exercises. Note how much more difficult it is to make slow motions gracefully and without jerking than rapid ones. See how slowly you can beat without stopping. Note that as you increase in speed your movements become shorter and more precise and you have to limit your arm more and more.

Exercise Nine

With a phonograph or, better still, a colleague taking turns with you at the piano, apply these exercises to such comparatively simple technical music as hymns, folk tunes, Mendelssohn's *Songs Without Words*, Tchaikovsky's *The Seasons*, Schumann's *Scenes from Childhood*, and the like. Go on to a collection of overtures by such composers as Suppé, Hérold, and Boïeldieu, and to collections of waltzes by the Strausses, Lanner, Waldteufel, Gungl, and Ziehrer. Practice the motions without looking at the music, by using your ears, with each hand alone and then with both hands together. Avoid the extremes of beating so many motions that the eye cannot follow easily, or of going so slowly that your beat stops or becomes jerky. Do not look at the time-signatures, or one of the main objects of this exercise will lose much of its value. This object is to accustom your hands to adopting the correct pulses when all knowledge of the music is conveyed to you via ears, not eyes.

Chapter Five

TWO BEATS TO THE BAR

THE POSITION OF THE HAND AND THE BODY

Form your right hand somewhat like a printer's fist, the palm downward and the thumb in a straight line with the inner lower arm. Insert the thick end of the baton into the center of the hand so that it gently touches the middle part of the palm, resting lightly on the first joint of the middle finger, poised between the index finger and the thumb. Close the fingers lightly yet firmly over the baton without making any other change in position. There should now be a straight line from the forearm, through the wrist and hand, to the tip of the stick. This is one good way to hold the baton. Another is to hold the thick end of the stick between the thumb and the index and middle fingers. Some conductors use both positions according to the passage, the former for heavy and *forte* passages and the latter for lighter, more precise, and softer passages. Such changes in position also help to relieve muscular tension in some cases. Experience will soon show the student what fits his special hand and style, and he will learn to make adjustments according to the volume, tempo, and mood of the music.

It is well to place your weight on your toes while conducting and to lean slightly forward, in order to establish better physical and psychological contact with your forces. As you stand before your music rack and imaginary orchestra, raise your whole arm so that your elbow juts out just a bit to the right, away from your body and a little below a straight line with your shoulder. If your strokes fall below this line, as is sometimes the case with short conductors, the performers will have trouble seeing anything but the top of your strokes unless they keep straining. Also, if you are short in stature, keep your strokes pretty well above your waist line, or the bottom of your strokes will give the performers trouble. If you are tall, see that your elbows keep on a line with your shoulder, or a gawky picture may result. Unless you are inordinately tall, conduct from a platform. If your position is correct, the angle formed by the upper part of your right arm and the line from your neck to the juncture at the shoulder should be about 135 degrees, or a right angle and a half.

Retaining this position for your elbow, raise your hand to the level of your eyes, extend it till the juncture at the elbow forms a right angle, and then turn the palm slightly outward. Now bring your left hand and arm to the same position as the right, keeping the arms far enough apart to allow complete independence and freedom of action in either hand and arm. It should be possible, in this position, for every member of the playing and singing group to see your face and every one of your movements; and for you to look directly into the eyes and countenance of each of your collaborators.

It is of the utmost importance that there always be a direct line of vision from your eyes through the tip of your baton into the eyes and countenance of each player and singer, so that he can lift his eyes from his music without squirming and follow you, and so that you can turn your own head toward any part of the pit or stage without straining. The position you now have is a natural one, quite simple to demonstrate, and far from being as complicated as it may seem from this necessarily detailed written description.

Two observations need to be made before we consider actual patterns for beating. First, unless otherwise specified, take it for granted that you beat *mezzo-forte*, *legato*, and *moderato*. Second, while an arithmetic order of patterns, that is, one, two, three, four, etc., beats to a bar, *seems* to be the most logical one to learn, it actually is so only from the point of view of one who has already been over the whole ground. Paradoxically, the easiest road for the student is the order followed here: two, three, one, four, six, five, and seven beats to a bar. The reason for this will be understood later.

Before considering time-beating in detail, let us present a telegraphic summary of some technical principles. The student must never forget that he is playing upon thinking human beings, in distinction to the instrumentalist, who plays upon an inanimate object. This statement has been made elsewhere and will be made again, because it contains the reasons for many of the principles here stressed. Many years of oral tradition and theoretical writings have been necessary to evolve these principles. They are not accidental or arbitrary, although they may be used in an individual and personal way. As in any other art, they conceal their art. And when a true balance is achieved between technique and individuality, the result is what we term, for want of a better word, re-creation.

The conductor should make enough motions to give his forces something to hold to at all times in even the slowest tempos, and yet not too many to confuse them in the most rapid ones. He should obtain maximum effect with minimum motion. Every gesture, pose, bodily attitude, and facial expression must be sincere and unaffected, a faithful translation of the mood and spirit of the music he is interpreting.

The important traditional technical principles may be summarized as follows. The first pulse of every measure is given downward; the last pulse is given upward at the right of the pattern; the secondary accent, when there is one, goes outward to the right; and the weaker pulses and subdivisions are filled into these broad outlines.

METHOD OF BEATING

The student must realize immediately that time-signatures do not necessarily determine the number of strokes to a measure for a pattern. The proper number of beats in a pattern is determined by what is comfortable to the conductor's hand and clear to the performers, i.e., there must be enough beats to keep the music flowing and not too many to confuse the watchers. Thus, a passage marked 2/4 may be taken two to the bar, one to the bar, with subdivisions, or with two bars as one. Stated baldly, any rhythm which can be comfortably beaten with two strokes to the bar should be so done.

Rhythms which are taken two to the bar form a fairly large class; they include such time-signatures as 2/4, 2/8, 4/4, 4/8, 4/16, 6/16, 6/2, 6/4, and 6/8. Note that this list includes both duple and triple pulses. *Alla breve* (¢) also belongs to this category and, often, so do classical works written in 4/4, *allegro* or *presto*. This class even includes very rapid quintuple and other combined pulses. A great deal of the most serious music, as well as a host of salon genres like intermezzi and caprices, comes under this heading. In general, any brisk duple (either simple or compound) rhythm in flowing tempo is beaten two to the bar.

In interpreting printed patterns in these discussions, remember that the *tip* of the baton is being outlined and that the printed page limits representation to two dimensions. The imagination of the reader, therefore, must add the third dimension. Similarly, where parts of a figure follow each other on the printed page, the reader must mentally superimpose them.

Fig. 13

Figure 13 will be found appropriate to a large number of *legato-moderato* cases calling for two to the bar. According to the usual rule, take the first stroke down and the last stroke up. Figure 14 is a suggested pattern for *staccato-marcato* passages. In the accompanying musical quotations (Exs. 1–6), wherever the attack begins on part of a measure, beat out a whole measure as preparation until after we have considered attacks in detail.

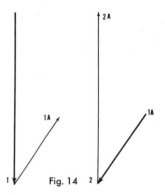

Fig. 14

Ex. 1.   Beethoven: Symphony No. 1

Ex. 2.   Haydn: Symphony No. 11, "Military"

Ex. 3.   Schumann: Symphony No. 1, "Spring"

Ex. 4.   Bruckner: Symphony No. 4, "Romantic"

Ex. 5.   Mozart: Marriage of Figaro Overture

Now apply these beating patterns to Examples 1 through 6. The greatest care should be exercised that the down beat is really down and does not swerve either to right or left. Orchestral players complain frequently and with justice that without a clear down beat they cannot count their measures or give a clear entrance, and thus they run the risk of coming in wrong in crucial places after long rests. The slightest indecision or raggedness in a down beat will be immediately reflected in the ensemble, even more in the winds than in the strings. Once the baton starts its downward course it must continue logically at a regular pace and straight down. Players, consciously or subconsciously, develop what may be termed a "time and space" sense, and they must be able to tell what is coming from what has gone before. A wavering or faltering beat, known among many orchestral players as a "corkscrew" beat, should not be added to their burdens.

In executing the down beat in two to the bar, keep the palm facing downward and the down beat vertical until about two-thirds or three-fourths of the length of the whole stroke has been reached. Then turn the palm away from the body and snap the wrist a bit outward and upward, allowing the lower arm to aid the motion a little. The resulting fairly deep curve will serve to separate the down and up strokes distinctly and will also prepare for the stroke upward, which is executed by reversing the previous motions: sweeping the palm inward and downward until it reaches the bottom of the stroke, and then bringing the baton back to the top of the stroke with a straight motion, mainly by the wrist. The ascending curve is not quite so deep as the descending one. Note that in order to make a new down beat for the succeeding measure, one must turn the wrist back and have the palm face downward once more, just as the top of the stroke is reached.

In reference again to Figures 13 and 14, note that when the bottom of the stroke is reached, the wrist makes what is virtually a rebound. As you will see later, this rebound is of great importance when more motions are beaten to the measure than in this instance. The rebound gives the beat resilience and allows the muscles to relax; it keeps the baton

Ex. 7. Rimsky-Korsakoff: *Scheherezade* (Copyright by M. P. Belaieff Editions. Used by permission of sole agents, Boosey & Hawkes.)

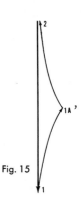

Fig. 15

moving between strokes in broad tempos which are not broad enough for subdivisions, and yet where lack of finish in the ensemble might result if the baton hesitated or waited for even a fraction of a second. It also prevents an exaggerated up-beat. Not the least function of the rebound is to impart visual grace to patterns. In Figure 15, there is the slight suggestion of a breath pause in the up stroke, marked by an apostrophe. Practice this pattern on Example 7.

THE ATTACK AND THE BREATH PAUSE

A moment's reflection will show that every signal given by a guide, a traffic policeman, or an orchestral conductor cannot be seized and acted upon at the same instant, and that the watchers, no matter how quick their reflexes, must inevitably come in afterward. This fact, applied to our situation, means that the conductor must signal what is to come next whenever the baton has stopped. When giving a signal for the orchestra to begin a passage, he must, therefore, show the *exact* point of entrance by giving a preparatory stroke toward the point where the music and the baton are to function together. The simplest case is that in which the music starts on the down beat. The general rule, to be adjusted to various circumstances, is to give the previous beat as preparation, in the same style (*legato*, *staccato*, etc.), speed, and volume as the beat it is introducing. This preparatory beat is shown in the diagrams by a dotted line. For a preparation on a *legato* down beat, use Figure 16. For more precise attacks, use Figure 17. Note that a breath pause may be made here, resembling a string player's bowing in such passages.

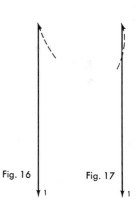

Fig. 16   Fig. 17

Now practice attacks on the down beat with Examples 1 through 6. Start on the first full measure when necessary.

When the entrance is exactly on the up beat (in this case for two to the bar, but applicable also to any up beat in any rhythm), the down beat, adjusted to the context, may be given as preparation. For soft, *legato*, and *moderato* passages, have the open palm face the point of entrance at the bottom of the beat (Fig. 18); for more precise and rapid

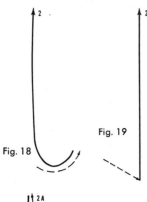

Fig. 18

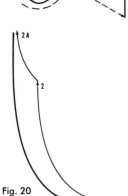

Fig. 19

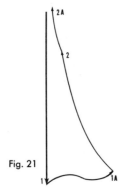

Fig. 20

Ex. 8. Haydn: "La Reine" Symphony

Allegretto (♩ = 116)

Ex. 9. Beethoven: Symphony No. 8

Allegro vivace (♩ = 132)

passages, point the back of the hand toward the bottom of the point of
entrance (Fig. 19). Note that in the latter pattern, again a breath pause
may be made. Practice on Examples 8 and 9.

SUBDIVISIONS

In executing subdivisions, use the wrist in contrast to the arm up
to the elbow, and the arm up to the elbow in contrast to the whole arm.
Keep all arm joints flexible, in somewhat the same manner as a swimmer

Ex. 10. Dvořák: Symphony No. 5, "New World" (Used by permission of the Oliver Ditson Company,
copyright owner.)

Adagio (♪ = 100)

Ex. 11. Borodin: Symphony No. 2

Animato assai   (♩ = 92)

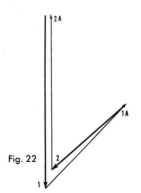

Fig. 21

Fig. 22

TWO BEATS TO THE BAR

executes a crawl stroke with his legs: one motion from the hip down but with the knees and ankles yielding.

Begin practicing subdivisions by beating two to the bar as slowly as you can. You will soon reach a point where indecision will result unless extra motions are added, i.e., subdivisions. When the pulses are duple, one subdivision after each main stroke must be added; when they are compound duple, as in slow 6/8, two subdivisions after each main stroke must be added. The chief aim should be to keep the main outlines of the pattern clear and the subdivisions unobtrusive. The wrist is to the conductor what the fingers are to the pianist. Use it for subdivisions in contrast to the arm, which beats the main lines of the patterns. The performers must never be in doubt about the main outlines. The sight of a conductor directing a delicate string passage with enough arm motion to control a huge choir and orchestra is not so infrequent as it should be.

For one subdivision, *legato*, after a main stroke, use Figure 20 and its variant, Figure 21, and practice on Example 10; for more precise passages, use Figure 22 and practice on Example 11.

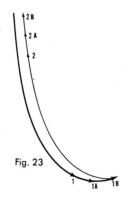

Fig. 23

Ex. 12. Rimsky-Korsakoff: *Scheherezade* (Copyright by M. P. Belaieff Editions. Used by permission of sole agents, Boosey & Hawkes.)

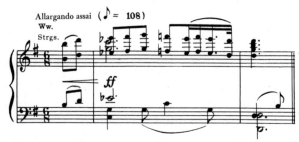

Fig. 24

Ex. 13. Tchaikovsky: *Italian Caprice*

Ex. 14. Wagner: *Tannhäuser*, "Evening Star"

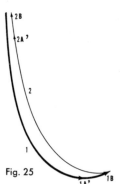

Fig. 25

The excerpt from Borodin's Symphony No. 2 (Ex. 11) illustrates a place where the baton beats two to the bar for strict tempo and goes into two with one subdivision for retards.

For two to the bar with one subdivision some conductors prefer to use a pattern which avoids two motions in the same direction. If Figures 20 and 21 seem uncomfortable after a reasonable trial, adopt Figure 43.

For two subdivisions after each main beat, in slow tempo, use Figure 23 (Ex. 12). Since the subdivisions proceed in the same direction as the main strokes, this pattern often proves uncomfortable when the tempo becomes fluid and brisk, as in Example 13. For such cases, Figure 24, with directions changing after each stroke, is more suitable. For tempos and melodic phrases where the second and fourth pulses are so weak as to be negligible, as in Example 14, Figure 25 is suggested. Note the breath pauses.

In some vocal passages, especially operatic, the freedom of the singer's interpretation is such that one must be prepared to give any of the patterns above in all sorts of contracted and extended forms. Such a case occurs in Mascagni's *Cavalleria Rusticana*, when Turiddu sings the first passages of the performance behind the scenes and adds to the conductor's problems by observing holds in certain places. Following a recording of this aria should prove excellent practice for a student. Usually the tenor places holds on the high *A* flat in the 19th bar (counting from the *andante*) and on the *E* natural in the 33rd bar; he gives each of the high *A* flats stentorian attention in the 39th bar, and holds the *F* in the 40th bar. The aria is usually beaten two to the bar for the first 33 bars and then six to the bar till the end. But a conductor can never count on beating it this way, since tenors often hold those notes which they think are their best. The value of the aria for practice lies in the fact that one never knows how the tenor will take it.

Another helpful example is the tenor Canio's "Vesti la giubba" from Leoncavallo's *Pagliacci*. Although this is taken in two to the bar generally, one must always watch for elongations calling for subdivisions. Measures 17 and 18, counting from the *adagio*, are sung *agitato*; measures 24 and 25 are beaten with one subdivision after each main stroke; measure 28 and the second half of measure 31 are beaten with two subdivisions after each main stroke. Again, some tenors seem to delight here in taxing the ingenuity of the conductor.

TWO MEASURES TAKEN AS ONE

This is a good place to consider an apparent exception to the rule that each measure should have its own down beat. Sometimes the tempo of

Ex. 15.   Beethoven: Symphony No. 5

Fig. 26

a piece is so rapid that the literal observance of this rule would confuse the watchers. In other places, especially at the end of some compositions, measures are grouped in phrases of two, which might easily have been written as one measure. In the oft-quoted examples from the *presto* of Beethoven's Fifth Symphony (Ex. 15), the strong pulses are obviously on the odd measures. Therefore, give the down beat for the first measure, the up beat for the second, and so on. Make the strokes as in Figure 26, that is, almost horizontal.

The beating of two measures as one gives a broader outline to phrases and will be practiced fairly often. It is useful in many Viennese waltzes where one feels the rhythm to be 6/4 rather than the written 3/4. At the ends of overtures where *forte* chords alternate with silent measures, this procedure should be followed. Giving strong beats on silent measures has been known to inveigle unwary players into embarrassing entrances. The conductor should give the chords with vigorous down beats and use the silent measures as up-beat preparations for the next entrance, a procedure which will result in obviously less tension.

Chapter Six

THREE BEATS TO THE BAR

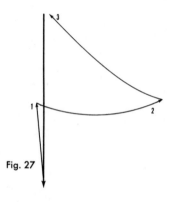

Fig. 27

METHOD OF BEATING

Triple rhythms, such as moderate 3/2, 3/4, 3/8, and brisk 9/8, i.e, rhythms which call for three strokes to the measure, are commonly beaten according to Figure 27. Practice on Examples 16 through 20.

In Figure 27 we have the usual down beat on the first stroke and up beat on the last, the third in this case. The second stroke fits into the pattern by going to the right, which direction immediately differentiates it from four to the bar, as we will see later. This distinction is most helpful when the rhythms shift from three to four or vice versa, because it shows the players the change in rhythm unmistakably.

Since the down beat has a special stress which may cause an unwanted accent or *sforzando*, a rebound is required. This brings the baton back to the center of the pattern and further serves to make the second and third strokes equal, though not so long as the down stroke. The palm faces downward in the rebound and turns a bit toward the beat it introduces, just before the center of the model is reached. Note that the rebound retraces half of the course of the down stroke through the air. The rebound itself swerves slightly *away from* the stroke it introduces, in

Ex. 16.   Brahms: Symphony No. 2

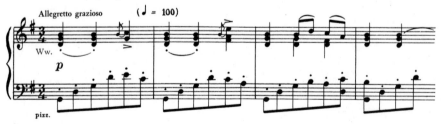

Ex. 17.   Schubert: "Unfinished" Symphony

Ex. 18.   Haydn: Symphony No. 6, "Surprise"

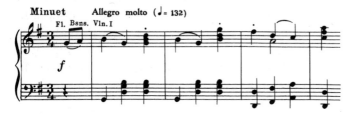

Ex. 19.   Tchaikovsky: Symphony No. 4

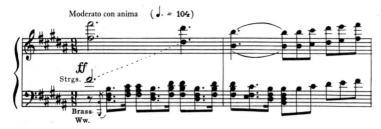

Ex. 20.   Mozart: Symphony in D, "Haffner"

this case going toward the left since the next stroke is going toward the right. Note that the rebound will diminish in length and stay nearer and nearer the bottom of the down beat as the music becomes more and more precise and *staccato*.

In the second and third strokes, the palm faces the ground, except in very *legato* and *adagio* passages, where it turns slightly toward the direction in which it is proceeding; and the curves of these strokes drop deeper and deeper below an imaginary straight line. In such cases, prepare the hand for the next stroke by connecting the motion gracefully with wrist turns.

Strive, by slow and careful practice, to obtain smooth connections between the strokes, seeing to it especially that the wrist and the palm do not turn before they should in the direction of the beat you are about to give. The chief danger in this pattern is that the wrist muscles may force the second stroke to bend upward somewhat, thus precipitating too short an up beat; the short up beat will then make the third beat look like a mere preparation for the next down beat, which development in turn causes the players to hurry and anticipate. Oddly enough, this tendency is far more common in the United States than abroad.

If special articulation is wanted on each stroke and the tempo is not quite broad enough for subdivisions, make a slight breath pause after each stroke, restoring the tempo by giving a slight preparation for the next stroke, as shown in Figure 28.

In certain types of compositions, for example, patriotic music and folk dances, the normal stresses are dislocated so that often the second or third beats become nearly as strong as the down beat. In some fluid waltzes, where one to the bar would be too rigid and where three to the bar as shown in Figure 27 would be too literal, the baton must execute a pattern where either the first and second beats, or the second and third beats, almost coalesce. In fairly rapid concert waltzes, there is no time for anything but a sort of combined one-two and three. In "The Ball" from Berlioz' "Fantastic" Symphony, the beat approaches more a one and two-three. For further examples of coalescent beats, see mazurkas, polonaises, and the like.

SUBDIVISIONS

In leisurely tempos calling for one subdivision after each main stroke in three to the bar (as in Examples 21 through 23), use Figure 29. This pattern may be varied by executing downward the first subdivision after the rebound of the down beat, returning at once to the center of the

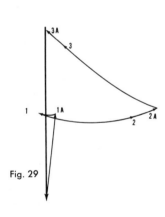

Fig. 28

Fig. 29

Ex. 21.   Beethoven: *Leonora Overture No. 3*

THREE BEATS TO THE BAR

Ex. 22.   Haydn: Symphony No. 4, "Clock"

Ex. 23.   Beethoven: Symphony No. 4

pattern. Breath pauses may also be observed when the phrasing implies them.

This is a good place to recall that, musically, beating three beats to the bar, each with one subdivision, is not the same procedure as beating two beats to the bar, each with two subdivisions, i.e., that three times two does *not* equal two times three *musically*. One of the best instances to illustrate this point occurs in the shifting time-signatures of the orchestral version of Ravel's *Alborado del Gracioso*, where the 6/8 is sometimes two times three and sometimes three times two, and where the interest rhythmically is heightened by the composer's use of 3/8 measures and also of 9/8 measures with accents on normally weak pulses.

See to it that the subdivisions are made with the wrist when the lower half of the arm is being used for the main beats, and with the lower half of the arm when the whole arm is being used for the main beats. There will otherwise be no contrast between the subdivisions and the main beats, and the performers may stress subordinate notes and phrases. Moreover, the whole effect will be hazy upon the eyes and hence the ears of those people in the audience who get many of their reactions by watching the conductor, as a sort of emotional guide pointing out to them what they are to look for.

To outline each main beat with two subdivisions in moderate tempos, as in 9/4, use Figure 30 (Ex. 24). For fluid tempos, use Figure 31 (Ex. 25). Figure 32 falls between them (Ex. 26).

In very fluid passages, Figure 31 will be found appropriate. The main strokes and subdivisions pass over each other back and forth in the

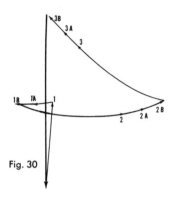

Fig. 30

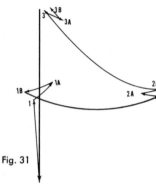

Fig. 31

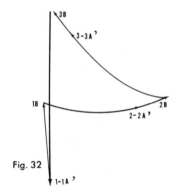

Fig. 32

Ex. 24. Wagner: *Tannhäuser Overture*

Ex. 25. Debussy: *L'Après-midi d'un faune* (Permission for reprint granted by Jean Jobert, Paris; Elkan-Vogel Co., Inc., U.S.A. copyright owners.)

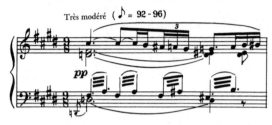

Ex. 26. Dukas: *The Sorcerer's Apprentice* (Permission for reprint granted by Durand et Cie, Paris, copyright owners; Elkan-Vogel Co., Inc., agents for U.S.A.)

air, and these changes in direction for each stroke, main and subordinate, make for clarity of pattern. Patterns can easily become confused when strokes go in the same direction in fairly rapid tempos and fluid phrasing. Figure 31 minimizes this danger.

In the comparatively rare cases where there are more than two subdivisions after a main stroke, simply add the necessary motions within the framework of the patterns already given. The principle to apply in such cases is this: where the number of subdivisions is odd (the main stroke is not being counted now), beat the main stroke and the first subdivision *away* from the next main stroke. In Figure 33 (Ex. 27) we have three subdivisions after the third main stroke. Give the third main stroke upward, the first and second subdivisions away and down, and the last subdivision up.

THREE BEATS TO THE BAR

Ex. 27.   Beethoven: Symphony No. 9

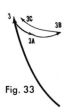

Fig. 33

When the number of subdivisions is even, again excluding the main stroke from the count, give the first subdivision *toward* the next main stroke. Such a case occurs in the final section of Hindemith's *Mathis der Maler*, where eight subdivisions follow the main stroke in four to the bar. This excerpt will be detailed later. Evolve patterns and practice these subdivisions when you reach four and six to the bar.

This device of swerving in the proper direction on the first subdivision, depending on whether the subdivisions total an odd or even number, will make the hand come out in the right place after the subdivisions so that it is prepared to give the next main stroke according to the proper pattern. It is also helpful to visualize patterns for three main beats in the following order: with one, three, and five subdivisions, and then with two, four, and six. Keeping these patterns in mind while practicing them will finally fix them in the hand, until they can be beaten automatically.

Complete measures with such subdivisions are rare, though passages requiring the outline of such subdivisions on part-measures do crop up occasionally. Therefore, practice patterns with subdivisions on some main beats and with no subdivisions on other main beats.

Chapter Seven

ONE BEAT TO THE BAR

DUPLE PULSES

Practically any rapid duple or triple rhythm may be taken one to the bar. The usual rhythms in this category are 2/4 and 3/4, though other pulses may be included. To execute single strokes to the bar neatly and to adapt them to varying odd and even pulses, changing phrases, syncopation, and shifting dynamics, are not such common accomplishments as one might expect from examining the seemingly simple outlines involved.

Figure 34 shows the common pattern for the duple pulse, one to the bar (practice on Examples 28 and 29). The strokes pass over each other in the air, of course. Similarity between models for two to the bar and one to the bar is only apparent, for while the upward stroke in one to the bar is a preparatory motion for the down beat, the second stroke for two to the bar is independent. In one to the bar the palm always faces the ground; in two to the bar the palm and wrist turn upward on the second stroke.

An unusual case for one to the bar occurs in the second movement of Borodin's Second Symphony (Ex. 30). The four notes reiterated on the horn and the subsequent syncopation (not reproduced here), often

Fig. 34

1

Ex. 28.   *Glinka: Russlan and Ludmilla Overture*

ONE BEAT TO THE BAR

Ex. 29.   Brahms: Symphony No. 2

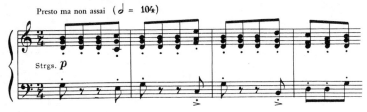

Ex. 30.   Borodin: Symphony No. 2. See also: Stravinsky, ''Firebird'' Suite (1919 version), ''Danse infernale du roi Kastcheï,'' the 6/4 at no. 33 in the score; Sibelius, Symphony No. 5, *Scherzo*.

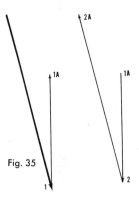

Fig. 35

preceded by a rest at the start of the measures, make this example very intriguing. Note that you are conducting two measures as one.

The tempo of this excerpt is fast enough to beat one to the bar comfortably, and the phrasing shows that two measures are grouped as one successively. To beat each bar at the designated speed and as a separate entity would dissect the line and give the phrasing an edgy *staccato*. By beating two bars as one (see Figure 35), the phrasing is expressed better, and the muscles of the arm and hand maintain their ease. In Figure 35, the main strokes rebound almost to the top of the pattern; both 1A's are at the same point. The two motions pass over the same places in the air, not as the two-dimensional lines of the printed page suggest. Make the odd strokes by *mentally* stressing the muscles of the hand and arm on the outside, and the even strokes by *mentally* stressing the muscles on the inside of the hand and arm, those closest to the body. The procedure is akin to changing fingers rapidly on the same note in pianoforte music. The alternation of muscles will make for grace. The players need not, of course, be aware that two bars are being conducted as one. The pace is so brisk and the strokes are so close together that performers will invariably interpret your beating as one to the bar. This procedure, beating groups of measures together as units, is of special importance in giving naturalness to the beat and clarity to phrases, and is of immense aid in memorizing.

Note the exciting effect which Stravinsky obtains toward the end of the "Danse infernale du roi Kastcheï" in the "Firebird" Suite (1919 version) by writing successively 3/4, 2/2, 6/4, and again 3/4. The 3/4 and 2/2 are taken one to the bar, as is the 6/4, and they may even be taken two bars in one stroke. The final eight bars in 4/4 of this section are cut in the concert version. From no. 37 in the score until the end, constituting twenty bars, one actually beats two bars to one stroke, or even two bars on a sweeping wide quasi down stroke and two bars on a wide sweeping quasi up stroke, making virtually four bars to one sweep. The passage offers a fascinating example of one to the bar with rising excitement.

SILENT BARS

In rapid tempos, for example at the ends of many overtures where smashing chords alternate with silent measures, there is always the danger of inadvertent entrances (Ex. 31). There is no opportunity for ambiguity if you give two measures as one, giving a strong beat on the chord and a weak one on the silent measure, with the suggestion that the latter is a preparatory up beat for the next chord, i.e., taking two bars as one.

TRIPLE PULSES

For brisk triple rhythms, one to the bar is also applicable, with certain differences, however, from the manner in which it is given for duple rhythms. In triple rhythms, the baton rests on the second pulse and

Ex. 32.   Brahms: *Symphony No. 2*

Fig. 36

↑ 3

↓ 1-2'

Ex. 33. Dvořák: Symphony No. 5, "New World" (By permission of the Oliver Ditson Company, copyright owner.)

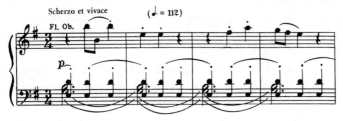

Ex. 34. Smetana: *Bartered Bride* Overture

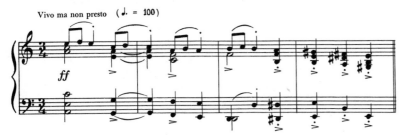

observes a breath pause, giving the third stroke as a preparation for the next down beat, i.e., as an inhalation for the exhalation which follows (Fig. 36). Letting the baton rebound to the top directly, without the breath pause, would cause the orchestra to try to catch the beat and hurry. Practice on Examples 32 and 33.

SHIFTED ACCENTS

In triple pulses with accents shifted away from the bar lines, as in Example 34, one may point up the accents by observing breath pauses at the ends of the strokes. This amounts in practice to an adaptation of Figure 35.

Waltzes in general, and Viennese waltzes in particular, should almost invariably be taken two bars as one, especially in *legato*. *Staccato* waltzes with accents on the start of each measure, of course, should be done one to the bar literally. Hum, for example, "The Merry Widow Waltz," which might easily have been written as 6/4 instead of 3/4; and note how the first and third bars, etc., have the strong accents, and the even bars, the secondary accents, thus forming two-bar groupings. In such cases, conduct two bars as one, with a pattern resembling an almost horizontal "figure 8," which imparts a swinging and lilting suggestion. Figure 37 illustrates the model, with Figure 38 showing more closely what meets the eye.

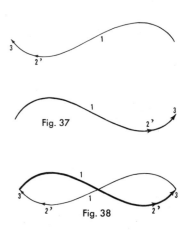

Fig. 37

Fig. 38

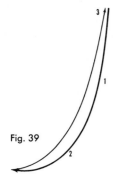

Fig. 39

The patterns for beating waltzes vary perhaps more than any other kind of pattern. The conductor must be prepared to bring out any of the three pulses, though he is virtually giving only one to the bar. Figure 39 suggests a method of shifting the emphasis to the second pulse, and Figures 40 and 41 to the third pulse.

Any of the waltzes by Waldteufel, Gungl, Ziehrer, Lehar, and the Strausses furnish many scores of examples of constantly shifting emphases in three-quarter time taken one to the bar. Practice them assiduously.

For rapid quintuple and even greater numbers of pulses taken one to the bar, see Chapter 11.

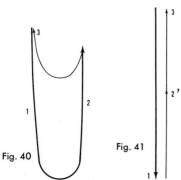

Fig. 40

Fig. 41

Chapter Eight

FOUR BEATS TO THE BAR

METHOD OF BEATING

Four strokes to the bar is used in moderate 4/4 or C, brisk 12/8, etc., wherever four pulses may be comfortably beaten to the measure (Exs. 35 and 36). The commonly accepted model is shown in Figure 42. Many passages in 2/4, taken at a leisurely pace and implying subdivision, may be appropriately taken according to Figure 43, adapted from Figure 42. Many conductors prefer to use Figure 43 in order to avoid two motions in the same direction (cf. Figures 20 and 21). Figure 43 is also especially useful when going from two to four strokes to the bar and vice versa.

   This is the first time we have considered a pattern going in all four directions, down, left, right, and up. Note the following points in this model. The rebound swerves slightly *away* from the stroke it precedes, this time toward the right, since the next stroke, the second, is to proceed toward the left. (Recall that it swerves toward the left in three to the bar.) This rebound in the opposite direction prepares the hand for the second stroke. All strokes except the first dip under an imaginary straight line connecting the extreme ends of the strokes. The third stroke dips under the second. The first and third strokes are practically equal in length, the third beat being slightly shorter than the first; while the two

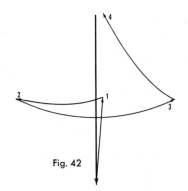

Fig. 42

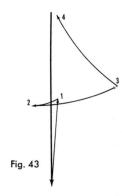

Fig. 43

Ex. 35.   Franck: Symphony in D Minor

Ex. 36. Schubert: Symphony No. 7, "Great"

weakest beats, the second and fourth, are almost equal in length to each other and are each about one half as long as the two strong beats.

The first stroke, as always, is down; the last is up. The third stroke, requiring underlining as the secondary stress in the rhythm, goes to the right, thus forcing the attention of the performers to it. (In former days it was often the practice to give the third stroke inward to the left, as is still done occasionally in Europe. Taking the third stroke to the left, how-ever, weakens its focusing power, especially in the theater pit, where many of the players find it difficult to see the baton against the body of the conductor in the usual dim lighting.) The principle of stressing the secondary accent by executing it to the right applies also with five, six, and seven beats to the bar. In four to the bar, this method leaves only one direction for the weak second beat, to the left.

This is an appropiate place to point out that a 4/4 rhythm is not to be conducted or played as if it were a combination of successive 2/4's. A 4/4 has one strong and one secondary stress for each measure; a 2/4 has alternating strong and weak stresses. This point may seem too simple to belabor, yet one occasionally hears the opening of Wagner's *Die Meister-singer* Overture with two accents to each bar, as if the time-signature were 2/4 instead of 4/4.

Beating *very* slow four to the bar looks easy. In reality, it is no simple matter to hold together a large group of players in any very slow tempo, for the baton tends to sag and to lose its power at the ends of beats. In many passages, subdivisions are not the solution because they would not translate the outline of the musical text. It is difficult to maintain vitality under such circumstances, especially when the tempo becomes almost,

FOUR BEATS TO THE BAR

though not quite, broad enough for subdivisions. The tendency of the wrist muscles is to force the first stroke slightly inward, the second stroke upward, the third upward (veering in the opposite direction, of course), and the last stroke downward, especially when the student desires a strong attack on the succeeding down beat. The resulting pattern, by no means uncommon, looks something like Figure 44.

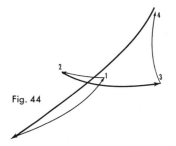

Fig. 44

To a watcher this succession of motions, when done briskly, seems to be alternating gesticulations almost up and down. When you realize that many instrumentalists who have long periods of rest count the number of their silent measures by the number of down beats they *think* they see, the danger of an unfortunate entrance becomes apparent. See to it that a pretty close plumb line is made on one, that two and three are practically horizontal, and that four ascends directly after the initial short curve under the imaginary straight line connecting the extremities of the stroke. It is far better to exaggerate the geometric outlines of Figure 42 at the start, and to strive gradually for grace, than to run the risk of slovenliness. Remember that knowing what you want and showing what you want are two very different matters.

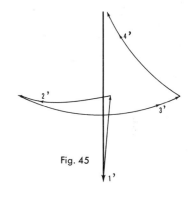

Fig. 45

Here are two suggestions for maintaining a steady pattern in four to the bar when no subdivisions are called for. The first suggestion is to make a breath pause near the end of each stroke and then to give a slight preparatory motion for the following stroke, as in Figure 45. This pattern is not to be confused with four strokes subdivided, i.e., eight pulses, where each stroke, main or subordinate, is independent.

The second suggestion, for very broad *legato,* is to give rounded lines for the strokes with rebounds for each (see Fig. 46). Here again the difficulty is that the baton moves so slowly that it is hard for the players to distinguish the ends of the strokes. This difficulty can be overcome by observing tiny breath pauses and a round rebound for each stroke. The rebound becomes in effect a preparatory motion for the next stroke. These breath pauses are not strictly stops; the players anticipate their length by means of their time and space sense, already oriented by the general context. To repeat: when the tempo is moderate, beating out a pattern at the same rate of speed keeps the music going naturally; but when the baton moves very slowly and no subdivisions are justified, tiny breath pauses and rounded rebound-preparatory motions give the players something to hold to, which they need. The end of the stroke in such cases is sometimes called the "click," as if the baton were touching an imaginary point. This click and the occasions when it is appropriate must be determined by each conductor for himself. It varies much with different texts and with individual temperaments.

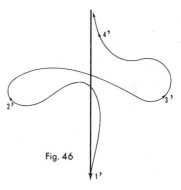

Fig. 46

SUBDIVISIONS, EIGHT PULSES

Some conductors take everything too rapidly, others too slowly. Still others take slow passages too slowly and rapid passages too rapidly. Sometimes the cause is temperamental; sometimes the transgressor is attempting to obtain contrast through exaggeration or is incapable of delicacy and nuance. In the same category are the conductors who apparently see no difference between *ff* and *fff* or between *pp* and *ppp*.

Another error is committed by conductors who overbeat by painfully indicating every unimportant sixteenth and thirty-second note, and who suggest a fencer in a funk. At the opposite extreme is the conductor who underbeats by leaving out subdivisions, a sign of mental laziness or undeveloped technique. The whole problem is one of knowing where to indicate subdivisions, so that the performers have guidance in crucial places, the main line is kept moving, and the clarity of the baton patterns is maintained.

Go over the passage you are to conduct; and decide whether it requires subdivisions anywhere to keep the baton moving so that the players have something to guide them, or whether subdivisions would confuse the pattern in rapid tempos so that the baton would move too rapidly for the players to follow. If you use subdivisions, see that they are given with the wrist and the main strokes with the arm, so that the pattern does not appear cluttered up.

For precise and pointed eight pulses to the bar, use Figure 47 (Ex. 37). For broad eight pulses, use Figure 48, noting that the first subdivision is near the center of the pattern (Ex. 38).

When you have flowing passages like Example 39, and when you and your orchestra know each other well, use as a variant Figure 49, which gives the first and third main strokes special prominence and relegates the other pulses to the background.

Ex. 37.   Weber: Oberon Overture

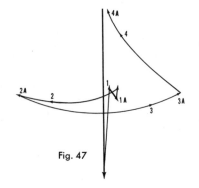

Fig. 47

Ex. 38. Brahms: Symphony No. 2. See also: Bach, Suite 1 in D ("G String Aria").

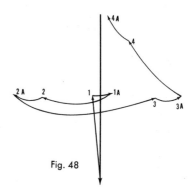

Fig. 48

STACCATO AND SYNCOPATION

The next pattern, Figure 50, is suitable for *staccato* and syncopated passages like Example 40. It stresses the rebound on the first stroke and the subdivisions themselves. To obtain a clearer outline, lower a bit the main strokes on two, three, and four (not on the first stroke, since it changes direction with its rebound) and come forward on the first part and inward on the second part of each stroke. Point the wrist in the same direction for each main beat and subdivisions thereof, to demarcate clearly the main pulses and their subdivisions.

In genuine beating of subdivisions, the wrist motions are not to be skimped as if they were merely preparatory uphooks (see Figure 45) for the succeeding main beats. Give them weight and body and full value.

Ex. 39. Beethoven: Symphony No. 1

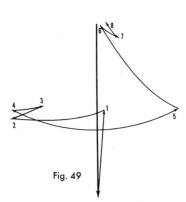

Fig. 49

Ex. 40. Wagner: *Rienzi Overture*

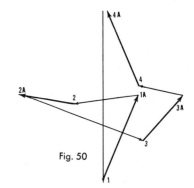

Fig. 50

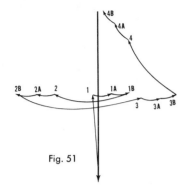

Fig. 51

The first subdivision after the main beat's short rebound may be given near the bottom of the first stroke and have its own rebound; or it may be given near the center of the pattern after the full rebound of the main stroke.

SUBDIVISIONS, TWELVE PULSES

For rhythms requiring that each main beat have two subdivisions, as in slow 12/8 (Ex. 41), use Figure 51. The first two subdivisions may come at the bottom of the stroke or near the center. They may also jut out from the center of the pattern toward the right. If they are given at the bottom of the pattern, each subdivision should have its own rebound.

Where the tempo is fluid but not quite rapid enough for main beats only (see Example 42), and where main beats and subdivisions going in the same direction (as in Figure 51) would appear too fast for the watcher's comfort, Figure 52 offers a neat solution. Using Figure 51 would give an impression of deliberation not suitable here. See to it that the *first* subdivision (1A) veers to the left, i.e., *toward* the next main beat (cf. Figure 31). It is important in this pattern that the main beats stand out in clear relief, a contrast which can be assured by using the wrist for the subdivisions and the hand and arm for the main beats.

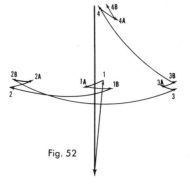

Fig. 52

Sometimes the first subdivision of each main beat is so slight and fluid that Figure 53 would translate it into the proper pattern (cf. Figure 25). Simply leave out the first subdivision of Figure 52 and observe a breath pause instead, with the second subdivision imparting a feeling of preparation for the next main stroke. Music for which this pattern is suitable usually occurs in *ritardandi* and *accelerandi*. It would require encyclopedic space to illustrate every variation as we go on from this point, and such detailed illustration is not needed or wise, for the student should now be able to apply a principle once it has been considered.

Other good examples in this genre of time-beating may be seen in the slow movements of Brahms's Second and Third Symphonies and at the start of Sibelius' Symphony No. 5.

In *grandioso, allargando,* and *staccatissimo* passages, all subdivisions as well as all main beats may be given their own rebounds. It should be gratuitous to add that such extremes are to be reserved for special occasions, or else anticlimaxes will result, especially in the music of composers like Tchaikovsky and Wagner.

In the exceptional cases where more than two subdivisions occur, adapt patterns as was done in Figure 33.

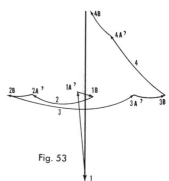

Fig. 53

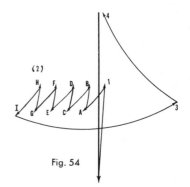

(2)

Fig. 54

Our final illustration of twelve pulses (Ex. 43) is taken from Hindemith's *Mathis der Maler,* in the "Versuchung des Heiligen Antonius," page 38 of the Schott small score. Beat according to Figure 54.

The passage is taken four to the bar. The down stroke returns at once to the center of the pattern, where it remains for the hold. At the right time, the baton executes the short subdivisions (nine in all) as part of the second stroke. The second note is the same as the first, and tied to it; hence a stroke to the left suffices to indicate it and the release simultaneously. The accent marks on the next eight notes show that the composer wants each note articulated. There are, then, nine parts to this second stroke. They are given simply by indicating the release to the *left* center (after the rebound of the down stroke to the center), the next eighth a bit to the right, the next a bit to the left, and so on, in orthodox fashion. Note again that the first stroke goes to the left, to make the hand and baton come out at the proper place to proceed as usual with the next stroke, in this case, to the right for the third pulse (see Chapter 6). Split the second beat in the third bar. The passage is reaffirmed on the next page and is executed similarly; the conductor has the added chore of bringing in the lower brass and strings by splitting the third stroke.

Measure 10 is done as was measure 1, except that here the trombones, cellos, and basses enter, with a hold of their own on the rebound of the down stroke, which they release on the last (ninth) subdivision. The third stroke may be split to show the trombones, cellos, and basses where they enter again. The first three pages of the small score offer an unusual example of practice in free orchestral utterance.

Ex. 44. Strauss: *Also sprach Zarathustra* (Reprinted with the permission of the copyright owner, C. F. Peters Corporation, New York.)

FOUR BEATS TO THE BAR

There is perhaps the danger, in the necessarily detailed and pigeon-holed remarks above, of forgetting that patterns are to the conductor merely what scales are to the instrumentalist, to be adapted rather than to be applied literally. A passage may require various combinations of patterns to translate successfully its mood and line. The more skillful and individual an interpreter becomes, the more accurately will he interpret the mood of his music, by applying the spirit and not the letter of these remarks and patterns.

The student is to devise his own patterns for the excerpt from Strauss's *Also sprach Zarathustra* (Ex. 44).

Chapter Nine

SIX BEATS TO THE BAR

METHOD OF BEATING

Patterns for beating six to the bar are among the most varied of all rhythmical patterns in practice. This is all to the good, for one pattern will often fit a particular musical text when none other would do quite so well. Such variants may be thought of in the same light as are different fingerings for instrumental passages, which individual interpreters take according to personal taste and training; the agility of their hands; their nationality and tradition; the preceding and succeeding passages; the mood, nuances, and phrasing of the music; and other qualifying factors.

Six to the bar, is, in a sense, four to the bar with weak beats added after the second and fourth strokes. The first stroke is down; the last is up; and the secondary accent (here on four) is to the right. The weak second and fourth beats naturally fit in toward the left, after the initial rebound, which veers toward the right *away from* the beat which follows; while the weak fifth beat fits in toward the right after the strong fourth beat. Figure 55 illustrates the commonly used pattern for slow *legato* passages like Example 45.

Ex. 45.   Brahms: Symphony No. 1. See also: Wagner, Prelude to *Parsifal*; Delius, *On Hearing the First Cuckoo in Spring.*

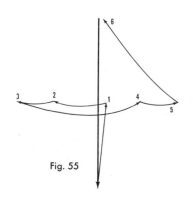

Fig. 55

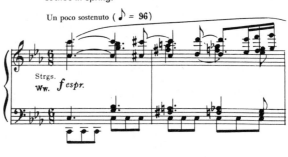

Ex. 46.   Berlioz: "Fantastic" Symphony

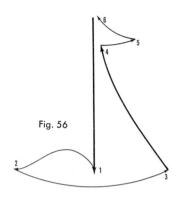

Fig. 56

When the tempo proceeds in a leisurely way but not quite so slowly as the premeditated pace which implies a strong full stroke on the second beat, give the second beat downward with its own rebound. It is often quite feasible to give the first three strokes all downward, each having its own rebound, in which case the second and third strokes are each half-length. Examples suitable for such procedure are to be found in the second movement of Brahms's Symphony No. 4, in the 6/8 movement of Mozart's "Linz" Symphony (K. 425), and in the closing sections of Strauss's *Ein Heldenleben*.

A pattern much used for fluid passages where one and four stand out in bold relief and the other beats are subordinated, like Example 46, is shown in Figure 56.

Note that Figure 56 is really a variant of Figure 23, and is used for two to the bar with two subdivisions after each main beat. It is of great service in bridging an *accelerando* from two to six to the bar, and vice versa. Much salon music lends itself to this sort of outline.

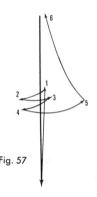

Fig. 57

When there are bars of unvarying "neutral" phrases, or bars where only the first and last strokes stand out and yet where the count should be kept going, Figure 57 may be used. Note again that in even pulses, as here, the second stroke goes to the right; in odd pulses (five and seven), it goes to the left in order to have the hand come out right for the last up beat. This pattern is of special value in operatic background music.

SYNCOPATION

In beating syncopation, where the accents temporarily come on one, three, and five instead of on the normal one and four (Ex. 47), use the pattern shown in Figure 58. Note that the strong pulses initiate new directions, an important principle to remember.

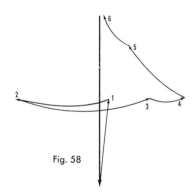

Fig. 58

In some passages, such as Example 48, the second and fifth beats are so subordinated that it is advisable to elide them in patterns. While this elision may be done on both up and down beats, it is often advisable to elide on one part of the measure while beating out the other part of the measure fully, or even, at times, to go from these elided patterns to two or six to the bar. Figures 59, 60, and 61 illustrate the usual combinations (cf. Figures 25 and 32).

Ex. 47. Debussy: *La Mer* (Permission for reprint granted by Durand et Cie, Paris, copyright owners; Elkan-Vogel Co., Inc., agents for U.S.A.) See also: Strauss, parts of *Ein Heldenleben*.

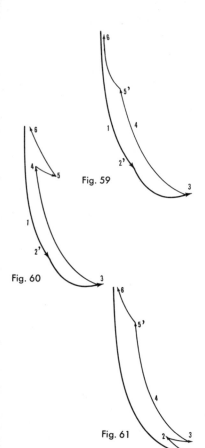

Fig. 59

Fig. 60

Fig. 61

Ex. 48. Thomas: *Mignon Overture*. See also: Offenbach, *Orpheus in Hades Overture*.

SUBDIVISIONS

Subdivisions for six to the bar are uncommon. Example 49 needs one subdivision, and Figure 62 gives a pattern for it. For two or more subdivisions, the student can evolve his own patterns, by applying suggestions given for such cases in four to the bar. The chief point to remember is that the number of motions going in the same direction should be reduced to a minimum.

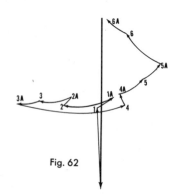

Fig. 62

Ex. 49. Delius: *Summer Night on the River* (By permission of Oxford University Press. World copyright transferred to Oxford University Press, 1930.)

SIX BEATS TO THE BAR

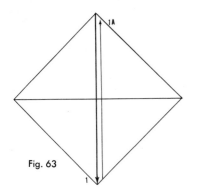

Fig. 63

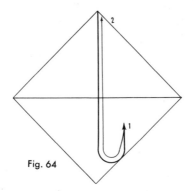

Fig. 64

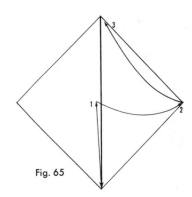

Fig. 65

REVIEW OF PATTERNS

This is a good place for the student to make a thorough review of all that has been presented up to this point and to fix again in his mind the principles outlined thus far. The student should have a clear mental picture of all the patterns presented and of their proper proportions. To this end, five representative patterns are inscribed within diamonds (Figs. 63 through 67). They should aid in visualization of what has been discussed.

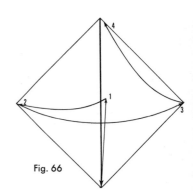

Fig. 66

The student should practice beating Example 50, as a further review. Detailed and unmistakable characterization of the note values should be the constant aim. Be sure that the motions of the baton which delineate the start of a new note have more body than other motions. Thus, when you beat the measure with four quarter notes, give each motion weight and body according to the main and secondary accents; but when you beat the measure with a half note between two quarters, give the third beat less body than the other beats. In the phrase consisting of dotted eighths followed by sixteenths, make the baton split each stroke so that the second part of the stroke points up the sixteenths, unlike the almost even splitting when eighths succeed each other. The student is here left to solve the other problems involved in beating patterns for the phrases in Example 50. He should make many additional examples in skeletal form, both of his own invention and from standard works.

Some of the best possible practice in clearly delineating note values may be obtained by conducting folk songs, hymns, and chorales.

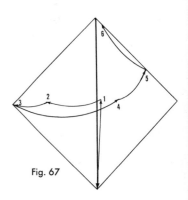

Fig. 67

Ex. 50

Chapter Ten

ATTACKS

ON THE BEAT

More than one famous conductor has been quoted as saying that the most difficult part of a conductor's technique is the attack, and most students are inclined to agree with this statement. It is not too much to say that a conductor's innate gift for leadership may best be gaged quickly by the results he achieves on attacks. Every musical work has a beginning, and it is of this beginning that auditors are most aware. The student, therefore, should pay special attention to this matter of attacks and entrances, which set the mood for subsequent reactions in both the orchestra and the audience.

It has already been said that a conductor must be mentally ahead of his players at all times. A corollary to this principle is that every time the baton stops (breath pauses excepted), some sort of preparatory motion *must* be given to the performers before they can enter again without ragged and frayed edges. This means that at the ends of holds and cut-offs, and at important changes in tempo, mood, time-signature, style, nuance, volume, instrumentation, etc., there *must* be warnings indicated in some definite, logical, and comprehensible manner to the executants. The performer is waiting, or he should be, for a signal of what is coming and for the *exact* point of entrance. It is the least he is entitled to. When such intimations are correctly given to the player or singer, he will imitate them and translate them into music.

To secure attention suddenly, and literally to jerk the players into tenseness, some conductors (though much more formerly than recently) are wont to dispense with the usual preparation. Instead, they poise the baton histrionically in the air until every eye in the orchestra and also in the audience is upon it, and then bring it down with tremendous drive,

thrusting it forward at the same time. At the end of the stroke, the performers catch the beat which waits there dramatically. Thereupon the
conductor executes a rebound, which serves simultaneously to cut off the
first stroke and to prepare the next one. This technique often proves
effective theater, but it should be reserved for experienced conductors
and the proper occasions.

Let us consider the case as you stand ready to start a musical performance. You raise your baton so that there is a direct line of vision from
your eyes through the tip of your baton into the eyes of the performers.
If your baton now descends without warning, the performers will come
in at various places *after* your baton has started. They have no possible
way of knowing what is coming in style, speed, and dynamics. Thus the
down beat itself will, in actual practice, become the preparation; and the
rebound will become the point of entrance. The case is the same when
the orchestra is playing and it is necessary to show a forthcoming change.
To avoid confusing the players under such conditions, the conductor
should continue as usual until the last pulse before the change, and then
use this last pulse, already established, to indicate the ensuing change.
By that time, it is too late for the performers to change on the "last"
pulse, so they will come in correctly on the next. The importance of this
psychological principle must be understood at the outset, for its applications are many, especially in sudden accents and *sforzandos*.

To repeat: after the baton has stopped, some sort of preparation *must*
be given if the orchestra is to start again with a clean attack. The stop
may be occasioned by holds; cut-offs (releases); breaks; ends of phrases,
sections, or movements; or other causes. Once the baton has stopped,
the situation is exactly the same as if the music had not been played
before at all, as if the motion were being made for the first time. The
players must be prepared for the next attack.

There are, obviously, only four general directions for the baton to
take: down, up, right, and left. Preparations for these directions should,
therefore, be applicable to any pattern. In theory, one should give the
preceding beat as preparation, in the same style, speed, and volume as
the actual point of entrance. In practice, the preceding beat is adapted
and adjusted in length and direction toward the actual point of entrance.
The preparation is of the nature of an inhalation, followed by an exhalation (the attack), with a breath pause between them, similar to a person's
actual breathing. The preparation must never be longer than one unit
of beating to the measure; for example, when there are two strokes in a
2/4, the preparatory motion consists of a quarter note; when there are
six strokes in a 6/8 passage, the preparation consists of an eighth note.

The essence of a good preparatory beat is to suggest so well the speed, style, and volume of the entrance that the performers subconsciously imitate. In effect, the conductor gives one unit of the actual entrance alone; there is a breath pause; then the players imitate as he beats the actual entrance with them.

At this point, review what has been said about attacks on the down and up beats in Chapter Five.

LEGATO AND STACCATO

In a *legato* preparation, the palm points to the entrance; in *staccato*, the back of the hand points to the entrance. The force and length of the preparatory stroke vary according to the beat it introduces. Do not forget that the preparatory stroke, the breath pause, and the attack literally imitate natural breathing.

The preparation for an up beat is essentially the same in any pattern and is given like an up-hook which drops slightly at the start. To give the whole down beat might trap unwary or overanxious players into a premature attack. The preparation here, which is really a down beat adjusted in length and direction and executed to suggest an inhalation, has a curve the depth of which is greater for *legato* than for *staccato*, more energetic for *forte* than for *staccato*, and more precise as the tempo quickens. During the preparation, one should point the back of the hand and the wrist toward the place where the up stroke starts, and then turn them upward for the entrance itself.

For entrances on a smooth beat to the left (the second beat in four, the second and third in six, etc.) or to the right (the second beat in three, the third in four, the fourth and fifth in six, etc.), use the half down beat and rebound as preparation (Figs. 68 and 69, Ex. 51).

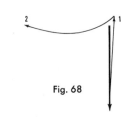

Fig. 68

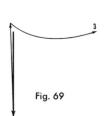

Fig. 69

Ex. 51.   Gluck: *Iphigenia in Aulis* Overture. See also: Berlioz, "Fantastic" Symphony, "Scenes in the Country," at start.

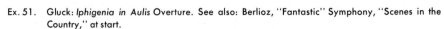

Adapt Figures 70 and 71 to *forte-staccato* passages like Example 52, to assure incisiveness in the attack. Point the back of the hand and wrist toward the entrance and change them when it is reached.

Ex. 52. Bizet: "L'Arlésienne" Suite, No. 1

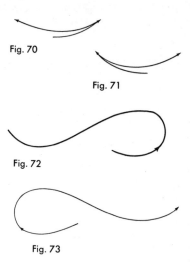

Fig. 70

Fig. 71

Fig. 72

Fig. 73

Some conductors give a half-length down beat to prepare this sort of entrance (see Figures 72 and 73). The curve at the entrance serves to suggest compulsion.

"FREE" ENTRANCES

Thus far, indications of entrances (at the beginning of strokes) have been fairly easy to give, but the problems become more demanding when we meet what are sometimes termed "free" entrances. Our first task is to decide how to indicate entrances which come on exactly half of a stroke. Since we cannot give more than one unit of beating in the whole measure as a preparation for an attack without giving the watchers a wholly false intimation of what is coming, we split our stroke so that one half serves as a preparation and one half as the point of actual entrance.

The first half of the stroke drops and goes slightly forward; the latter half retraces the path of the first half. The first half of the stroke is weak and short and like an exhalation; the latter half is of equal length, but strong and like an inhalation. The next attack is, of course, another exhalation. The split stroke ends in the center of the pattern, where it is in position to proceed in any of four directions: right, left, down, or up. Figures 74 through 77 show four representative entrances exactly on the half stroke: within the down beat, within a stroke to the left, within a stroke to the right, and within the up beat. Practice these patterns on Examples 53 through 56 respectively.

Note that the preparation for an attack within the up beat is made at the top of the stroke; preparations for the other types, at the usual places in the patterns. Note further that the preparation for the half

Ex. 53. Schumann: *Manfred Overture*

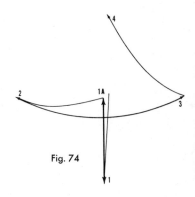

Fig. 74

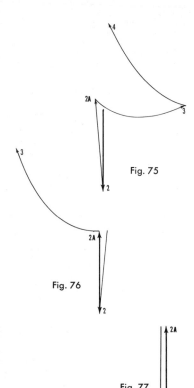

Fig. 75

Fig. 76

Fig. 77

Ex. 54. Alexander: *Morning Prayer* (By permission of the composer.)

Ex. 55. Mendelssohn: Symphony No. 4

Ex. 56. Goldmark: *Rustic Wedding*

beat and the entering note should not take more time *together* than any of the other strokes. The introductory strokes may go slightly in the direction where they would normally go in the pattern and dip forward at the same time.

WITHIN STROKES

The indication of entrances within a stroke depends as much upon suggestive powers as upon actual technical procedures. Such powers naturally cannot be translated into written directions; they usually come with experience. The general technical rule is to give the whole stroke of which the actual entrance is part.

In practice, the stroke is adjusted to the special circumstances of the case. The baton is thrust toward the actual point of entrance, with a precise motion as if it were tapping an object at the actual point of entrance. The conductor at that point is actually beating beforehand the note or group of notes which comprise the part-entrance. He then observes a breath pause of exactly the same length as this stroke. The players imitate his motion on the breath pause. Thereupon, at the attack the

Ex. 57.   Beethoven: Symphony No. 6

Ex. 58.   Rimsky-Korsakoff: *Scheherezade* (Copyright by M. P. Belaieff Editions. Used by permission of sole agents, Boosey & Hawkes.) See also: "La Marseillaise"; Rossini, *Barber of Seville* Overture.

baton and the orchestra function together. In other words, the conductor has given one unit of beating, which is comprised in his motion and the breath pause. If this sounds too complicated in description, it will be found not nearly so in actual practice.

In giving preparations where one third, two thirds, etc., of a stroke are concerned, a conductor further uses the principle of imitation. (For one third of a stroke, practice on Example 57; for two thirds, on Example 58.) Thus, in bringing in an entrance on the third part of a stroke, as one does in so many beginnings of symphonic *scherzi*, one should thrust the baton upward in exactly the length of time taken up by the entering note, observe a breath pause of the same length to allow the players to imitate the thrust as they enter, and then bring down the baton for the next measure with the players. This procedure applies, of course, to similar "free" entrances on any stroke.

In each case, the duration of the preparatory stroke should be the same as if the conductor had given the whole stroke of which the entrance is part. To put the matter into other words, he beats the entrance once; he waits for the instrumentalists to play it; then both proceed to the next measure together.

It is suggested here that theory of time-beating should rarely be presented to orchestra players. The beat should be so suggestive and *seem* so logical and inevitable that they will rarely have questions. Instrumentalists are practical; they want to execute and follow and are usually impatient of explanations. These should be needless except under unusual circumstances. This generalization holds especially in the case of prep-

Ex. 59.   Mozart: *Magic Flute Overture*

Ex. 60.   Mozart: *Magic Flute Overture*

arations. If the attack is not knife-edged, the fault will probably lie in your own technique. Cast about and analyze it, and try to discover why it has failed to achieve the results you are after.

The opening measures from Mozart's overture to *The Magic Flute* (Ex. 59) and also measures 97–102 just before the *Allegro* (Ex. 60) often cause concern. In Example 59, give the usual preparation for a down beat; then give the strong down beat with a rebound to the center of the pattern; hold the baton motionless for a bit to accentuate the tension; execute the second stroke to the left as though you were cutting off; and underline the suggestion by a slight downward motion of the left hand, *immediately* giving the third beat to the right for the quarter rest. Now hold the baton motionless for as long as you wish to observe the hold, which, from the conductor's point of view, comes between two rests. Preclude a premature attack by holding up the open left palm in a warning attitude. Since one rest follows another here, beat the first rest *immediately*, or some one may be drawn into a premature attack.

Now prepare for the sixteenth-note entrance by letting the baton drop and rebound in exactly the length of time of the sixteenth note;

observe a breath pause of the same length; and give the next down stroke with the players. The players should enter directly after your rebound, while you are observing the breath pause. Drop the baton as the players proceed to the second measure. If your preparatory motion for the sixteenth note has been executed with conviction, the players will imitate it, and you will all reach the next attack at the same time. Repeat the procedure for the second measure. In the third measure, the first violins play the thirty-second note triplet group, and they must be brought in together. Again, drop your baton and make it rebound in the same length of time as their attack. During your breath pause the violins will enter, imitating your preparatory motion. You next give the down beat *with* the players for the start of the fourth measure, which is taken four to the bar.

An excellent exercise may be made by changing the length of the sixteenth notes here and practicing the different preparatory strokes made necessary by each change. Write out the excerpt so that the sixteenth notes are successively eighths, thirty-seconds, and sixty-fourths; and make every effort to give your preparations so that each one translates its entrances accurately. Since this sort of attack depends as much upon psychological factors as upon technical, try to have a pianist follow you. Better still, try to practice on a few players, including preferably at least one representative of each section of the orchestra. If necessary, rearrange the chords so that they are complete. To inveigle players, alternate as a player yourself and let the others take turns conducting the passage. Include in your rehearsal the *adagio* before the *allegro* (Ex. 60).

Give the first stroke in Example 60 with a short, light beat to indicate the quarter rest, and observe a breath pause. Thrust the second stroke toward the left, as if you were tapping an imaginary object at its end. The next two strokes are orthodox. In the second bar, give the first stroke downward, the second to the right top of the pattern. Wait there to indicate the hold. In the third measure, indicate the rest on the first quarter with a light beat. The rest of the passage has precedents in the previous measures of these two excerpts.

Ex. 61.   Beethoven: Symphony No. 7

In measures 298–300 of the first movement of Beethoven's Seventh Symphony (Ex. 61), the entrances to the two successive holds offer another example of places requiring neat attacks, which were found very difficult not only by Beethoven himself but also by many a conductor after him. Part of the difficulty arises from the fact that the sixteenth notes just before the holds are in the wood winds and are *piano*.

At this stage, do not trouble yourself about the technique of holds. Concentrate on their preparation. Conduct the passage without the holds. Two to the bar is the correct beat for the passage. Practice further by transforming the sixteenth notes successively into eighths, thirty-seconds, and sixty-fourths. Return to this exercise later on when holds are being considered, and practice it then with your added technique.

DIRECTLY AFTER THE STROKE

Attacks coming directly after the stroke has started are among the most instructive and interesting in the whole domain of conducting technique. The opening motif of Beethoven's Fifth Symphony (Ex. 62) is probably the most famous example of this type of attack.

The beat here is one to the bar (really, two bars taken as one). The initial downward thrust of the baton (on the rest), which immediately rebounds to the top of the pattern ready for the next measure, gives the players the unit of measurement for *each* of the succeeding eighth notes. The baton observes a breath pause while the players sound the three eighth notes. Thereupon, the baton starts beating again, while the players proceed to the second measure. Continue to disregard the holds and practice this passage as if they were not there.

It was formerly the practice, and it is one seen even today, for a conductor on occasion to beat out a few measures silently in order to insure a clean attack on this passage. Such procedure admits lack of adequate baton technique and suggestive control of the players. An orchestra of the requisite standard to play Beethoven's Fifth Symphony needs no such babying.

Another procedure sometimes encountered is that a conductor holds

Ex. 62. Beethoven: Symphony No. 5

ATTACKS

his hands aloft, beats a preparatory motion with his left hand alone, and then brings both hands down, thus giving *two* preparations, which are unjustified. If the conductor gives the proper preparation on the first eighth rest, with the necessary inner conviction, assurance, and authority, the attack should be clean. But since some orchestras have been wrongly trained in this passage, they may have some trouble in "un-learning" it.

Of Examples 63 through 66, which are for the student to mull over, the one from Richard Strauss's *Don Juan* (Ex. 63) may be taken as representative. For this excerpt, thrust the baton upward and forward as a preparation and as a means of shocking the players into attention, keeping the baton near the center of the pattern. Time this forward-upward stroke to make it exactly the tempo at which you want the players to execute *each* of the following sixteenths. Observe a breath pause to allow the players to give these sixteenths. Then bring the baton still higher for the up beat on the second half of the measure. Proceed with the players on the down beat, in orthodox fashion.

Ex. 63. Strauss: *Don Juan* (Reprinted with the permission of the copyright owner, C. F. Peters Corporation, New York.)

Ex. 64. Wagner: *Flying Dutchman Overture*

Ex. 65. Weber: *Oberon Overture*

Ex. 66.   Sibelius: Symphony No. 5 (By permission of Wilhelm Hansen, Copenhagen, and G. Schirmer, Inc., New York.)

Ex. 67.   Beethoven: Symphony No. 9

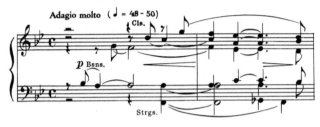

INVOLVING RESTS

Attacks involving rests which take up a whole unit of beating are treacherous, unless one uses the rest itself as part of the attack. If a preparation is given for the rest itself, there is always danger that some unwary player will enter before he should, especially during orchestral accompaniment to recitative and solo instruments. To illustrate, at the beginning of the slow movement of Beethoven's Ninth Symphony (Ex. 67), which is beaten in four subdivided as eight, give the down beat as the preparatory motion and bring in the second bassoon on the first subdivision.

In the overture to Wagner's *Rienzi*, at the tenth measure before the change of time-signature to *alla breve*, there is a drum roll (Ex. 68). This measure brings in the bassoons, trombones, and tuba on the second stroke (four to the bar) after a quarter rest on the first beat. The safest procedure

Ex. 68.   Wagner: *Rienzi Overture*

here is to beat this measure by giving a strong beat with an equally long rebound back to the top of the stroke, holding the baton ostentatiously high in the air with the wrist pointing upward, so that the players can see that a down beat is next. The drum roll thus becomes a quasi hold. When you are ready, give the down beat (which occupies the rest) for the bassoon, trombone, and tuba, as a preparation for their entrances on the second beat. Repeat this procedure in the seventh measure before the *alla breve*.

The wrong way to conduct this passage is to beat out the first measure in Example 68 and finish the fourth stroke near the bottom of the pattern. It is now necessary to bring the baton up to give the next down beat, and at this point some player may break through, interpreting the up beat as a preparation for an attack. We repeat: bring the baton *immediately* to the top of the pattern, where it is ready to descend, with the quarter rest serving as the preparation.

FOR DIFFERENT INSTRUMENTS

A few words about practical approaches in obtaining clean attacks from different instruments may appropriately bring this part of the discussion to a close. Where strings are concerned, obtaining a clean attack is easiest of all, for their bows can usually catch even the most erratic thrust of the baton and can move just about as fast as any baton. With double reeds in general and with oboes in particular, however, the conductor had better be more diplomatic. With the French horn, above all, he should be most understanding. If he has ever tried to play this noblest of instruments, he will not indicate a rapid attack without some sort of proportionate breath pause. If he tries to, the result will probably be so perturbing that he will not repeat such procedure. A few sessions in the rehearsal room will also bear out the warnings of Berlioz and Weingartner that many trumpet, trombone, tuba, and timpani players have an aristocratic tendency toward late entrance, especially in figures containing reiterated notes.

A sensible method is to put yourself mentally in the place of the players, inhaling for the preparation and exhaling for the attack. In a little time, you should begin to feel instinctively the differences in attack of string, wood-wind, brass, and percussion instruments. Add to this list a very important group: singers. To bring in the several parts of a wood-wind choir with a knife-edged attack, or to bring in a brass section as one man on a *pianissimo*, *legato*, *adagio* entrance are feats not quite so easy as they appear when done under experienced and musical hands. A successful result is certainly due as much to psychological as to technical resources.

REVIEW

As a review of the principles involving attacks and their preparations, practice Example 69 in various tempos, with different time-signatures and strokes to the bar, in *legato* and in *staccato*, and with different instrumental combinations in mind.

Ex. 69

Chapter Eleven

COMBINATION PULSES

FIVE BEATS TO THE BAR WITH DIFFERENT SPEEDS AND ACCENTS

The beating of measures containing combinations of duple and triple rhythms, such as five and seven beats in a measure, is a fairly recent innovation. Formerly, it was often the custom to break up these pulses into smaller units and to give two down beats a measure. Any difficulty involved in mastering these patterns is rarely technical, for they are just as easy to beat as the more usual ones. Such difficulty is usually due to the fact that, except for members of certain Slavic and other races, most people do not habitually think in five and seven pulses. It is said that people of nations which have many words in their spoken language with such rhythmic combinations can play these pulses easily and naturally. If the student makes such pulses part of his own thinking processes, he should not have the slightest difficulty in beating them correctly.

There was a time when composers were somewhat diffident about writing five and seven to the bar and evaded the issue by putting down alternating two's and three's, four's and three's, etc. (Note the disguised quintuple pulse in Sibelius' *Finlandia*.) Today, a composer who writes these pulses means what he says: one strong accent to the bar and one secondary accent. There are still conductors who continue to evade the issue by giving two down beats. Of course, if players are told beforehand what is being done, almost anything *can* be done, no matter how illogical and unmusical it may be. Even when players have been informed, however, someone who is counting his rests during a long wait may break through sooner or later with a wrong entrance. Such illogical beating, moreover, distorts the composer's intentions. The tendency to consider five beats to the bar as four plus one or as six minus one must also be guarded against.

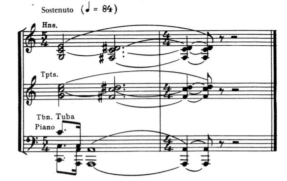

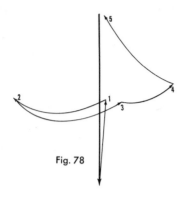

Fig. 78

The two chief considerations which determine the choice of patterns for beating five and seven to the bar are, first, the tempo of the passage, and second, the distribution of the main accents. For ordinary purposes, the general run of such quintuple passages may be divided into three speeds, slow, medium, and fast. The usual accents are either ONE, two, THREE, four, five; or ONE, two, three, FOUR, five.

Let us first consider music slow enough to be taken in five separate strokes. As in all our patterns, the first stroke is down and the last is up. The secondary accent, almost invariably on the third or fourth beat, is to the right. The weak beats are then fitted into these patterns. Thus, when the rhythm has the strong accents on ONE and THREE, use Figure 78. (Practice on Example 70.) Here the rebound of the down beat swerves to the right to introduce the second stroke, which goes to the left. The fourth stroke naturally goes in the same direction. It is a good principle to avoid giving more than one stroke upward whenever possible, to permit an unencumbered preparation for the down stroke.

When the tempo is slightly more brisk and the second pulse is weak, the second beat may be given downward with its own rebound which swerves to the left. THREE and four go to the right as before, and five goes up.

Ex. 71.   Wagner: *Tristan and Isolde.* See also: Debussy, *Six épigraphes antiques,* Part 2 (Ansermet arrangement).

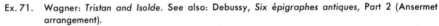

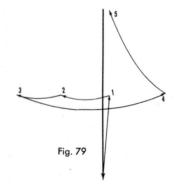

Fig. 79

When the main accents are ONE, two, three, FOUR, five, use the pattern shown in Figure 79 and practice on Example 71. Here, too, the second and even the third beats may each be given with its own rebound.

One occasionally finds the main accents on ONE and TWO (Fig. 80, Ex. 72), an arrangement which amounts in practice to one plus four; or the main accents on ONE and FIVE (Fig. 81, Ex. 73), an arrangement which amounts in practice to four plus one. Note in Figure 80 that the second down beat on two is half-length, and in Figure 81 that the fifth stroke (the second up stroke) is executed with the back of the hand pointing toward the top of the stroke, to differentiate it from the fourth (the first up) stroke.

For very brisk five pulses (three plus two), where each pulse must be articulated, use Figure 82 and practice on Example 74. When the accents are brisk two plus three, give an up and down beat and then a small triangle at the top of the stroke, all in wrist motions.

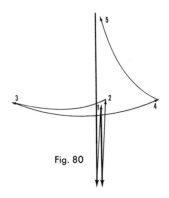

Fig. 80

Ex. 72.   Copland: *Appalachian Spring* (By permission of the copyright owner, Boosey & Hawkes Inc.)

Ex. 73.   Bloch: *America* (Used by special permission of C. C. Birchard & Company, Boston, Massachusetts.)

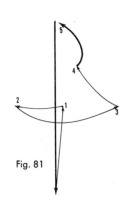

Fig. 81

Ex. 74.   Ravel: *Daphnis and Chloë*, Suite 2 (Permission for reprint granted by Durand et Cie, Paris, copyright owners; Elkan-Vogel Co., Inc., agents for U.S.A.)

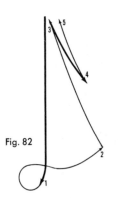

Fig. 82

Ex. 75.　Rimsky-Korsakoff: *Russian Easter* Overture

Ex. 76.　Barber: *Second Essay for Orchestra* (Copyright, 1945, by G. Schirmer, Inc., used by permission of publisher.)

Two interesting adaptations of five pulses to the bar in the music of Rimsky-Korsakoff and Samuel Barber are shown in Examples 75 and 76. Take two strokes down, then one stroke to the left, one right, and one up.

In Rimsky-Korsakoff's *The Snow Maiden* (see Example 77), there are five main pulses, one on each half note with an extra quarter note added to the second main pulse. Patterns in Figures 83 or 84 are suggested.

It has already been noted that time-signatures do not necessarily determine the number of strokes to the bar. In Example 78, an excerpt in 11/4 from Stravinsky's *Le Sacre du Printemps*, we can simply give the first beat down and the last up, with the other beats in the center of the pattern after the initial rebound (see Figure 85). Note that in this case the second stroke is to the right, to bring the hand to the proper place for the final up beat on the eleventh pulse. This "neutral" pattern is very useful in such places. Accents and stresses may be suggested by bringing the baton and left hand forward when necessary.

In moderate and flowing tempos, five separate strokes for each measure would obviously clutter up the pattern; it is, therefore, wise to excise

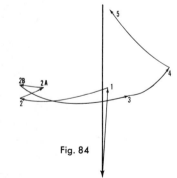

Fig. 83

Fig. 84

Ex. 77.　Rimsky-Korsakoff: *Snow Maiden* (By permission of W. Bessel & Cie, Paris.)

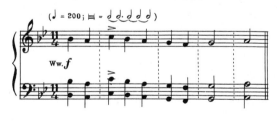

COMBINATION PULSES

Ex. 78.   Stravinsky: *Le Sacre du Printemps* (By permission of the copyright owner, Boosey & Hawkes Inc.)

Ex. 79.   Tchaikovsky: Symphony No. 6

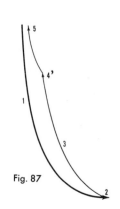

Fig. 85

Fig. 86

the weaker beats when possible. In Example 79 the opportunity presents itself to utilize the rebound as a stroke, the breath pause coming on that part of the bar which has the three-part pulse. Thus, in two plus three beats to the bar, use Figure 86.

When the accents are three plus two, use a pattern in which the breath pause comes on the second pulse. Here give the down beat on one; then observe the breath pause; the rebound comes on three; take the fourth stroke to the right, and the fifth stroke upward.

When quintuple pulses go fast enough for two to the bar, as in Examples 80 and 81, take two on the down stroke and three on the up stroke, or vice versa, as the passage happens to require (Figs. 87 and 88). On the stroke delineating three pulses, whether it is up or down, observe a hovering breath pause for the middle pulse.

Where precise one to the bar is called for, as in Example 82, observe the breath pause at the bottom of the stroke on the middle pulse (three). Group two bars as one, mentally, counting ten pulses to each group whenever phrasing permits (Fig. 89).

Ex. 80.   Stravinsky: *Histoire du soldat* (By permission of J. & W. Chester, Ltd., London and of G. Schirmer, Inc., New York.)

Fig. 87

FIVE BEATS TO THE BAR

Ex. 81.   Copland: *Appalachian Spring* (By permission of the copyright owner, Boosey & Hawkes Inc.)

Ex. 82.   Stravinsky: *Petrouchka* (By permission of the copyright owner, Boosey & Hawkes Inc.) See also: Stravinsky, *Histoire du soldat* (5/16).

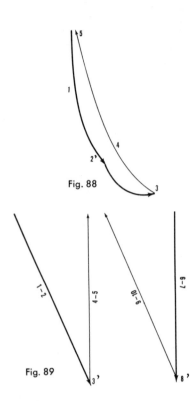

Fig. 88

Fig. 89

SEVEN BEATS TO THE BAR

Patterns for seven beats to the bar are also determined by speed of tempo and distribution of accents. For slow ONE, two, three, FOUR, five, six, seven, use Figure 90. Berlioz, incidentally, originally wrote the movement quoted in Example 83 as three plus four, only later as seven. For the accents ONE, two, three, four, FIVE, six, seven, and for other combinations, the student should evolve his own appropriate patterns.

The principle of using a new stroke for each strong accent may be applied to the unusual cases where accents shift from measure to measure. Excerpts from Stravinsky's "Firebird" Suite (Ex. 84) furnish illustrations of such a case. The time-signature is 7/4 and grows naturally out of a previous 3/2 (quasi 6/4). The accents are either three, two, two; or two, two, three. A purist might conceivably insist that the phrasing demands that two-bar groupings make the rhythm 14/4. This interpretation is left to those who want to beat it so. It is here suggested that each main

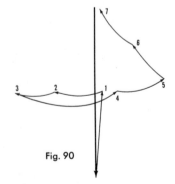

Fig. 90

Ex. 83.   Berlioz: *L'Enfance du Christ*

COMBINATION PULSES

Ex. 84.   Stravinsky: "Firebird" Suite (By permission of J. & W. Chester, Ltd., London and of G. Schirmer, Inc., New York.)

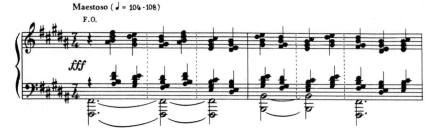

pulse be beat in a different direction in the pattern, as shown in Figures 91 and 92.

This passage from the "Firebird" Suite should be memorized and its beating patterns practiced until they become automatic. The following skeletal scheme should help the student. Each small "x" represents a quarter note; each large "X" represents the repeated entrance of the tuba and timpano.

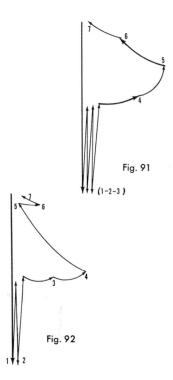

Fig. 91

Fig. 92

Key

B	X xx xx xx	xx xx xxx
	X xx xx xx	xx xx xxx
C	X xx xx xx	
	X xx xx xx	
	X xx xx xx	xx xx xxx
		xx xx xxx
	X xx xx xx	
B	X xx xx xx	xx xx xxx
	X xx xx xx	xx xx xxx
		xx xx xxx
		xx xx xxx

When the tempo becomes too fast for a separate stroke on each pulse, elide the weak beats and give a stroke in a new direction for each group of pulses (duple and triple), as was suggested for quintuple pulses. See to it that the length and duration of the strokes accurately indicate the musical text (Fig. 93, Ex. 85).

Seven pulses to the bar may be taken in three beats, two beats, or even one beat to the bar when the tempo is rapid enough. The student should now be able to evolve his own patterns, similar to those suggested for five beats to the bar.

Subdivisions in septuple pulses, obviously rare, nevertheless serve as excellent practice material. The student should evolve patterns for some of these himself.

Now review once more all the patterns studied thus far, practicing them with either hand alone; with both hands together; in various tempos, styles, and degrees of volume; and with various stresses.

Ex. 85. Falla: *El Amor Brujo* (By permission of J. & W. Chester, Ltd., London and of G. Schirmer, Inc., New York.) See also: Copland, *Appalachian Spring* (7/8); Barber, *Second Essay for Orchestra* (7/4); Stravinsky, *Histoire du soldat* (7/16).

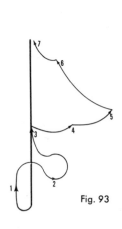

Fig. 93

Chapter Twelve

THE LEFT HAND

USES AND EXERCISES

The student will have had considerable practice by this time in the skills a conductor must acquire for proper use of his right hand, whose main task is to indicate rhythmic pulses and tempos. We come, now, to the use of the left hand, whose main tasks are to indicate contrast, shading, nuance, emphasis, and volume; to cue in; and, most homely and necessary task of all, to turn pages if a score is used.

When we speak of right hand and left hand, we mean literally right hand and left hand, since practically all conductors conduct "right-handed" whether or not they are so in other activities. History records that an occasional conductor (Siegfried Wagner, for example) has conducted "left-handed"; but the chances for confusion, should a conductor place his baton in his left hand, are apparently greater than modern conductors have cared to face. For the record, though, let us mention the fact that a well-known string quartet recently included a left-handed first violinist, who rearranged his strings and gave excellent interpretations of chamber music; and it is quite possible that a left-handed conductor may some day follow suit and rearrange the seating of the orchestra.

It has been said, and with no little truth, that the conductor's right hand is the artisan, his left hand the artist. While the aphorism is not to be taken too literally, it does tend to point out the main distinction between the two hands. The left hand, in performing its many tasks, should be manipulated in a natural and artistic way, but the way will vary from one individual to another, for it is an intensely personal matter. The art of the left hand is very difficult to write about. Obviously it is easier to train the artisan hand than the artist, and the apprentice conductor is almost always recognizable by his wooden left hand. This awkwardness may stem from natural ineptitude, but it often results from lack of proper understanding of the functions of the left hand, coupled with lack of proper preparation and training.

The amount of a conductor's experience can usually be gaged by watching his left hand in action. In no other part of his technique is gaucherie more quickly apparent. This fact leads one to suspect that at least some of the conductors who affect the one-hand technique do so to hide innate stiffness and awkwardness in their left hands. A few decades ago, Wagnerian conductors frequently conducted an entire evening with their left hands in their trouser pockets, implying that their authority and control were so complete that they needed but one hand for the task. It it true that the right hand alone can do very much; but it cannot do everything, and in conducting it was never meant to. The inevitable result of one-hand conducting is partial ankylosis and atrophy of the left hand.

The opposite extreme, in which a conductor threshes about using both arms like flails, is equally objectionable and reveals a lack of sensitivity to the need for contrast. The two hands have separate functions and should be used independently. This fact does not prevent the hands from interchanging functions. On many occasions such interchange is the best way to interpret music. Simultaneous use of both hands making the same gestures should, however, be reserved for climax and contrast; overuse of this device lessens its effect and makes for anticlimax.

Mishaps in turning pages during a performance are likely to be irritating. A little practice in this homely chore will repay the few moments consumed. Find out whether turning the top or the bottom of the pages comes more naturally to your hand. Learn to separate pages between the thumb and the first two fingers of your left hand, so that you become skilled in turning only one page at a time. Learn to turn backward quickly for repeats. Practice these tricks while beating time. Be sure that you have a detailed mental picture of the score both at the beginnings and endings of pages, and at places where there are sudden changes and important cues.

In overcoming awkwardness in the left hand, the student must carry through his first task carefully, methodically, and conscientiously. It is to practice slowly and repeatedly, first with his left hand alone and then with both hands together, *every* pattern presented thus far in this book. In doing so, he will note that the left hand beats to the right at places where the right hand beats to the left, and vice versa. In other words, when the hands beat together, they are always approaching or leaving

THE LEFT HAND

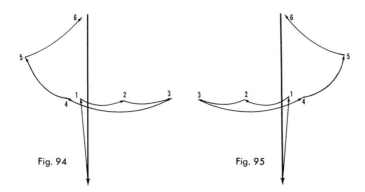

Fig. 94   Fig. 95

each other except on down and up beats. Figures 94 and 95, patterns for beating six to the bar, represent the procedure to be followed for every pattern which precedes them thus far.

When one begins to use this exercise, and for some time afterwards, for that matter (until the left hand is thoroughly worked in), practice cannot be too slow. At first the left hand will seem awkward, not only because it really is so with most people, but also because it will seem even more so in comparison with the relatively adept and practiced right hand. One should strive for grace, coupled with firmness and body.

When you feel that you can beat all the patterns considered thus far with almost equal facility in either hand, practice beating part of a measure with one hand and completing it with the other. This exercise can be varied in many ways, and it is a most helpful aid in the development of the independence of the hands.

An occasional exception to the usual pattern of contrary motion in the hands may occur when the conductor wishes to obtain a tremendous climax, or a swinging *accelerando* against the tendency of his performers to drag, or a *ritardando* when they tend to hurry. Under these circumstances, he may swing both hands in the same direction, thus compelling his unresponsive players to follow, through sheer force. This procedure can easily be overdone and should be resorted to very sparingly.

After you have practiced all the exercises with each hand alone, with both hands together, and with each hand sharing parts of measures; go over the exercises again and check to make sure that the patterns of your two hands do not overlap when the hands approach each other. If they do, the clarity of the outline will be blurred to the watchers. It is a good plan to divide with a vertical line the mirror before which you practice, so that you can easily see when either hand goes out of bounds. Next, practice with each hand alone holding a baton; and finally, practice with both hands together, one empty and one holding a baton. The empty hand will develop smoothness and fluidity, and the hand with the baton will develop firmness and precision.

The appearance of the left hand should be checked, to avoid any suggestion of strain and artificiality. A natural manner of holding it is much like our old printer's index sign. The forefinger points more or less prominently forward like a small baton and serves to fix the watcher's attention. This position is common *in action*, and it should, of course, be adapted to variations in style, tempo, volume, and so on. Opening or closing the fingers of the left hand, with variation in muscular tension, suggests a change in volume. Thrusting the open palm suddenly outward serves with many conductors to suggest *pianissimo*. The infinite positions which may be assumed by the left hand to indicate nuance, shading, and mood hardly admit of description and cataloguing. When it is not in action, as it should be most of the time, do not allow it to hang limply at your side with no suggestion of vitality. But do not pose it ostentatiously on your hip, with pseudo-nonchalance. If you *must* imitate a certain great Italian conductor, begin with his lofty and uncompromising artistic integrity, not his idiosyncrasies.

CUING IN

One of the most important functions of the left hand is to cue in, i.e., to indicate entrances, and by extension, to indicate changes in volume, style, mood, and tempo during the actual progress of the music. In other words, an impending entrance or change must be indicated to the player or section affected, while the other players continue with their parts. It is very difficult for a solo voice, instrument, or section to come in at exactly the right place and in the right mood without disturbing the ensemble, especially in operatic music. Very often, for example, brass and percussion players have long waits during which the tempo and rhythm of the music vary. They have a fair right to receive an assisting signal from the conductor, and it should be given them. But there is an even more important reason why entrances should be indicated by the conductor instead of being left to the mood of the players. The mathematics of the players may be right, but one directing will must unify both the entrance and the interpretation. Even when imitative or antiphonal passages call for differences among players in style and interpretation, coördination of such passages is a task for the conductor, not for the individual instrumentalists.

It is quite possible for an experienced conductor, with routined players who are familiar with each other and their music, to cue in one section of the orchestra with merely a nod or a slight forward-beckoning motion of the right hand alone. This sort of cue should be given as if the ensuing entrance were starting the composition: the head rises for preparation and descends on the actual entrance; or the right hand, while beating, gives the preparation for the ensuing entrance, according to principles suggested in the chapter on attacks. Both head and right hand may work together. Such a preparation should be given just *before* the attack. Since the music is going on and the passage which is about to end has been established in mood and tempo, the men who are already playing cannot possibly change when the conductor cues in the new section; they will continue in their own parts and ignore directions not meant for them. Remember that players are always literally *following* a conductor. By the time the new signal has been given, it is too late for the functioning players to change the music they have just been playing. Moreover, from the conductor's attention to a special section, it should be obvious to them that they are not concerned with this change. Except under the ideal conditions described here, however, it is far better to use the left hand to cue in, i.e., first to warn, and then to signal the point of entrance for the important instrumental or vocal solo or section which the conductor wishes to bring out in the musical texture.

Giving a left-hand cue presupposes the ability to perform two completely separate actions at the same time, one with each hand. For while the right hand continues to beat time, the left hand must alternate between remaining motionless and signifying preparations, beginning and stopping at any point desired, all the while entirely independent of what the right hand is doing.

Let us assume that the orchestra is playing and that a single instrument is about to be brought in. The right hand is beating time. The incoming instrument must now be treated by the left hand as if it were going to play for the first time, which, from its own practical point of view, it really is doing. The left hand, therefore, gives it a preparation and a cue just as if the other instruments were not and had not been playing.

As an initial exercise in cuing in, review attacks on beats, on split beats, and within beats, in every pattern thus far, for the left hand alone. Now practice in the following manner. Hold the left hand motionless slightly above the right, with the index finger extended and pointing first in one direction of the orchestra pit and stage and then in another. Beat out the various patterns with the right hand and signal attacks with the left hand, on and within various strokes. The left hand should remain motionless until it is ready to give the preparation; then it invites the soloist or section to enter. The head may also beckon. The tension and position of the left hand should show the volume and mood desired in the newcomer's execution. Once the new part has been established, the left hand may become motionless again or concern itself with other tasks.

Excellent exercises for developing ease in cuing in may be found in the open score edition of Bach's *Inventions and Fugues* (London, Charles Vincent); *The Forty-Eight Fugues in Color* (ed. by Boeckelmann, Breitkopf and Härtel); *The Art of Fugue* (ed. by Graeser, Breitkopf and Härtel), and in James Higgs's *Fugue* (London, Novello), which reprints five fugues by Bach and one by Kirnberger in open score. If difficulty is experienced in obtaining these scores, the student might copy a few fugues from the piano edition into open score. Practice in cuing in on these works should prove of special value in developing polyphonic thinking. Try to have a pianist play the fugues. Whether he uses piano or open score is of no moment; but the conductor should use open score only, or much of the value of this training will be lost. Now memorize and practice cuing in the entrances in measures 514–535 of Beethoven's *Leonora* Overture No. 3. In this music, avoid at all costs phrasing according to the bar lines. Make your right-hand patterns translate the composer's phrasing. Next, browse through all your scores and practice cuing in on various beats and parts of beats, e.g., the opening measures of Beethoven's First Symphony and the entrances therein of the first violin, the viola and violoncello, the bassoon and contrabass, and the flute, oboe and first violin; also the opening measures of the *andante* in Mozart's G Minor Symphony (K. 550).

Discussion of other functions of the left hand must be left for later consideration. The student's task at this time is to accustom the left hand to act gracefully and independently. Unfortunately, apprentice conductors are often recognizable not only because their left hands are so difficult to control, but also because their conducting suggests that they have two left hands.

The beating of holds, technically termed fermatas or coronas, often puzzles students out of all proportion to the difficulties involved, since each type of hold yields to analysis and logical practice. It is helpful, when confronted by a passage with holds which seems troublesome, to beat through the text without the holds to get the main line of the musical thought, and then to add the holds. This simple approach will suggest solutions for many problems.

A hold is merely a cessation in the flow of the music, the length of which depends upon the surrounding context. The poignant hold in the third movement of Brahms's Second Symphony (on the bar line between measures 22 and 23) is at least as long as a full measure. The length of the sublime hold on the word "God" in Beethoven's Ninth Symphony is limited only by the breath of the singers.

One should not assume that the only holds to be observed are those clearly indicated. For an example of implied holds, consider the opening statement of the passacaglia theme in the last movement of Brahms's Fourth Symphony, where a succession of quasi holds is certainly implied. Often, when notes or chords are stressed and broadened, they become virtual holds and heighten the effect of the musical declamation.

In its simplest form, the hold indicates a cessation in the flow of the music, a stopping place, after which the music proceeds *without* a break. A hold is shown by the cessation of motion in the baton. It is a good general principle never to move the baton on a hold.

After the baton has stopped on the hold, matters are left as if the music had never begun; consequently some sort of preparation must be given the watchers in order to have them enter cleanly on the next attack. What the baton then does is to cue in, according to principles already detailed. The difference at this point from an ordinary cue is that the movement of the baton indicating re-entrance must be joined logically to its last movement preceding the hold, in such manner that the main outline of the pattern remains clear and unchanged.

In holds, the performer must be shown two things: when the hold is to end, and when the music is to re-enter. When there is no break between the hold and the ensuing music, the signal to end the hold and the preparation for the next entrance are combined into a single motion. This combined cessation-preparatory motion is differentiated from the usual single-purpose preparation by its slightly more premeditated character. It should be given toward the point of entrance of the next attack.

To summarize the foregoing instructions: the baton is moving with the music; it stops on the hold; it continues on its way to the next stroke as part of the usual pattern, this motion serving also as preparation for the next entrance. In curtest terms, a stroke is interrupted by a hold; it stops; it continues on its way toward the next stroke. The theory is simple enough; the practice presents enough variation to justify detailed analysis of representative categories.

ON ENTIRE MEASURES

A hold occupying an entire measure is the prototype of all holds. Figures 96 through 98 present various patterns for beating it. Dotted lines signify preparations for attacks or combined cessation-preparatory motions. Practice on Examples 86 and 87.

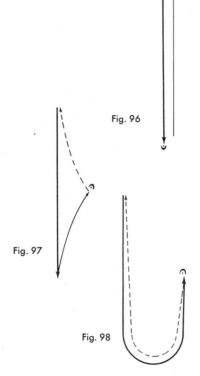

Fig. 96

Fig. 97

Fig. 98

Ex. 86.   Mendelssohn: *Midsummer Night's Dream Overture*

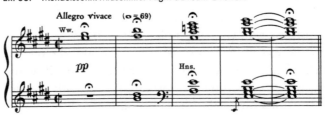

Ex. 87.   Rimsky-Korsakoff: *Scheherezade* (Copyright by M. P. Belaieff Editions. Used by permission of sole agents, Boosey & Hawkes.)

Ex. 88

Ex. 89

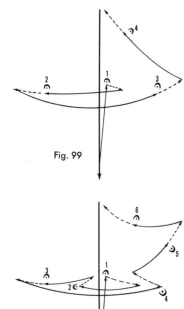

Fig. 99

Fig. 100

Technically translated, such a series of holds is a succession of down beats going into down beats. The baton stops at the bottom of the stroke, then uses the rebound as the cessation-preparatory motion; or the baton takes its rebound to the center of the pattern, and then proceeds toward the next stroke.

ON DIFFERENT STROKES

There are, as has already been observed, only four general directions for the baton to move in: down, up, left, and right. Since holds may come at any point of any stroke going in any of these directions, there are theoretically sixteen basic combinations. In practice, however, it is simply a matter of adjusting the length and direction of the combination cessation-preparatory stroke so that the baton can reach the entrance point of the next attack without changing the main lines of the basic pattern. Figure 99 illustrates motions for a hold on each stroke of four to the bar. Apply the principles here to Example 88.

IN THE SAME DIRECTION

The cessation-preparatory motion undergoes a slight modification when the hold occurs in a pattern which has two strokes going successively in the same direction, e.g., the second and fourth strokes of slow six to the bar. In such cases, the cessation-preparatory motion should be taken slightly up and away from the main beats in order to allow the main pattern to stand out in bold relief. Otherwise, the succession of beats in the same direction will confuse the watchers. This procedure is suggested also for holds on subdivisions (Fig. 100, Ex. 89).

IN DIFFERENT DIRECTIONS

Typical instances of holds taking up more than one pulse and stroke in different directions are illustrated in Example 90. To avoid any possible ambiguity in the minds of the watchers, observe the principle of

Ex. 90

holding on the first beating unit and using the next stroke as the cessation-preparatory motion.

In bar one, give the down beat with a rebound to the center of the model and hold. Then give the second stroke to signify simultaneously the end of the hold and the preparation for the third stroke. Give the third stroke and hold. The fourth stroke shows that the hold is over and that you are preparing for the down beat.

In bar two, give the first and second strokes and hold. Use the third stroke as a cessation-preparatory motion for the next up beat.

In bar three, give the down beat with its rebound and then hold. When you are ready, give the cessation-preparatory stroke lightly to the right; then bring in the last stroke.

In bar four, give the down beat for the first quarter note, the second stroke to the right, and hold. Use the left hand if you wish to show the passing pulses. When you are ready, give the cessation-preparatory stroke up to the top of the pattern, where the baton is prepared for the next down beat.

Bach chorales, e.g., "Wie schön leuchtet der Morgenstern," offer good practice for similar holds.

To repeat a warning: do *not* move the baton on a hold, or some unwary player may break through. Some conductors hold the baton aloft motionless, while showing the passing pulses with unobtrusive beats in the left hand.

The student should now work out models for beating Examples 91 and 92, and he should also devise other examples of holds involving rests,

Ex. 91

Ex. 92

THE HOLD

Ex. 93　　　　　　Ex. 94

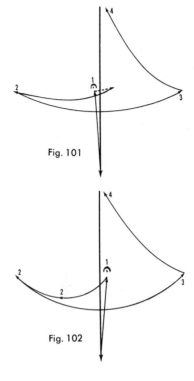

Fig. 101

solving the time-beating problems in ways suggested by examples already cited. He should use examples in various tempos.

FOLLOWED BY THE SAME NOTE AND BY DIFFERENT NOTES

Our next problem concerns holds followed by the same note repeated, in contrast to holds followed by different notes. Note the procedure outlined in Figure 101 for Example 93, where the hold is succeeded by a note of different pitch. In this case the hold must be broken by a stroke away from the next main beat. But in Example 94 (Fig. 102), the hold is tied to a note of the same pitch, and must be broken by using the stroke for the tied note as a cessation-preparatory stroke. To give a special cessation-preparatory stroke might invite a premature entrance, for it would suggest change, and here the pitch does not change.

The principle may be put into other words. Holds written on a note whose duration is longer than one unit of beating to the bar should be thought of as ending on a full stroke. Thus, there is a dotted quarter note at the beginning of Beethoven's Symphony No. 2 (Ex. 95), and it should be beaten according to Figure 103. If this passage were conducted according to Figure 104, some players might be trapped into playing the *F* sharp when they should be finishing the third eighth, which is still part of the hold. Think of this passage as written in Example 96.

Fig. 102

Ex. 95.　Beethoven: Symphony No. 2

Ex. 96.　Beethoven: Symphony No. 2 (adapted)

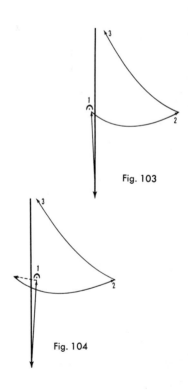

Fig. 103

Fig. 104

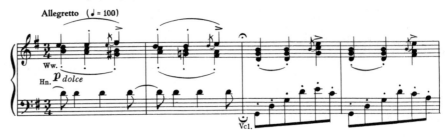

In beating Example 95, one makes the baton rebound after the down stroke and observe the hold. The second stroke proceeds in the regular pattern because there is no change in pitch; it is slightly split and given the suggestion of a breath pause, in order to show the players (oboes and bassoons) where the third eighth enters. If this third eighth differed in pitch from the previous eighths within the hold, it would be necessary to beat the passage as in Figure 104. But to give that extra motion of Figure 104 in this case would almost certainly draw in a premature attack.

ON BAR LINES AND RESTS

Holds over a bar line sometimes tempt a conductor to indicate the start of the new measure, a practice which may bring in incautious players (see Example 97). Beat up to the hold, ending the stroke preceding it with a downward flick of the baton to suggest cessation and with the left palm held open and high as an added warning. After the hold, bring in the next attack with an upward flick of the baton. Some conductors vary the practice by giving this preparatory flick with the left hand only, and the down stroke with both hands. Such precaution is perhaps leaning over backwards to be safe.

When a rest is to be held, stop before the rest and hold the baton motionless. Use the beat on the rest as a preparation for the next attack (Exs. 98 and 99).

Ex. 98.   Kodaly: "Hary Janos" Suite, *Intermezzo*

Ex. 99. Kodaly: "Hary Janos" Suite, *Intermezzo*

IMPLIED HOLDS

Climactic ends of compositions often contain instances of implied holds. Sometimes in other cases the music presents measures of unchanging chords which virtually form a long hold. The first measure may then be given as usual, and the other measures in the group indicated with small wrist motions with the left hand, to show the passage of time and to keep the music going (Ex. 100).

THE CUT–OFF AND END BEATS

When a hold is followed by a break, a new motion is needed to insure a clean finish, in the same manner that a preparatory motion is needed to insure a clean attack. What we want to know about a hold followed by a break is, first, in what direction is the baton going when indicating the holds; and second, where does the next entrance begin, i.e., in what direction must the baton move while indicating the break in order to come out at the right place to give the next attack? The principle is that the baton gives the cut-off (release) in the general direction of the next entrance. We have, then, the following succession of motions: the hold, the cut-off to show the break, the preparation for the succeeding attack, and the new entrance.

In its simplest form, a hold on a down beat is followed by a break and is succeeded by another down beat. Examples 86 and 87 may now

Ex. 100. Delius: *On Hearing the First Cuckoo in Spring* (By permission of Oxford University Press. World copyright transferred to Oxford University Press, 1930.)

be profitably practiced with breaks between each hold. The sequence of motions consists of the preparation for the down beat (not forgetting the breath pause at the top to insure a clean entrance), the cessation in movement to signify the hold, the preparation for the cut-off, and finally, the cut-off proper. In this case the cut-off goes a bit to the right so that the hand will be ready for another preparation to a down beat.

Failure to get the baton to the right place at the right time, ready to give the proper preparation for the next attack, is one of the most embarrassing contretemps an inexperienced conductor meets. What happens in many instances is that the unwary conductor makes the cut-off, only to find immediately that his hand is in the wrong place. He thereupon makes a slight motion, with the idea that he will *then* be in position to give the real preparation. He has, in effect, prepared the preparation, and he usually drags in some players too early, in the process. One such mishap usually suffices to convince the conductor that he should never make more than one preparation for an attack. He learns to decide before the cut-off where his baton must be in order to give correctly the preparatory motion for the next beat, and he sees to it that the cut-off motion gets his hand and baton to the right place. Figure 105 shows a hold on

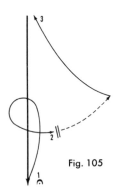

Fig. 105

Ex. 101.   Haydn: Symphony No. 5, "London No. 2"

Ex. 102.   Bach: *Christus, der ist mein Leben*

THE HOLD

the down beat followed by a cut-off to the right, and then a preparation for an ensuing up beat.

The student should at this point, for an exercise, determine ways to beat Examples 101 through 107.

Ex. 103.   Liszt: *Hamlet*

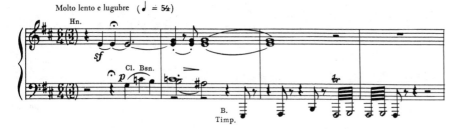

Ex. 104.   Bloch: *America* (Used by special permission of C. C. Birchard & Company, Boston, Massachu-setts.)

Ex. 105.   Mahler: Symphony No. 2 (Used by permission of Universal Edition [London] Limited and Univer-sal Edition A.G., Vienna.)

Ex. 106.   Borodin: Symphony No. 2

Ex. 107. Rimsky-Korsakoff: *Scheherezade* (Copyright by M. P. Belaieff Editions. Used by permission of sole agents, Boosey & Hawkes.)

SIMULTANEOUS HOLDS

When one part of the ensemble holds a note while other parts proceed, indicate the hold with one hand held aloft motionless, and keep the moving parts going with the other hand. When the moving hand has reached the last stroke before the hold is to be terminated, both hands proceed together to signify the end of the simultaneous holds. Practice Examples 108 and 109 with the right hand motionless and the left hand moving, and vice versa. Examples 110, 111, and 112 are for the student's own solution.

Here are two instructive passages (Exs. 113 and 114) from Schumann's Symphony No. 4, which are easy to confuse in execution by the very nature of their similarities.

In Example 113 (Philharmonia pocket score, page 24, bar 5), beat two strokes for the first measure and hold at the top of the pattern with both hands. Terminate the hold by an upward flick of the left hand alone and by having both hands descend at once for the attack in the second measure. If the right hand alone were to give the end of the hold, some players might break through, since a rest follows in the next measure. Keep the right hand motionless on the hold while the left hand terminates it. Then bring both hands down.

In the third measure of Example 114 (Philharmonia pocket score, page 36, last bar), hold the baton at the end of the down beat. At the right moment, give the flick upward with the left hand alone to indicate the end of the hold, and then have both hands ascend to bring in the

Ex. 108.   Weber: *Oberon Overture*

Ex. 109.   Bach: *Ach, Gott und Herr*

Ex. 110.   Strauss: *Don Quixote* (Reprinted with the permission of the copyright owners, C. F. Peters Corporation, New York.)

Ex. 111.   Brahms: Symphony No. 4

SIMULTANEOUS HOLDS

Ex. 112. Haydn: Symphony No. 12 (Breitkopf & Härtel No. 104)

Ex. 113. Schumann: Symphony No. 4

Ex. 114. Schumann: Symphony No. 4

last sixteenth of the measure; or give the flick with the right hand while maintaining the left hand in an attitude of warning. In either procedure, take the ascent on the rest immediately, to preclude premature entrance or break-through. The various places in this movement which are almost identical often confuse players.

BREATH PAUSES AND END BEATS

Breath pauses, technically known as caesuras, are to music what commas and semicolons are to the spoken language. They literally give breathing space between phrases and they clarify the text. Many composers of the past rarely used them; although on the other hand, one composer, Gustav Mahler, used so many that he has been quoted as questioning toward the end of his life the practical effectiveness of such detailed punctuation. Breath pauses are often implied in music, and correct use of them reveals the taste and artistry of the conductor. In

Strauss's *Don Juan*, the characteristic opening measures imply a breath pause, which should be observed almost every time the figure is heard (Ex. 115).

An implied breath pause sometimes occurs just before a striking modulation or a *subito pp*. It prepares the auditors' ears for a sudden change and is effective if not overdone (Ex. 116).

Study the opening section of Dvořák's *Scherzo Capriccioso*, and note that its measures are grouped in a way that implies tiny breath pauses between each group. To omit the breath pauses would metamorphose a passage which now gives the effect of improvisation into a banal succession of fenced-in measures.

Breath pauses are indicated like miniature cut-offs, by a tiny flick of the wrist in the direction of the next attack. They end with a tiny inward or outward hook, which should be executed *on* the stroke containing the breath pause, not later. In theory, an indication of a breath pause contains both a cut-off and a preparatory motion for the next attack, but in actual practice these two motions coalesce. The length of a breath pause depends upon the context of the passage in which it occurs.

"End beats," as they have been termed, are beats which terminate a phrase or section, especially where such beats are followed by tiny pauses. End beats are often implied before measures with part or full rests, by means of a slanted line that cuts across the top of the staff, or the apostrophe sign, or the letters G.P. (Grand Pause).

Ex. 115. Strauss: *Don Juan* (Reprinted with the permission of the copyright owners, C. F. Peters Corporation, New York.) See also: Charpentier, *Impressions of Italy;* Mahler, Symphony No. 1, Slow Movement.

Ex. 116. Beethoven: Symphony No. 7

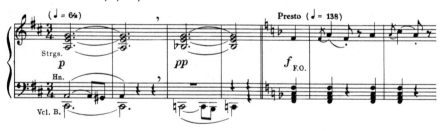

Ex. 117. Brahms: Symphony No. 2

Ex. 118. Brahms: Symphony No. 4

Ex. 119. Beethoven: *Missa Solemnis*

To insure a clean ending and to prevent someone from breaking through the beat, make the end beat with a definitive hook which suggests cessation. The motion consists of a miniature cut-off and then a slight inward or outward hook. The direction of this motion, made mainly with the wrist, varies according to the individual. Both hands may be used for emphasis. In principle, the end beat is a cut-off on the last note, not after it. If you conduct the last note and add an end beat, the players will as often as not tack on the extra length to the last note and quit it with a wrench. If rests follow the end beat, do not beat them. You may, of course, count them silently, and use the last rest before the next attack for a preparatory motion.

An end beat may be given in any direction. We suggest that it proceed to the center of the beating pattern, where the baton will be able to give the next preparation in any direction. When either end beats or breath pauses are followed by a break, arrange to have the pattern end in the center, so that your baton will be in position to give a preparation toward any direction easily. Figures 106, 107, 108, and 109 present suggested patterns for application to the examples cited in this chapter. Examples 117, 118, and 119 present various problems for the student's own solution.

The opening measures of the last movement of Beethoven's Symphony No. 1 (Ex. 120) offer splendid instances of holds, implied breath pauses, and attacks before rests; and they serve to summarize principles already considered. It is most important to remember that when a rest follows another rest, you must stop moving your hand *immediately,* after the first rest. Then on the second rest, make a preparatory motion for the next attack. If your hand rests before the first rest, and then you beat it, many players will interpret the motion as a preparation for the next played note and will come in too soon.

In Example 120, execute the first measure by giving a down stroke and rebound to the center, where the baton remains to indicate the hold (which should be thought of as coming on the first quarter). When you are ready, give the combination cessation-preparatory stroke to the right as an end beat with a tiny breath pause, and join it almost at once to the up beat, a procedure which takes care of the dotted sixteenth and thirty-second. Beat the second, third, and fourth measures four strokes to the bar. Immediately after the down stroke, make an end beat to the left to show the eighth rest. Observe the breath pause here for as long as you wish. If the baton makes the breath pause after the down stroke, and then makes a motion, players might break through. With the third stroke, bring in at will the scale mosaics in these measures. The principle involved in this passage is to beat the eighth rests *at once.*

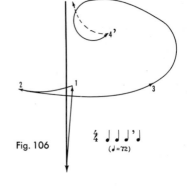

Fig. 106

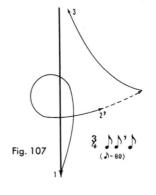

Fig. 107

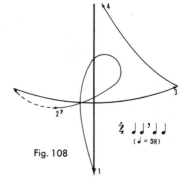

Fig. 108

Ex. 120.   Beethoven: Symphony No. 1

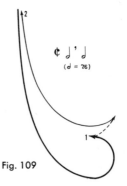

Fig. 109

Some conductors indicate subdivisions, implied breath pauses, and *ritenuto* on the thirty-second notes in the fourth measure, but this practice may easily degenerate into affectation unless one is very careful.

Terminate the hold on the fourth line *F* in the sixth measure by a release to center right, which puts the baton in position to give the up-beat preparation for the down beat in the following measure. Do not beat the second eighth in the seventh measure. Great care must be exercised here to give the up beat the character of a strong inhalation and the seventh-measure down beat that of a strong exhalation, or the players may tend to stress the first note of the ascending scale and confuse the whole rhythmic scheme of the passage. Note that the last three sixteenths of measure six and all of measure seven belong to the new tempo; consequently, take them two to the bar. Memorize the passage. As an added exercise, study the last twelve measures of Beethoven's Fourth Symphony.

A helpful exercise is to practice the patterns in the early chapters of this volume first by inserting breath pauses after various strokes, and then by omitting one, two, and three strokes from the end of the pattern and indicating end beats on the last stroke given. Vary the tempos and volume as much as possible. Another exercise is to beat out passages from any good hymn book, using the same procedure. Bach's chorales offer excellent material for this study. Find a friendly organist to play them, but avoid use of the pianoforte here, since it cannot sustain notes.

Return again to the careful study of beating medleys and potpourris of folk songs, operettas, and operas; for these contain successions of shifting time-signatures, breath pauses, breaks, holds, and changes in tempo, and they are very difficult to do with the requisite lilt, grace, and ease.

Chapter Fourteen

VOLUME, ACCENTS, *LEGATO*

AND *STACCATO*

VOLUME

Even mediocre interpreters usually recognize and try to show differences in extremes of shading, such as *piano* and *forte*; but not every interpreter succeeds in obtaining convincing and artistic differences between such comparatively closely related indications as *pp* and *ppp*, or *mp* and *p*. Another common fault is to ignore the fact that all terms describing volume (and for that matter, speed also) are relative. Thus, a *sforzando* in one passage may be a mere *piano*; in another, a weighty *forte*, depending upon the context. A third fairly common fault in orchestras is the tendency to retard on *diminuendo* and to diminish in volume in descending passages, and of course, the reverse: to accelerate when making *crescendo* and to increase in volume when ascending. The conductor should watch for signs of these deviations during rehearsal. It is also wise for him to remember that *ff* sounds much louder directly after a *piano* than after a *forte*, just as *pp* sounds much softer directly after an *f* than just after a *p*. This is especially true in the case of accents and *sforzandos*.

Indulging in anticlimaxes is still another common fault of conductors. Series of *fortissimos* or *pianissimos* lose most of their effect unless they are graded in intensity. Map out the over-all dynamic plan of one of Wagner's or Tchaikovsky's overtures, by making a simple graph. Mark the changes in volume by letters on the side of the page, and use a rising and falling line to indicate the course of these throughout the work. This will give you a perspective of the climaxes and show you how to plan in order not to spoil the real climaxes by previous exaggeration.

Changes in volume may be shown to the orchestra by beating in various planes, i.e., by bringing the baton upward for greater and downward for less volume. Some conductors bring the baton forward and upward for increase in volume, and downward and inward for decrease. Indicating changes in volume is one of the special provinces of the left hand, which should be much employed in this category of conducting technique. Use of the left hand demands that it be completely independent of the right hand, which keeps beating patterns while the left hand indicates desired nuances. This independence is not easy to achieve and requires much practice and experience. Although each conductor must develop his individual methods, certain motions have found more or less general acceptance.

As an example of the independent use of both hands, let us consider the hairpin *crescendo* and *decrescendo* on the hold, in the opening trumpet solo of the overture to Wagner's *Rienzi*. Give the entrance with both hands, and keep the right hand motionless to show the hold. Let the left hand ascend with palm facing upward to show the swell, and then descend with palm toward the ground to show the fading of the tone. Although ordinarily the baton should not move on a hold, it is possible here to stop it just for a moment to show the hold and then to proceed with it up and down. It is even feasible here to beckon the trumpet for the attack and let him play the call alone on his *A*. Another example of this type of dynamic change is found at the beginning of the overture to Boïeldieu's *La Dame blanche*.

Some orchestras, incidentally, tend to make a *decrescendo* on holds. A corrective is to tell the wind players to save their breath and string players to save their bows. While the right hand remains motionless, bring up the left hand to indicate the duration of the hold and to keep the volume steady.

Many motions which show changes in volume are obviously primitive in origin and almost self-explanatory. The clenched left fist proceeding upward and outward is easily interpreted as pantomime for *crescendo*, and the reverse for *decrescendo*. Holding the left hand high with the forefinger extended in a warning attitude is a general signal for special attention of the players. Tenseness of the hands and body suggests loudness; repose suggests quiet and serenity. The clenched left fist thrust suddenly forward indicates an accent; the open left hand, held high and suddenly brought forward, demands *piano subito*. The left hand open and executing a rocking motion, as if the palm were wiping something, suggests lessening of tension and volume, and is especially useful in securing balance between parts. To make this last motion while continuing to point the left hand toward various parts of the orchestra, and to beat time in regular patterns with the right hand, usually requires much practice; or one hand will inveigle the other into imitation. The hands must be wholly independent.

Beethoven's Symphony No. 7 offers some of the greatest instances in musical literature of Jovian impacts of sounds, both in *crescendo* and *decrescendo*. Note especially page 18, bar 10, to page 19, bar 8 in the Breitkopf and Härtel edition.

As we have already pointed out, many orchestras tend to play loudly when there is a *crescendo* sign and to play softly when there is a *decrescendo* sign. They must be made to realize that, paradoxically, a *crescendo* sign means less volume at the start and that a *decrescendo* sign means more volume at the start, to allow for gradual change. It is not easy for an orchestra to play a gradual *crescendo* or the reverse, and it usually takes long and patient training. Recall how late in the history of the art it was before an orchestra like that at Mannheim was able to achieve this in a manner which aroused the enthusiasm of the chief musicians of the times. Orchestras must be taught to avoid reaching the maximum of volume too soon. An effect like that of Figure 110 instead of Figure 111 is all too common.

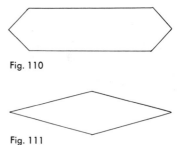

Fig. 110

Fig. 111

Wind players should be warned often that they must save their breath, or unjustified *decrescendos* will result. String players must be told repeatedly to save their bows in down bows, because the upper half does not have the same pressure and volume as the lower half. For this reason down bows are good for decrease of volume and up bows for increase.

With stringed instruments, change of string for a passage often results in a more mellow tone. Thus, on the violin, the *A* string may often be better for a passage than the *E*, and the *D* better than the *G*. The *G* string may be used in the higher positions for sonority and be made to sound almost like a cello. The principle of changing strings for special effects may be applied to all stringed instruments, though with diminishing returns as one descends.

It may be pointed out here that open notes on stringed instruments are likely to obtrude in slow and moderate tempos because of their differences in tone color. Direct the players to use other fingerings (stopped notes).

By this time the student should be able to evolve his own exercises to overcome any technical problems in dynamics discussed thus far. One suggested here, dry but helpful, is to beat through the usual patterns with each hand in various speeds from slow to fast and from fast to slow, and with various combinations of volume from soft to loud and from loud to soft.

An intriguing exercise is to try to show increase in volume in one hand and the reverse in the other. This requires the utmost independence of the hands, and especial pliancy and powers of suggestion. If one degree of dynamics has already been established, hold it with the baton hand and show the new dynamics with the left hand. Facial expressions and the eyes darting from one section to another should aid the players greatly.

When two degrees of dynamics confront the conductor simultaneously, he should warn beforehand the sections to be affected. Conducting with one hand held high for the louder section and the other hand moving below it for the softer section should meet the situation. The hand held high may descend gradually to signify decrease in volume for one section, and the hand below may rise slowly to signify increase in volume for the other section, if such changes occur.

ACCENTS

Accents and other sudden outbursts in volume must be prepared. When the tempo is slow enough, give the preparation on the previous stroke. A good example occurs in the 21st and 22nd measures of Weber's overture to *Oberon*. The 21st measure, with the violas holding a whole note on a major second, suggests resolution. This effect can be heightened by holding the measure somewhat longer than the measures preceding it, a procedure which also gives the violins time to take off their mutes. A *decrescendo* to *ppp* is most effective here. On the fourth stroke of the 21st measure, prepare the explosive *tutti ff* chord on the 22nd measure; and make the character of the preparation imply the ensuing musical pistol shot. There is no danger that the players will anticipate the *ff* and spoil the *pp*, for the baton moves so rapidly that they will have just enough time to catch the explosion.

When the tempo is fairly rapid, however, there is usually no time to give a complete stroke as preparation except by awkward overbeating. This is especially true when an accent or a *sforzando* comes within a stroke. The procedure in that case is to give the accent at the start of the stroke in which it occurs, and the players will imitate it in the next split second. There is no danger that the players will anticipate the new gradation in volume; the tempo is going too fast for them to do so. All they can do is to imitate the conductor's signal for an accent or *sforzando,* and by the time they have done so, the music with the new dynamic is upon them. Just which cases need a warning for accents on the previous stroke and which on the stroke itself, will soon be learned in practice. In general, in medium tempo, an accent on a stroke is prepared on the previous stroke; in rapid tempo, an accent within a stroke is prepared at the beginning of the stroke itself.

Strauss's *Till Eulenspiegel*, with its oft-repeated characteristic figure first announced by the clarinet in the 47th measure, offers an interesting example of a warning *on* the stroke itself. The first note of this figure must be enunciated with special clarity amounting to a *spiccato* tick. It is prepared each time *on* the stroke with a forward thrust of the baton. The players imitate this, and by the time they have played the figure, the baton has gone on to succeeding notes. This technical device of indicating an accent within a stroke by cuing it in with the stroke itself, recalls the procedure of attacks, i.e., it is carried out just as if the orchestra were starting on the accent with nothing behind it.

Beethoven's music affords, among its many other facets, incomparable instances of violent contrasts in volume. The student cannot do better than to study the second movement of his Symphony No. 8 from this point of view. In the ninth measure, an *ff* is followed by an *sf* and then by a *p*, and these must all be shown to the players beforehand. Of course the players have the directions before them and will approximate the dynamic changes no matter what the conductor does, but the result of directionless playing would hardly have the unified certainty and spirit which characterize the response to an authoritative conductor. Beat the ninth measure two quasi four. The *ff* comes within the second stroke; show it at the beginning of the stroke. To try to split the stroke would be useless; there is no time. Prepare the *sf* on the third stroke by lifting the previous stroke in order to allow for a downward thrust of the baton. Prepare the *p* on the fourth stroke by a warning sign in the left hand before it arrives.

LEGATO AND STACCATO

A distinction must at once be made between indications of purely physical changes such as *legato, staccato, spiccato,* and *martellato;* and indications of the spirit of the notes such as *con brio, scherzando, maestoso,* and the like. The first sort depend largely upon technique; the second largely upon suggestion.

An analysis of the musical styles of some conductors will reveal that they may often be classified as either *legato* or *staccato* interpreters. Many of the younger ones tend toward *staccato;* the older toward *legato.* Conductors who can maintain a broad and elevated *legato* are not common. This is due as much to lack of spiritual serenity as to any technical faults. The spiritual remedy lies beyond the province of the present discussion.

Legato and related styles are suggested by the repose of the eyes, face, and hands. The baton moves in curves and loops with at least the lower arm taking part in the motions. In *staccato, marcato,* and related styles, the baton moves very much like a bow under similar circumstances, jerking to the end of the stroke and observing a wait there before proceeding to the next stroke. The hands, face, and eyes do their part by their comparative tautness, and the wrist and even the fingers take on the character of the detached style. *Staccato* elides all unnecessary motions and may be termed the style of economy; *legato* connotes connecting lines and evokes the feeling of fullness. In *legato,* rebounds are much in evidence; in *staccato,* they are reduced to a minimum. *Legato* is associated more with long phrases than with short ones and with moderate rather than with fast tempos. Therefore, when *legato* is desired in brisk passages, group the measures according to phrases, and let your baton indicate the over-all phrasing rather than each measure in detail.

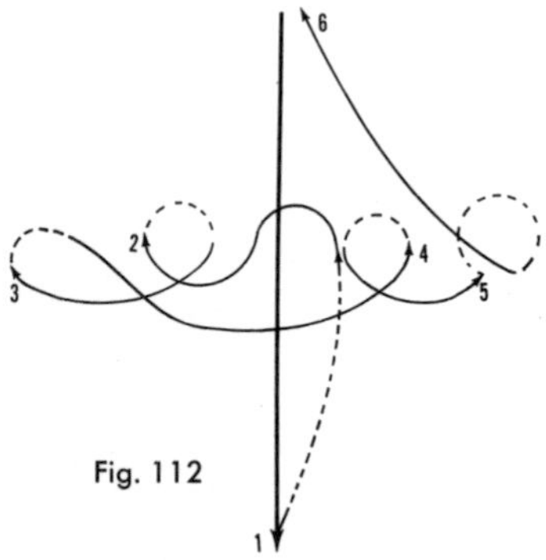

Figure 112 is a linear approximation for six to the bar, *legatissimo;* and Figure 113 is the same, *staccatissimo.* Note the "click" at the start of each *legato* stroke where the players enter.

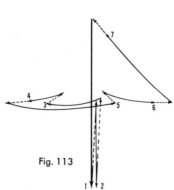

Fig. 112

Fig. 113

These two patterns illustrate one of the most important principles in baton technique. In *staccato,* the players catch the baton at the start of each stroke after a tiny breath pause and miniature rebound; in *legato,* they catch the baton on the "click," which comes after the combined rebound and stroke. In *staccato,* there is no genuine stop; the baton does observe a miniature breath pause but its length is in proportion to the time and space of the whole pattern; in *legato,* the baton may stop and observe the "click," that is, stop at a point where the baton seems to impinge lightly upon an imaginary spot of cessation. The baton then executes the rebound and makes another "click." The rebound and following stroke coalesce. In *staccato,* the time and space sense of the players maintains the ensemble; in *legato,* it is the "click" which does so.

It should be recalled again that *staccato* does not necessarily mean *forte* or *accelerando,* and that similarly, *legato* does not necessarily connote *piano* and *ritardando.* As a check against the tendency to associate these stylistic and dynamic elements, practice *staccato-pianissimo, ritardando;* and *legato-fortissimo, accelerando.* In addition, practice *staccato* and *legato* in strict time. Some conductors have even been known to practice simultaneously *staccato* in one hand and *legato* in the other.

Excellent training in all these branches of technique may be obtained by conducting Beethoven's pianoforte sonatas and Bach's *Forty-Eight* with the aid of a friendly pianist. In this practice, see to it that your baton and left hand always reflect the main lines: rhythmic, melodic, phrasal, thematic, and other ideas. Do not wrench to indicate the syncopations.

A summary of feasible changes in the motions of the baton from extreme *legato* to extreme *staccato* follows. As *legato* increases, the strokes dip; they tend to become round and looped; the baton glides and flows; and the rebounds are much in evidence; in *staccato,* the strokes tend to straighten out; subdivisions extend beyond the main strokes; breath pauses come at the end of strokes, as in bowing; rebounds are minimized; and the baton is thrust forward.

Chapter Fifteen

TECHNIQUES OF RHYTHM

POETRY AND MUSIC

A study of poetry and its relation to music, especially from the point of view of rhythm, should prove of great aid to the student of conducting. To this end the following works are recommended: C. F. Abdy Williams' *The Rhythm of Song* (London, Methuen); Edmonstoune Duncan's *Melodies and How to Harmonize Them* (London, Vincent Music Company); Raymond MacDonald Alden's *Introduction to Poetry* and *English Verse* (both, New York, Henry Holt). A practical approach would be to analyze and to beat out poems in *The Oxford Book of English Verse,* in Palgrave's *Golden Treasury,* and in similar compilations.

PROSE RHYTHMS

The conductor sometimes meets passages whose melodic lines are free and close to prose utterance. This sort of musical speech often occurs in older choral works, though instances are also found in recent orchestral works. To conduct such passages with justice to the subtlety of the rhythmic line and yet to maintain clarity of form is a balance not easy to achieve.

The first task a student has, upon inspecting such prose rhythms, is to note where the strong and the weak pulses come. These can be marked in the score with dotted lines and time-signatures if desired. The general principle in such passages is to beat each strong pulse in a new direction.

Let us consider the prose rhythm of Example 121. The up beat and measure of four are obvious. The two measures of music set to the words "Father, and the only begotten Son," are what now interest us. In the measure with "Father, and the," give two strokes down, one to the right, and two up; in the next measure give two strokes down, three to the right, and two up. But delineate with the freedom of prose, not in rigid patterns.

Ex. 121. Arkhangelsky: *Day of Judgment* (By permission of the copyright owners, J. Fischer & Bro.)

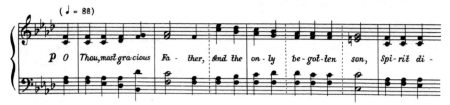

A practical method of treating many prose rhythms is to mark the strong pulses by giving the first beat down and the last up, with the strokes between to the left and right alternately, or vice versa, according to the *total* number of strokes involved. When the total number of strokes is odd, take the second stroke to the right (when there are three, five, and seven strokes, etc.); when the total number is even (four, six, and eight strokes, etc.), take the second stroke to the left. This procedure will make the last stroke come out on the right-hand side of the pattern in either count, ready for the up beat. Note also that a rebound to the center of the pattern serves to make it possible for all beats between the initial down and final up beats to be equal in length. The rebound swerves *away from* the direction of the stroke it introduces. When you want to stress any stroke, thrust the baton outward and forward and in this way attract the attention of the performers to it. All strokes except the down and up overlap in the air, of course, and do not appear as they have to be pictured, in only two dimensions (see Figure 57).

Example 122 is another illustration of the free melodic line. A modern composer might have written this in rather slow 2/2 with bar lines. What concerns us here is to determine the main stresses and breath pauses and to indicate them with the baton.

For historical examples, consult such works as Hugo Riemann's *Musikgeschichte in Beispielen* (Leipzig, E. A. Seemann); *Historical Anthology of Music* by A. T. Davison and W. Apel (Cambridge, Harvard University Press); Arnold Schering's *Geschichte der Musik in Beispielen* (Leipzig, Breitkopf and Härtel); and the Desclée edition of *Gregorian Chant in Modern Notation* (Tournai, Belgium).

Ex. 122. Old German Song, transcribed by Kurt Thomas (From *Lehrbuch der Chorleitung* by Kurt Thomas, published by Breitkopf & Härtel; used by permission of Associated Music Publishers, Inc.)

PROSE RHYTHMS   105

Ex. 123. Vaughan Williams: "Pastoral" Symphony (By permission of J. Curwen & Sons Ltd., London, and of G. Schirmer, Inc., New York.)

Practice Example 123, a modern work containing barless melodic musical speech. Place dotted lines to separate the main phrases, and use patterns which change directions on the main accents.

A REVIEW OF RHYTHMIC PATTERNS

It is suggested at this point that a review be made once more of rhythmic patterns. Variety may be obtained by making it a daily practice to run through a number of pages of the musical excerpts contained in such books as Sigmund Spaeth's *Guide to Great Orchestral Music* (New York, Modern Library); Hermann Kretzschmar's *Führer durch den Konzertsaal* (Leipzig, Breitkopf and Härtel); Percy Goetschius' *Masters of the Symphony* (Boston, Oliver Ditson Company); Charles O'Connell's *The Victor Book of Symphonies* (New York, Simon and Schuster); *Reference Book of Miniature Scores with Thematic List* (London, J. and W. Chester); Eulenburg's

Kleine Partitur-Ausgabe—Thematisches Verzeichnis (London and Zurich, Eulenburg); the Burrows-Redmond compilation, *Symphony Themes* (New York, Simon and Schuster); and the Barlow-Morgenstern *A Dictionary of Musical Themes* (New York, Crown Publishers).

This routine may be lightened somewhat by beating through daily some folk songs in such collections as *The Botsford Collection of Folk Songs* (New York, Schirmer); Möller's *Das Lied der Völker* (Schott); and Rimsky-Korsakoff's *100 chants nationaux russes* (Paris, Bessel). For American examples, consult the article on folk music in the Dodd Mead *International Cyclopedia of Music and Musicians.*

Supplement this sight-reading with medleys and potpourris of operettas by such composers as Victor Herbert, Franz Lehar, and Suppé, and of operas in the standard repertory. In beating through several pages (which should be done with the help of a pianist), do not stop; avoid spending a measure or two getting into a new tempo. Beat through the piece without pause in correct tempo, and return, at another time, to make any needed corrections.

The objects of this daily routine are to quicken the student's ability to translate into patterns the printed page and to improve his sight-reading powers. Close application to a subject often has the effect of causing one's mind to overemphasize details. This sort of routine should act as a balance to such a tendency.

SHIFTING RHYTHMS

The idea that bar lines are merely general guideposts should be recalled when we find many passages whose main pulses do not at all coincide with the beginnings of the bar lines. Slavish adherence to the bar line often inveigles the student conductor into monotonous accentuation and geometric repetition of rigid patterns. Translate the excerpts in Examples 124–131 so that their pulses are brought out into correct relief. The chief precept to remember in such cases is that a clear down stroke is not necessarily strong and long. The length and strength of each stroke should depend upon the context of each passage.

Ex. 124.   Brahms: Symphony No. 1

Ex. 125. Ravel: *Spanish Rhapsody* (Permission for reprint granted by Durand et Cie, Paris, copyright owners; Elkan-Vogel Co., Inc., agents for U.S.A.)

Ex. 126. Offenbach: *Tales of Hoffmann*

Ex. 127. Stravinsky: *Petrouchka* (By permission of the copyright owners, Boosey & Hawkes Inc.)

Ex. 128. Sibelius: Symphony No. 5 (By permission of Wilhelm Hansen, Copenhagen, and G. Schirmer, Inc., New York.)

Ex. 129. Copland: *Appalachian Spring* (By permission of the copyright owners, Boosey & Hawkes Inc.)

TECHNIQUES OF RHYTHM

Ex. 130. Beethoven: Symphony No. 6

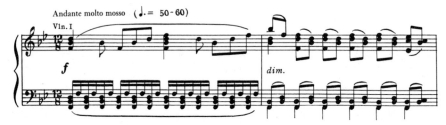

Ex. 131. Beethoven: Leonora Overture No. 3

INTERPOLATED MEASURES

A single measure of a time-signature different from the surrounding measures, suggesting an aside or reiteration, will be met from time to time. Often such a measure gives the reader the feeling of an extra inhalation. Meyerbeer termed such interpolated measures "petites mesures." According to writers of a past generation, these "petites mesures" were supposed to have occasioned some difficulties in time-beating, though it is puzzling to see just why. Deldevez, in his *L'Art du chef d'orchestre*, pays special attention to them at no little length and quotes four examples by Meyerbeer. In essence, these isolated measures are simply parts of the contiguous measures and might have been separated from their parent measures by broken instead of the usual heavy bar lines. They are beaten quite simply by maintaining the same pulsation as the surrounding measures; or, to state this in other words, an eighth equals an eighth, a quarter equals a quarter, and so on, and the same number of strokes is apportioned to each unit as in the surrounding bars. To beat them so,

Ex. 132.   Meyerbeer: *L'Africaine*

Ex. 133.   Strauss: *Don Juan* (Reprinted with the permission of the copyright owners, C. F. Peters Corporation, New York.)

Ex. 134.   Strauss: *Don Juan* (Reprinted with the permission of the copyright owners, C. F. Peters Corporation, New York.)

TECHNIQUES OF RHYTHM

Ex. 135. Hindemith: *Mathis der Maler* (Published by Schott, Mainz; used by permission of Associated Music Publishers, Inc.)

Ex. 136. Hanson: Symphony No. 3 (Published by Carl Fischer Company; used by permission of copyright owners, Eastman School of Music.)

Ex. 137. Strauss: *Also sprach Zarathustra* (Reprinted with the permission of the copyright owners, C. F. Peters Corporation, New York.)

Ex. 138. Sibelius: Symphony No. 5 (By permission of Wilhelm Hansen, Copenhagen, and G. Schirmer, Inc., New York.)

INTERPOLATED MEASURES

111

Ex. 139.   Chausson: Symphony in B Flat

of course, one must be prepared to change patterns quickly for the changing signatures, always keeping the pulse-units equal. Practice with Examples 132–136.

Examples 137–139 must not be confused with interpolated measures. Triplets in these examples cause some players and conductors erroneously to retard. One should observe strict time. Split the middle note of the triplet mentally, giving the first half to one pulse and the second half to the next pulse, but tied as one note, of course.

The preceding examples illustrate passages where the unit of tempo remains constant. Easily confused with them are those passages in which the tempo of the whole measure remains constant. Look at Example

Ex. 140.   Beethoven: Symphony No. 9

140, from the *scherzo* of Beethoven's Symphony No. 9. After the measures in 3/4, there follows a *presto* (*alla breve*). Beat one to the bar throughout; phrase two bars as one; and keep each bar of the 3/4 and *alla breve* equal in length of time. Study also the similar place in the *scherzo* of the same composer's Symphony No. 3, just before the *finale*.

RAPIDLY CHANGING RHYTHMS

It is suggested that the student, in order to acquire facility in conducting rapid successions of changing rhythmic patterns, prepare a pack of cards, writing on each a different time-signature. Include cards for each time-signature in slow, medium, and rapid tempos, and also for subdivisions. Shuffle the pack, and a different routine of time-beating is ready for each day. At the start, repeat each card a few times until you achieve assurance in it. Then take each time-signature once only, in succession according to the order of the day. Admittedly, this is not the most romantic approach to conducting; neither is the practice of pianoforte chromatic thirds and octaves romantic; yet both are necessary for a well-grounded technique. When this conducting game gives the student no special trouble any more, he may copy a few bars of appropriate music on each card and continue his setting-up exercises every day with actual living music.

Consider the following summaries of time-signatures in works by Igor Stravinsky, the variety of which seems to point to some sort of record. In many instances in his music, the use of cross-accents and combined rhythms, together with the complexity of the tone-color combinations, serves to heighten the interest. Consult, for example, *Petrouchka*, in which the following time-signatures occur: 2/4, 3/4, 4/4, 6/4, 2/8, 3/8, 4/8, 5/8, 6/8, 7/8, 9/8.

Write each time-signature in this list on a separate card and you again have a good exercise in changing pulses, which may be varied by shuffling the cards. Practice the same procedure with each time-signature in the *Histoire du soldat* and in *Le Sacre du Printemps* listed below.

Example 141, typical of many passages in Stravinsky's music which contain frequent changes in time-signatures, is taken from the 1912 edition, page 16 of the Kalmus small score. Take the 3/8 in fast three, the 4/8 in two, and the 2/8 in one (up and down). You may beat the 5/8 bars either in slow one or in two so that the last third of the down beat and the first third of the up beat take care of the middle eighth. At the next *stringendo* on page 26 of the same score, think of the preceding 1/4 as a 2/8. See that the unit of pulse, the eighth, remains the same in time value.

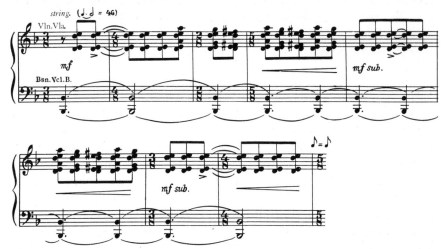

In Example 142, the same excerpt as Example 141 but adapted from the composer's own four-hand piano arrangement in the *Edition russe de musique* (*Russischer Verlag*), we find interesting differences in time-signatures.

In the next excerpt (Ex. 143), taken from the composer's 1948 revised version (Boosey and Hawkes edition), we find still more evidence that the composer seems to like to change versions as well as to shift time-signatures.

Ex. 142.   Stravinsky: *Petrouchka* (pianoforte arrangement) (By permission of the copyright owner, Boosey & Hawkes Inc.)

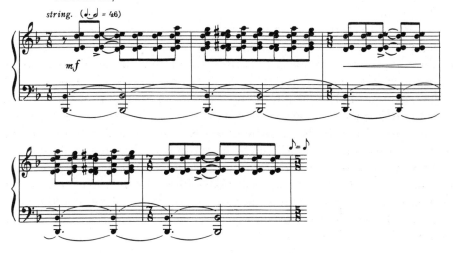

TECHNIQUES OF RHYTHM

Ex. 143. Stravinsky: *Petrouchka* (1948 edition) (By permission of the copyright owner, Boosey & Hawkes Inc.)

Examples 141–143 and many other passages in scores of Stravinsky's offer excellent exercises for the student to solve. Adapt the patterns already given and practice them until the hand automatically beats the shifting pulses with ease and conviction. To repeat a warning: see to it that the unit of pulse, in this instance, the eighth, remains constant in time value. When you have mastered this problem, introduce the *stringendo*. A good passage for practice in maintaining the unit of pulse occurs in *Le Sacre du Printemps* at the start of the "Rondes printanières," page 38 of the Boosey and Hawkes full score edition. Here fairly slow 5/4, 7/4, 6/4, and 5/4 succeed each other. Indeed, Stravinsky's "Firebird" Suite, *Petrouchka,* and *Le Sacre du Printemps* should be the student's constant companions since they constitute in themselves an unparalleled set of exercises in fluid pulsation, unique in the history of music.

Note in Example 141 that a 3/8, 4/8, 5/8 group is repeated except that the first group has an interpolated 2/8 bar, a kind of momentary recollection of the 1/4 bar a little before. Such juxtapositions of similarities and dissimilarities of phrase groups often help one to grasp a passage as a whole and to memorize it.

Go over this passage repeatedly while humming a vowel or tapping a pencil upon the table. Be careful to keep the eighths uniform in length regardless of the length of the strokes. It is very easy to be deceived and to elongate five beats to the bar into six or contract it into four. It is wise to use a metronome at the start and to let each click represent an eighth. When you can beat this passage automatically, observe the *stringendo* leading to the 3/4.

RAPIDLY CHANGING RHYTHMS   115

Consult also *Histoire du soldat:* 3/8, 4/8, 5/8, 6/8, 7/8, 3/16, 4/16, 5/16, 7/16, 8/16; and the rhythmic kaleidoscopes in *Le Sacre du Printemps:* 2/2, 3/2, 2/4, 3/4, 4/4, 5/4, 6/4, 7/4, 11/4, 2/8, 3/8, 4/8, 5/8, 6/8, 7/8, 9/8, 2/16, 3/16, 4/16, 5/16, 9/16.

The works in the following list provide instructive exercises in training the mind and hand to adapt themselves to continually changing rhythmic patterns. It should be stressed that the only safe way to acquire assurance and conviction in this branch of conducting technique is to know the music so well that the hand, already trained to execute varying patterns with facility, automatically translates the successive time-signatures into the appropriate designs. Trying to memorize the time-signatures first, and by this means, to adapt the patterns, results almost inevitably in stilted performance. One must know the music really well before starting to beat it. Here is a selection of works, chosen because they can help to develop feeling and technique for fluid patterns.

A PRACTICE LIST OF KALEIDOSCOPIC RHYTHMS

Barber: *Essay for Orchestra; Second Essay for Orchestra.*
Bartok: *Concerto for Orchestra,* Part IV, "Intermezzo Interrotto."
Bax: Symphony No. 3, Third Movement.
Bloch: "America" Symphony; *Concerto Grosso.*
Borodin: Symphony No. 2.
Copland: *Appalachian Spring;* "Dance" Symphony, Third Movement.
Debussy: *L'Après-midi d'un faune; La Mer,* Part I; *Six épigraphes antiques* (arranged by Ansermet).
d'Indy: "Symphony on a French Mountain Theme."
Hanson: "Nordic" Symphony, Third Movement; *Pan and the Priest.*
Harris, Roy: Symphonies No. 2 and No. 3.
Hill, E. B.: Symphony No. 3, Third Movement.
Holst: *The Hymn to Jesus; The Perfect Fool* (ballet music).
Koechlin: *Five Chorales in Middle Age Modes.*
Liadoff: *Eight Russian Folk Songs,* No. 2, "Christmas Song"; *Ballade de l'Apocalypse.*
Mahler: Symphony No. 2, Fourth Movement; Symphony No. 4, Slow Movement.
Miaskovsky: Symphony No. 7.
Mussorgsky: *The Feast* (or "Banquet"), 33 changes in 38 measures; *The Ragamuffin,* 24 changes in 76 measures. (These last two are for piano and voice originally.)
Mussorgsky-Ravel: *Pictures at an Exhibition,* the recurring "Promenade."

Rachmaninoff: *Isle of the Dead.*

Ravel: *Daphnis and Chloë; Miroirs* (for pianoforte); *Mother Goose* Suite, No. 2; String Quartet, Third Movement.

Rimsky-Korsakoff: *Mlada; Russian Easter; Tsar Saltan.*

Schoenberg: *Von Heute auf Morgen.*

Strauss: "Alpine" Symphony.

Stravinsky: *Histoire du soldat; Petrouchka; Le Sacre du Printemps; Renard.*

Tchaikovsky: *Oxana's Caprices.*

Vaughan Williams: "Pastoral" Symphony.

Walton: *Portsmouth Point* Overture.

Weiner, Leo: Orchestra Suite of Hungarian Folk Dances, Part 4.

SIMPLIFYING COMPLICATED TIME-SIGNATURES

Any consideration of the desirability of simplifying musical notation brings in its train other debatable issues, which the student may well consider carefully at this time. One of these, unnecessary subdivision of pulses, is illustrated in Stravinsky's *Le Sacre du Printemps* (see the Boosey and Hawkes large or small editions, which have the same pagination).

Just as many composers seemed afraid to write quintuple and septuple time-signatures until fairly recently, and set down instead successions of binary and ternary pulses or vice versa; so we find some recent and contemporary composers, among them Stravinsky, writing minute subdivisions of pulses, which easily could and should have been written in larger units. Another minor but appreciable source of irritation in Stravinsky's music is his habit of frequently having a 2/16 followed by a 2/8 instead of a 4/16.

In many places in the score of *Le Sacre du Printemps,* the composer uses bar lines at almost every conceivable opportunity and then proceeds virtually to contradict himself by connecting larger units with tails. He has, moreover, contradicted his own microscopic time-signatures in certain performances which he has himself conducted. In fact the Boosey and Hawkes score, on the fly leaf, actually makes a recommendation in one instance that some of the small units be combined into one large one. The notation of the score in this respect is as logical as it would be to show a 9/4 bar as a succession of three bars, each of 3/4; or a 12/8 as a succession of four bars, each of 3/8.

It is suggested that, in order to make a Stravinsky score simpler to read in time-beating, the student edit many of the small bars into larger units and beat them so. Here are a few examples from the "Danse sacrale."

At page 115, brace 1, no. 149: combine bars 1 and 2 (beating three

Ex. 144.   Florent Schmitt: *La Tragédie de Salomé*, "Danse des éclairs" (From *Le Chef d'orchestre et son équipe* by D. E. Inghelbrecht, used by permission of the publisher and copyright owner, René Juliard, Paris.)

Ex. 145.   Inghelbrecht: *Pour le jour de la première neige au vieux Japon* (From *Le Chef d'orchestre et son équipe* by D. E. Inghelbrecht, used by permission of the publisher and copyright owner, René Juliard, Paris.)

Ex. 146.   Inghelbrecht: *Pour le jour de la première neige au vieux Japon* (rewritten) (From *Le Chef d'orchestre et son équipe* by D. E. Inghelbrecht, used by permission of the publisher and copyright owner, René Juliard, Paris.)

plus two); bars 3 and 4 (two plus two); and bars 5 and 6 (two plus two). At no. 150: combine bars 7 through 9 (three plus two plus two); and bars 10 and 11 (two plus three). At brace 2: combine bars 1 and 2 (two plus two). At no. 151: combine bars 3 through 5 (two plus three plus three); and bars 6 and 7 (two plus two).

The student may now go on and apply this principle to the following passages: pages 116 through 122, pages 125 through 128, and pages 136 to the end of the score.

A related procedure, very helpful in certain modern works which contain a welter of changes in time-signatures, is suggested by D. E. Inghelbrecht in his *Le Chef d'orchestre et son équipe* (Paris, René Julliard, 1949; translated by G. Prerauer and S. Malcolm Kirk, *The Conductor's World*, London, P. Nevill, 1953). He quotes from Florent Schmitt's *La Tragédie de Salomé* a passage which confused instrumentalists in 1908 and which, it may be added, might confuse some even today. The passage is here reproduced in Example 144. On one occasion, the conductor announced simply that he was beating the passage as if it were written in 7/8. The pattern, of course, is two down, two to the right, and three up. Compare this passage to the 7/4 in Stravinsky's "Firebird" Suite near the end of the score, and this pattern with Figures 91 and 92.

M. Inghelbrecht goes on to recall a conversation with his colleague, M. Chevillard, back in 1906, concerning the beating of a passage from M. Inghelbrecht's own work. The original version is given in Example 145; he rewrote it later as Example 146.

Ex. 147.   Inghelbrecht: *El Greco* (From *Le Chef d'orchestre et son équipe* by D. E. Inghelbrecht, used by
permission of the publisher and copyright owner, René Juliard, Paris.)

The pattern in the second version should be three down, three to
the right, and two up for the first bar, and the same for the second bar.
But M. Chevillard was adamant about the method of beating he pre-
ferred, writes M. Inghelbrecht. "This measure," asserted M. Chevillard
stoutly (this was in 1906), "is an 8/8, that is to say, a 4/4. I will therefore beat it so." M. Inghelbrecht adds wryly that his colleague's system
of beating gave the passage "an exotic flavor."

Writing such passages with indications in the time-signatures not
only for the number of pulses but also for the main accents, and even
with numbers under the phrases, might save a lot of time and confusion
in rehearsal.

In the next quotation by M. Inghelbrecht (Ex. 147), which he aptly
terms "permutations of terno-binary and bino-ternary," the notation
for both conductor and player has been greatly simplified by the numbers placed under the notes to show the small pulse-units, by the number
after the time-signature, and by the dotted lines to show the main pulses.
The student should now be able to evolve his own patterns for Example
147 and similar passages. The units of time should carefully be maintained, e.g., an eighth should remain an eighth regardless of duple or
triple combinations. Do not, in other words, make two eighths equal
three eighths.

This part of the discussion may close with the reflection that some
composers, like some philosophers, seem to delight in expressing the simplest thoughts in the most complicated manner possible.

Chapter Sixteen

COMBINED RHYTHMS

The difficulty of beating combined rhythms has been greatly exaggerated. Any difficulty arising in the performance of such combinations is almost always due to the playing, not to the beating of these passages. Conviction in playing such passages springs more from the routine of the players, the conductor's mental grasp of the music, and his pedagogical talents, than from any baton technique.

There have been advocates of beating simultaneous rhythms with different patterns in each hand, but just what the conductor is to do with only two hands when there are three or more conflicting rhythms, these advocates have never satisfactorily explained. Even when only two patterns are involved, the spectacle of one hand contradicting the other is apt to look like prestidigitation to some members of the audience. As for the instrumentalists, there is the ever present danger that a section of the orchestra meant to be influenced by only one of the hands may be attracted by a conflicting pattern in the other hand, especially when varying rhythmic figures dart about the orchestra pit. The recommendation is here given that only one pattern be beaten at any one time, regardless of the number of rhythmic figures in the music. This recommendation, however, does not nullify the idea that the left hand can and should aid the right hand by indicating entrances, end beats, phrasing, subdivisions, style, mood, and so on.

In so far as time-beating is concerned, simultaneous rhythmic patterns should cause the conductor no more trouble *kinetically* than one rhythmic pattern. When difficulties arise, and admittedly they do arise sometimes, they are usually due to the players' inability to feel the varying pulses. Remedying this defect is a matter of rehearsing. The conductor must come to the first rehearsal so prepared, with the music so clearly ana-

Ex. 148.   Debussy: *L'Après-midi d'un faune* (Permission for reprint granted by Jean Jobert, Paris; Elkan-Vogel Co., Inc., U.S.A. copyright owners.)

lyzed, and knowing so exactly what he wants and how to explain his wishes in orchestral parlance, that nothing remains but to iron out the details.

Some passages, like Examples 148, 155, and 156, really contain conflicting pulses. We must, however, again recall the truism that time-signatures do not in themselves determine the number of strokes to the bar; the speed of the music and the coincidence or lack of coincidence of the main pulses are the determining factors. When one part of the orchestra has only main accents to another part's main accents plus subdivisions, it can hardly be said that genuinely conflicting rhythms are involved, however the time-signatures are written. This fact applies to two against four, four against eight, six against twelve, two against six, three against six, three against nine, four against twelve, etc. Even when one group of instruments has rapid two against three or multiples thereof (as six against nine or eight against twelve), a single stroke takes care of each unit of two against three. In such cases each stroke may be split and a slight breath pause observed, so that the players of both duple and triple figures may interpret the stroke to suit their own parts (Exs. 149, 150).

Ex. 149.   Rimsky-Korsakoff: *Scheherezade* (Copyright by M. P. Belaieff Editions. Used by permission of sole agents, Boosey & Hawkes.)

It is helpful to remember certain principles in the execution of simultaneous rhythmic patterns. The first is that when main pulses coincide,
two different time-signatures do not necessarily increase the conductor's
difficulty. Brisk 2/4 and 6/8, for example, are beaten two to the bar
whether they sound together or in succession. In Example 149, from
Rimsky-Korsakoff's *Scheherezade,* Part 4, the time-signature reads 2/8
(6/16 3/8). Part of the orchestra plays duple, part triple pulse. The
conductor has only to beat one to the bar, and each part interprets this
pattern to fit its own music. The music shifts back and forth here from
two to three pulses to the bar, but the conductor continues beating one
to the bar whether the different pulses follow each other or are played
together. Tchaikovsky's Fourth Symphony, first movement, at "P" in
the Breitkopf and Härtel edition (Example 150) shows the trumpets in
3/4 against 9/8 in the timpani. The main pulses coincide, so the conductor simply beats three to the bar for all players.

The next principle to remember is that the players have their own
notes before them, and also that they have developed what has already
been referred to as a "time and space sense." This means that they can
easily fit into one or two strokes (and with a good orchestra into even
more strokes) any number of notes, so that each note in the group is
proportionate. Thus, when the baton makes a single stroke, players automatically fit into this motion groups of five notes, as in the "Storm
Scene" of Beethoven's Sixth Symphony; groups of five against six, as in
the second movement of Bruckner's First Symphony; groups of seven,
as in Ravel's Second "Daphnis and Chloë" Suite (at no. 187, Durand
et Fils, small score); or, for that matter, a handful of notes done *glissando*
on the harp, as in the final four bars of "Danse infernale du roi Kastcheï"
in Stravinsky's "Firebird" Suite. In Stravinsky's *Petrouchka* (Kalmus
score, page 114), there are groups of five done in single strokes, four to
the bar, where five- and seven-note groups oppose each other. Then
follow groups of five opposing groups of four done to six strokes to the

Ex. 151. Stravinsky: *Petrouchka* (By permission of the copyright owner, Boosey & Hawkes Inc.) See also: Berlioz, *Romeo and Juliet* (Eulenburg edition, page 271, brace 2, until *l'istesso tempo* on the following page), where a simple one to the bar (or two bars as one) holds together four pulses against three.

bar. The players do not have the slightest trouble playing all this, because of their time and space sense.

By means of the same faculty, players can also fit any number of notes into two strokes, regardless of the number of opposing groupings. Thus in Honegger's *Pacific 231* (Philharmonia, small score, page 8, bar 4), there is a group of five notes done to two strokes. On page 9, bar 2, there is a group of seven notes played to two strokes. In each case the players fit in the middle note with ease. A keyboard player or harpist has a real task in such combination passages; but in the orchestra each player is responsible for only one rhythmic pattern. If any difficulty arises, each part may be rehearsed alone and the rhythm drummed in until it becomes a habit, before the parts are played together.

ONE TO THE BAR

A general principle for combined rhythms is to take as few strokes as possible. The simplest case is naturally one stroke to the bar, which is illustrated by Example 151, from *Petrouchka* (Kalmus, small score, page 84, 12th bar after the *allegretto*). We have here a waltz, one to the bar, into which a 2/4 intrudes. It would make no difference at all if other time-signatures and pulses were tacked on, so long as the conductor continued to beat one to the bar. To simplify the phrasing, he should think of this passage as composed of two-measure groups. The players, of course, need not know anything about this technique. They see, or think they see, one stroke to the bar; whereas the conductor, if he wishes,

Ex. 152. Berlioz: *Roman Carnival* Overture

may beat two measures as one: one stroke down slightly to the right and up, and one down again, slightly to the left and up. The odd measures (1, 3, 5, etc.) have the real down beat, the even measures (2, 4, 6, etc.) the adjusted up stroke, but beaten so closely together that detection depends almost upon explicit knowledge of what the conductor is doing.

TWO TO THE BAR

It is an easy step from beating two bars as one to considering passages with two different rhythmic patterns which may be beaten two to the bar. Thus, in Berlioz' *Roman Carnival* Overture (Ex. 152), we have a time-signature of 6/8. The trombones have accents of ONE two THREE four FIVE six, against ONE two three FOUR five six in the French horns, i.e., there are three against two pulses in each measure. This conflict is characteristic of some Spanish music and of music of nations and composers under Spanish influence. Other examples occur in Ravel's *Spanish Rhapsody,* Debussy's *La Mer,* and Chabrier's *España.* Two to the bar is the proper rhythm pattern, though the baton may split the last third of the down stroke and the first third of the up stroke to aid the players having the triple pulse. Some conductors actually change from two to three and vice versa when these accents are consecutive, maintaining the equality of the unit of time-beating, i.e., eighths equal eighths, quarters equal quarters, etc.

Two pulses versus three should be taken in the smaller number of strokes when possible. In *Petrouchka* (Kalmus, small score, at no. 13), we have 2/4 taken two to the bar. At no. 14, fifteen measures later (Ex. 153), the oboes join the violins and violas with a triplet figure. Two strokes to the bar continues.

Two versus three pulses may also be taken in three strokes to the bar, in which case the instrumentalists with duple pulses take the down beat and the first half of the second beat for their first pulse, and the second

COMBINED RHYTHMS

Ex. 153.   Stravinsky: *Petrouchka* (By permission of the copyright owner, Boosey & Hawkes Inc.)

half of the second beat and the up beat for their second pulse. The conductor may split the second stroke to aid the players. Such cases do occur, as in Example 154, where the preceding music has established the triple pulse so firmly that a change might endanger the ensemble. In general, however, one should choose to beat the smallest number of strokes possible.

TWO TO THE BAR   125

Ex. 154. Strauss: *Ein Heldenleben* (Published by F. E. C. Leuckhart; used by permission of Associated Music Publishers, Inc.)

The finale of the Mussorgsky-Ravel *Pictures at an Exhibition* ("La Grande Porte de Kiev") and measures 14–17 (counting from the end) of Berlioz' *Harold in Italy* offer two more good examples of places where two to the bar is kept up though the prevailing pulse is triple.

It is easy to maintain a firm ensemble with two strokes to the bar against any other pulse, combination of pulses, or groupings of notes, provided that two strokes to the bar is sufficient to keep the tempo flowing. Thus in *Petrouchka*, page 11, bars 3 and 4 (Kalmus, small score), there is 5/8 against 2/4 (4/8). Already established is the whirling figure in the violins, a sort of inverted *basso ostinato,* which acts as musical pivot. The players with the four eighths take two on the down stroke and two on the up; those with the five eighths fit in the third eighth without any trouble. On page 98, last bar of the same work, the time signature is 6/8 (12/16) against the two piccolo-oboe five-note groups. Two strokes to the bar will give all the support the players need for a firm ensemble at this place.

Rimsky-Korsakoff's "Golden Cockerel" Suite at bar 21, Part 2, "King Dodon on the Battlefield," presents 4/4 against 6/4 in *alla breve.* Here there are four eighth notes against three quarter notes to each stroke; and since the measure divides exactly into half, two strokes to the bar solves the problem simply.

In the same composer's *Russian Easter,* each of the four measures before the *allegro agitato* (Kalmus, small score, page 12) contains fifteen notes in the harp part against eight eighth notes in the clarinet. Again, two to the bar is sufficient. The harp plays seven notes on each stroke and fits in the middle one between strokes.

FOUR TO THE BAR

From two strokes to the bar against three pulses, we proceed to four to the bar against six pulses, a fairly common combination (Exs. 155 and 156). Again we take the smaller number of strokes, four. The players

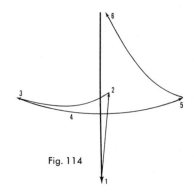

Fig. 114

Ex. 156.   Wagner: Prelude to *Parsifal*

with four pulses take one pulse for each stroke; those with the six pulses take three pulses to each two strokes. In other words, we beat six *as* four (see Figure 114). This maneuver often impresses auditors as being quite intricate and difficult.

When the music calls for four units against six and the six pulse has been already well established before the four pulse enters, it is sometimes the better part of valor to adopt some sort of six pattern, or better still, a simple two pattern subdivided into six (Figs. 23 and 24). The elementary mathematics involved should cause no reasonably good ensemble any concern. For instance, in Example 157, from Bruckner's Second Symphony, the oboe solo enters with four pulses to the bar after a string

Ex. 157.   Bruckner: Symphony No. 2. See also: Strauss, *Also sprach Zarathustra;* Chabrier, *Gwendoline* Overture; Wagner, *Siegfried,* "Forest Murmurs."

pizzicato has already established a six pattern. The conductor beats two subdivided as six. The oboe holds the first half note for the down beat and its subdivisions; it plays the subsequent quarter note on the second stroke and half the next subdivision, and the last quarter note of the bar on the second half of the subdivision just delineated and through the last subdivision of the up beat. The second bar of the quotation may be done the same way.

It was the quaint custom of some conductors in central Europe, until at least the early 1920's, to conduct this passage beating four to the bar with one hand and six with the other. This is not only unnecessary but may easily cause confusion when orchestral eyes looking at one pattern stray to the other. A few minutes of proper rehearsing should iron out any uncertainty in the passage.

THREE TO THE BAR

Measures containing three pulses with other pulses against them and calling for three strokes to the bar present little more difficulty than the cases considered heretofore.

Beethoven's Ninth Symphony, at the last measure before the double

Ex. 158.   Beethoven: Symphony No. 9

fugue in 6/4 (page 239 of the Breitkopf and Härtel edition), offers a case of eight sixteenths against three quarters, three times. Consider the second measure of the 3/2 in Example 158, which is being done three to the bar. The duple pulse of the sixteenths in the strings and especially on the low *A* roll in the timpano, coupled with the implied *calando* and *ritenuto*, calls for the utmost clarity and precision. It is suggested here that the first beat be given so that the down stroke and rebound imply subdivisions, that the second stroke be split into two parts, and that the third stroke be actually given as two detailed parts, each part split with a breath pause. The players with the duple pulses will, of course, have no trouble following this splitting into equal parts of the strokes; the wood winds, playing triplets on each stroke, may be aided by a breath pause between the quasi subdivisions. The conductor should execute the split beats in as straight a line as possible, to give the players the impression that he is still giving the stroke as a whole.

When three pulses play against six, nine, or twelve, they may be treated simply as main beats with subdivisions and there is then no problem, of course. But when three pulses are played against seven, as in *Petrouchka* (pages 10, 18, and 28, Kalmus small score), we have a choice of two courses. The easier way is to have the main pulses coincide by making three of the notes in the seven group a triplet. This the composer has kindly done for us, and he has so arranged the first three notes as to leave the last four for the two final pulses, which happily coincide with the prevailing accents elsewhere. If this solution had not been possible, and the composer had written his music to call for seven *equal* pulses against the rest of the context, the only alternative would have been to give three strokes and to train the players to divide the seven notes into this pattern through their time and space sense. This alternative, frankly, would not be comfortable, and a very good orchestra indeed would be required to execute it convincingly. Three strokes against four, or vice versa, presents the same problem and requires the same solution.

Also in *Petrouchka,* page 11, last bar, there are eight eighth notes against three quarter notes (12/16). Beat three strokes, splitting the second stroke in the center so that the group having eight notes apportions four notes to the down beat and the first half of the second beat, and the other four notes to the last half of the second beat and the up beat. In *Le Sacre du Printemps* (Kalmus, small score, page 63, bar 2), there is a *basso ostinato,* three beats to the bar with a five-note group taking up the last two strokes. Another such case may be found in Ravel's *Spanish Rhapsody* on page 62 in the miniature score (Durand et Fils). Note the five-pulse bar in the solo clarinet against the three pulses elsewhere.

Ex. 159. Berlioz: *Damnation of Faust*

MULTIPLE BARS TAKEN AS ONE

Hector Berlioz, in his book *Art of the Conductor*, discusses an excerpt from his own *The Damnation of Faust,* here reproduced in Example 159.

The principle to be extracted from this passage is that, when possible, one should combine several single measures into one large group and think of them in the resultant new time-signature. In this excerpt we may consider the three short bars as one long bar in 18/8. We proceed to beat this long bar as three subdivided into six, and each section of the orchestra interprets the pattern to suit its own musical text (see Figure 29). Thus, the 6/8 (18/8) players get one subdivided pulse for each three eighths, while the 3/4 players get one main pulse for each quarter.

In considering his next excerpt from his own "Harold" Symphony (Ex. 160), Berlioz expresses the fear that giving subdivisions might confuse the players. Obviously, orchestras of his time were not what they might have been; this procedure would cause no ripple among players today. The passage is beaten in two subdivided (adapted to *legato* so that each subdivision splits and has a tiny breath pause).

An interesting excerpt from Spohr's *The Birth of Music* (quoted in Deldevez's *L'Art du chef d'orchestre*), which is presented here in Example

Ex. 160. Berlioz: *Harold in Italy*

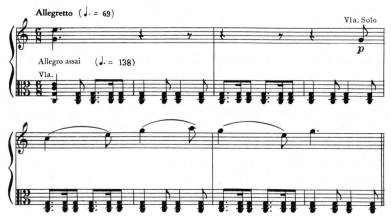

161, yields easily enough to analysis. Spohr himself suggested that the conductor (or violinist-director) mark each sixteenth note with up and down beats of the baton or bow. While this primitive solution may be feasible, it is far better to think of the passage as "edited" like Example 162, and to beat it simply in broad two to the bar. With the slight revisions in the second version, the tempo is nothing more complicated than two against three, with a held *B* flat; the players can interpret the beat in any desired manner.

The waltz in Stravinsky's *Histoire du soldat* offers an apt illustration in this connection (no. 22, page 45, Chester small score). The solo pianoforte arrangement (Ex. 163) has two staves, with 4/4 in the upper staff and 3/4 in the lower staff, for twelve bars until "Ragtime." The small score (Ex. 164), however, has everything neatly done in 3/4, with accents to

Ex. 162.   Spohr: *The Birth of Music* (edited)

Ex. 163. Stravinsky: *Histoire du soldat* (By permission of J. & W. Chester, Ltd., London and of G. Schirmer, Inc., New York.)

show where the conflicting pulses come. (In the quoted excerpt here one staff is omitted, that of the *cornet à pistons,* which enters later.)

As the music is written in the official pianoforte arrangement, one should consider the over-all time-signature as being 12/4 (consisting of three 4/4 and four 3/4 measures), which may be beaten four down, four to the right, and four up. The passage might easily have been written more simply, as it was in the small score. In the latter, the over-all time-signature is 12/4 (but this time four against three). It may now be beaten simply with four main strokes subdivided as twelve, i.e., three 4/4 measures equal four 3/4 measures, making one large 12/4 measure. The part playing the waltz will follow naturally; the part with the four quarter notes in the original measures may be aided with slight stresses of the baton where the accents occur.

The principle to be extracted from this excerpt is that in such cases it is wise to make one over-all measure from enough measures of the conflicting rhythmic patterns so that each of the conflicting rhythmic patterns can be divided evenly into it, i.e., the large measure contains enough small measures to constitute the least common denominator. Pierre Monteux and other conductors have followed this system of

Ex. 164. Stravinsky: *Histoire du soldat* (edited) (By permission of J. & W. Chester, Ltd., London and of G. Schirmer, Inc., New York.)

Ex. 165. Brahms: Symphony No. 2

Ex. 166. Brahms: Symphony No. 2 (edited)

simplification on more than one occasion in conducting Stravinsky's works. Stravinsky himself has been known to "simplify" his scores (or permit his editors to do so for him), and he has certainly practiced similar procedures in conducting his own music. There is, therefore, nothing disrespectful about this principle. It is, of course, very useful for all combinations of multiple rhythms; for instance, in combined 5/8 and 3/8, one may think of the passage as in 15/8.

In this discussion of the way some composers habitually use the most complicated notation possible, there comes to mind the famous passage from the last movement of Brahms's Symphony No. 2, which occurs the first time at bar 130, the second time at bar 333 (see Example 165). Can one say that his music has lost anything by keeping the notation simple, when he might have written something like Example 166?

MORE THAN TWO SIMULTANEOUS PATTERNS

Many passages which at first glance seem to have more than two simultaneous patterns reveal after inspection that this is not really so from the point of view of the conductor. Thus, a glance at Example 167, the oft-quoted passage from the "Ballroom Scene" in Mozart's *Don Giovanni* (pages 172–173, Peters edition), usually considered as containing three distinct rhythmic patterns, will show that three measures of 3/8 may be considered simply as one measure in 9/8, and that the main pulses of this long measure coincide with those in the single 3/4 measure. We have now left nothing more formidable than a duple pulse in 2/4 against a triple pulse in 3/4. The traditional solution is to give all down beats. It is recommended here that this procedure be followed, with the qualification that the first stroke of every three be of full length with a long rebound and that the following two strokes be taken down also, but shorter in length. This passage usually intrigues auditors, who think it is very difficult to conduct, especially because the action calls for dancing and stage business. It is really quite simple.

The passage may easily be rewritten or thought of with the 2/4 as a 3/4, and accents placed where the bar lines formerly showed the beginning of the measures. The passage could then be taken three to the bar without any mental confusion whatever (see Example 168).

Giving all down beats a measure in this fashion is also helpful in holding together amateur and educational organizations, which often need exaggerated motions to keep them from swaying. A neat device consists of giving the regular patterns of a measure with the right hand alone and at the same time giving all down beats with the left hand raised high above the right. Here too, the down beat is to be longer than the other strokes in the measure. The right hand may be reserved for the orchestra players; the left aimed at the stage singers to comfort, reassure, encourage, exhort, and console.

DEBUSSY'S *LA MER*

Three passages of unusual rhythmic interest, which at times have caused concern, may now be considered in some detail. The first occurs in Debussy's *La Mer* (Durand et Fils, small score, page 17). The length of the quotations considered in this section makes it impossible to include them in this volume; so the student is referred to the scores themselves. The two pages preceding this passage have already established a rhythm of six to the bar. On page 17, this six pulse is maintained by the flutes, oboes, English horn, clarinets, French horns, and violins. The bassoons and contrabasses have three quarter notes to the measure, which should

COMBINED RHYTHMS

Ex. 167.   Mozart: *Don Giovanni*

Ex. 168.   Mozart: *Don Giovanni* (edited)

hardly cause any added concern, for it merely means a case of conflicting accents already considered: ONE two three FOUR five six against ONE two THREE four FIVE six. The muted trumpet (sometimes tripled here to bring out its line in the orchestral web) has three eighth notes for the first half of bars one and three, and two dotted eighth notes for the last half of the first measure, with quarter notes in the second measure.

Beaten six to the bar, as is the usual practice, the trumpet has only to play one eighth note to each stroke of the baton, one dotted eighth for a stroke and a half, and one quarter for two strokes. The other parts have no trouble in following a six to the bar pattern, except the harps, violas, and cellos, which all have eight notes to the measure. This means that these players must fit in four notes for each half measure to three strokes of the baton. It requires a very good orchestra indeed to perform this feat with neatness, for it very rarely comes off with conviction and ease.

The usual reason given for beating six to the bar here is that the preceding pages have so firmly established the six pulse in the minds of the players that any change might endanger the ensemble. Nevertheless, I recommend that this excerpt be taken four to the bar, and that the four pulse be started one bar early (at no. 8, the last bar on page 16), a precaution which should serve to establish the change in pattern. Care should be taken to make the four pulses equal in duration to the preceding six. The whole passage, then, is only another example of our old friend, four against six. The first bar on page 18 is taken in three subdivided as six (see Figure 29).

STRAVINSKY'S *LE SACRE DU PRINTEMPS*

The second passage for detailed consideration occurs in Stravinsky's *Le Sacre* on pages 60–61 (full score) at no. 70. The signature, 6/4, has grown naturally out of the preceding 4/4. The composer continues the four pulse in the percussion section (timpani, bass drum, tam-tam, and guëro), against the six pulse elsewhere. To add to the possibility of indecision, some of the players execute a neutral succession of six quarter notes, while others (especially the brass) play ONE two THREE four FIVE six, a sort of 3/2.

Again we have what amounts to a four pulse against a six pulse, and it is quite possible to beat it as such. The texture is so complex, however, that I recommend that the usual four-beat pattern be given *as six,* adapted to look like a straight line to the watchers, as much as possible (see Figure 115). This procedure gives the players the illusion they are seeing a kind of two to the bar. In such involved passages, the aim should

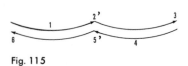

Fig. 115

be to give the simplest pattern possible in the fewest number of strokes, pairing as many motions in the same direction as possible, in order to give the players every aid in using their time and space sense. The players having the duple pulse will interpret the four strokes easily enough to suit their parts, while the players having six pulses will play half the measure to the down and half to the up stroke, i.e., three pulses to each subdivision. Once the players know this routine, it may be quite feasible to try beating slow four as six. The time-signature may be thought of as 12/8 rather than the written 6/4. A helpful device, also, is to run a dotted line down the two pages, cutting each measure in half. The players will then feel they are merely playing four against six twice in the same measure.

Our third special passage for detailed consideration occurs at no. 134, pages 106–107, also in *Le Sacre*. The preceding measure, the last on page 105, is taken in three subdivided into six, and it establishes the pattern for the two succeeding pages. Four horns with their bells in the air and three oboes are carrying the main melodic line, and the attention of the conductor is naturally concentrated on them. On page 107, two flutes, an echoing piccolo, and the first violins play twelve notes to each stroke. The third flute, the alto flute in *G*, the clarinets, and the second violins have four notes to each stroke. The other players have to be content with two and even only one note to each stroke. Stripped of running figures and written out in skeletal notation, the rhythmic simplicity of the arabesque pages emerges. If the pages are taken in three subdivided, slowly and distinctly, the ensemble should be quite firm. Figure 29 may be adapted to this passage by giving the down beat with a rebound to the center, the first subdivision again down with its own rebound, and the second and third beats of the model each divided in the center of their strokes.

A passage in this category, already referred to, occurs in the "Feria" of Ravel's *Spanish Rhapsody* (last bar, page 62, Durand small score), where the solo clarinet plays five pulses against three in the rest of the orchestra. The conductor maintains the established three to the bar, taking care to make the model as round as possible and creating an illusion of one continuous line. This enables the players to measure mentally the start and end of the model and make use of their time and space sense.

Another interesting passage with combined pulses occurs in Richard Strauss's *Salome,* where the orchestra is in 3/4 while the voice part, in 4/4, sings "Und brutale ungeschlachte Römer mit ihrer plumpen Sprache." The voice part might also have been written in 3/4, using appropriate dotted lines and accents, with no loss in effect. As it is written, if taken three to the bar it should cause no trouble. Another passage worth close study by the student is the last scene of Wagner's *Götterdammerung,* in which three different time-signatures occur simultaneously.

Although the usual rhythmic problems which a conductor meets in his ordinary routine have been considered in this chapter, it is quite possible to run across music which suggests cunningly wrought acoustical juxtapositions rather than emotional urge. It is admittedly conceivable to put on paper rhythmic combinations which could tax the ingenuity and technical powers of any conductor or orchestra, and which might even produce interesting intellectual results. Passages more complicated than those here considered may perhaps be encountered, though such a contingency is doubtful; for although more mathematical complication than we have studied is indeed possible, such passages would suggest "eye" rather than "ear" music.

Part Two

STYLE AND INTERPRETATION

TEMPO

The whole duty of a conductor is comprised in his ability always to indicate the right tempo. His choice of tempos will show whether he understands the piece or not. With good players, moreover, the true tempo induces correct phrasing and expression; and conversely, with a conductor, the idea of appropriate phrasing will induce the conception of the true tempo. This, however, is by no means so simple a matter as it appears.

Richard Wagner, *On Conducting*, 1869

We come now to the application of the techniques and physical skills we have been studying to the interpretative demands of music. One of the most vexing questions confronting the student at this stage of his work is, "How can one determine the correct tempo of a given passage?" On the answer to this question depends the choice of pattern, and failure to recognize the correct tempo and consequently the correct pattern lies at the root of much confused interpretation. The problem is especially acute in music of past generations. Yet it cannot be solved for the student by a categorical answer to his question.

In moderate tempos it is quite possible, metronomically speaking, to beat two or four, three or six, four or eight, in exactly the same number of seconds. One conductor may take a given passage with fewer beats than another; a third conductor may use subdivisions. Musically the result is quite different to the eye and ear, upon both performers and auditors, and is at once apparent.

FASHION AND TRADITION IN TEMPO

Many think tempos in general are somewhat faster today than they were a generation ago. It is a fact that some nations "feel" music faster or slower than do other national groups. One has but to listen to a

Beethoven, Debussy, or Tchaikovsky composition successively interpreted by French, German, Italian, and Russian conductors to realize how strikingly different are their conceptions of tempo. Different orchestras of different nationalities have varying reflexes, as do even orchestras in different cities of the same country. The same conductor has been known to vary in tempo and beating in successive performances of the same work.

Fashions change. Fritz Recktenwald's *Ueber das Dirigieren,* written in Vienna in 1929, contains the following revealing passage. "Thirty years ago it was the fashion to interpret Bach with all the eighths beaten out. The *allegros* in Beethoven's First and Second Symphonies were still beaten in four to the bar. This does not enter anyone's head nowadays . . . The *allegros* are now taken two to the bar, the Bach music in slow four, and here and there, as the melodic line broadens, the eighths are articulated. Similarly, the Storm Scene (despite Beethoven's *alla breve* directions), used to be given in rather slow four. This is no longer necessary, for even choral societies (with few exceptions) have got away from the beating of each subdivision." Perusal of literature on musical interpretation of half a century ago will reveal many similar instances of varying conceptions in tempos and time-beating.

Advice to students to go to tradition for guidance is fairly common. But is so-called tradition always, or even generally, safe? Has it not a facility for easy accretion? Is it not sometimes the result of the questionable taste or egocentricity or even megalomania of some conductors who were worshipped temporarily? Many of Weingartner's strictures on von Bülow in the former's *On Conducting* were largely justified. Finally, there is the understandable liability of honest error in oral and aural transmission.

COMPOSERS' AND CONDUCTORS' TEMPOS

Shall we rely always upon the composer's own words or performances? An experience concerning Dukas' *The Sorcerer's Apprentice* and Arturo Toscanini shows that this is not always wise, even when it is possible. Dukas, who had written in the metronome marks himself, attended a performance of the work under Toscanini's direction in Paris some years ago. After the performance he expressed his puzzlement at what he thought was the conductor's excessive speed in some places. The conductor's reply was to point to the metronome marks. The composer subsequently admitted, at least indirectly, that either his original marks were wrong or that he had changed his mind. A short time after this episode, the publishers of the work issued a badly mimeographed note with many changes in tempo, even suppressing the direction "rhythme ternaire."

Here follows the publisher's corrected version.

Page 1—*Assez lent*.................... ♪ = 90 to 103 instead of ♩ = 44
Page 2—*Vif*..................... ♪ = 168   instead of ♪ = 176
Page 3—*Ier mouvt*.................... ♪ = 103   instead of ♩ = 44
    Vif.................... ♪. = 168   instead of ♪ = 176
Page 5—*Vif*..................... ♩ = 116   instead of ♩ = 126

(Elide the "ryhthme ternaire.")

Page 41—*Plus animé*........... add....................... ♩. = 120
Page 48—*Très vif*.............. add....................... ♩. = 146
Page 49—*Retenu*.............. add....................... ♩ = 80
Page 50—*Plus retenu*........... 68 instead of................. ♩. = 80
Page 51—*A tempo*............. add....................... ♩. = 116
Page 59—*8th Measure*........... add "Très legerement retenu"
Page 60—*A tempo*............. add....................... ♩. = 116

(N.B. The Celeste may replace the Glockenspiel)

As a finishing touch, let us add that the emendated version issued by the publishers also contains obvious errors and that even French conductors differ in their ideas of tempo in this work, e.g., this writer has heard the dotted-eighth measures on page 50 and at no. 42 vary from metronome markings 50 to 70.

On one occasion Ravel, after hearing his *Bolero* conducted by Toscanini, made it quite evident that he did not agree with the tempos adopted. Stravinsky conducts his own works at certain tempos and has been known occasionally to criticize another conductor for taking the same tempos. George Bernard Shaw, in an interview with this writer, which was published in the *New York Herald Tribune* on June 25, 1939, recalled that "Siegfried Wagner once bored his listeners almost to anesthesia in the *Meistersinger* Prelude by his unconscionably dragging tempos. Toward the end of the piece, when the critics had long since departed, he achieved the apparently impossible by slowing up still more, and the audience became electrified and gave him an ovation." Now if the son of a composer, who had an unparalleled opportunity to absorb traditional tempos first-hand, so erred (and this has been affirmed by other competent hearers), what are we to say about tradition?

In related vein, we find these lines in Alfred Pochon's *Musique d'autrefois—Interprétation d'aujourd'hui* (Geneva, Henn, 1943). "It is known as a matter of fact that the three great orchestral conductors: Hans Richter, Hermann Levi, and Felix Mottl, each received all tempo and other indications in the conducting of the *Siegfried Idyl* first-hand *from Wagner himself*. And yet testimony of irreproachable authority relates that these three interpretations differed one from the other quite sensibly."

And so we have a variety of episodes occurring at different epochs; Ravel and Toscanini, Stravinsky and other interpreters of his works, George Bernard Shaw and Siegfried Wagner, all pointing up the extreme difficulty of agreeing on tempo indications, of the subjective elements involved, and even of accepting so-called traditional tempos.

Are recordings to be trusted? More than one conductor has expressed astonishment upon hearing his playbacks. Performing before a living audience produces different mental and emotional conditions from performing in an empty studio. Conductors have been known to vary tempos of the same composition in the recording studio, before audiences, and over the air.

TEMPOS IN BEETHOVEN'S FOURTH SYMPHONY

What are we to say when famous conductors depart from printed directions and deviate from each other, not in a small degree but in fundamentals? A comparison of tempos by two of the greatest conductors of recent times (Weingartner and Toscanini), in a work like Beethoven's Symphony No. 4 (the choice might have been almost any classical or romantic symphony) reveals surprising divergences. Yet the two interpretations are each the result of the deepest sincerity, the most careful and humble study, and a lifetime of experience. Here is the comparative table.

Beethoven's Fourth Symphony

Movement	Score marking	Weingartner	Toscanini
1. Introduction, *Adagio*	♩ = 66	♩ = 58	♩ = 44–46
Allegro vivace	𝅗𝅥 = 80	♩ = 126	♩ = 150
2. *Adagio*	♪ = 84	♪ = 72	♪. = 76
3. *Allegro vivace*	𝅗𝅥. = 100	. . . . . .	𝅗𝅥. = 118
4. *Allegro ma non troppo*	♩ = 80	♩ = 126	♩ = 140–142

Felix Weingartner, in his invaluable commentary, *On the Performance of Beethoven's Symphonies,* explains his own tempos for this symphony. Here follow representative excerpts.

First Movement: *Adagio*

Instead of the very quick metronome mark, ♩=66, I have adopted ♩=58. The transition to the *Allegro* produces the most natural effect if the half bars are played twice as fast as the quarter notes in the introduction. The corresponding metronome mark for the *Allegro* is ♩=126. The prescribed mark, 𝅗𝅥=80, gives an absolutely impossible speed.

Second Movement: *Adagio*

I have found here the metronome mark, ♩=84. This is, of course, a misprint; it must mean ♪=84. But this mark is also too quick, so I should recommend ♪=72, or thereabouts.

Scherzo and *Trio*

The extreme limit of speed for the *Trio* seems to me to be about ♩.=76; the tempo prescribed, ♩.=88, would cause an overhastening of this graceful piece. It should be noted also that ♩.=100 for the main section does not denote a very rapid tempo. It is a great error, and unfortunately a very common one, to play all of Beethoven's Scherzos quasi *presto*.

Finale

The *Finale* is marked *Allegro, ma non troppo*. The humor of this delightful piece is quite destroyed, however, if the *ma non troppo* is not observed, and if the movement is played like one of Haydn's final symphony movements. Not only must it be started with a comparatively quiet tempo, but this tempo must be maintained throughout so that the piquant play of the sixteenth notes does not degenerate into an exercise, or the pleasing melody of the secondary theme become a mere commonplace phrase. The great charm of the movement lies in just this contrast between the moderate tempo and the animated figuration. It gives an impression of speed without being played quickly. The metronome mark, ♩=80, does not in the least agree with the time signature. I should think that ♩=126 would be about right.

A similarly detailed analysis of tempos in any other symphony, as taken by the chief conductors of our time, would undoubtedly reveal equally disconcerting differences. Mengelberg adopted what sometimes seemed to the eye unusually slow tempos, yet to many hearers his tempos did not drag, so nobly were they sustained. Toscanini, in some instances, notably in Beethoven's Seventh Symphony, has adopted faster tempos than some of his contemporaries. Yet the frames of both conductors' interpretations have always seemed, at least to this hearer, to be logical and to result from inner compulsion. The point might be labored. The conclusion to be drawn from this discussion is that metronomic considerations yield to personality, sincerity, and conviction.

THE STUDENT'S APPROACH TO TEMPO

The answer to the student's question concerning correct tempos, then, is anything but absolute. The burden of the final decision lies upon each individual interpreter. Get whatever tradition you can first-hand. Hear as many interpretations by authoritative conductors as you can. Read what you can find about the works under consideration. Then decide for yourself. That you may and probably will change your conceptions of tempos from time to time until you die will only parallel the experiences of most searchers for the truth.

A metronomic check of some well-known interpreters reveals that many soon deviate from the tempos they adopt at the start of a work, despite the musical demands for a steady pulse. This deviation is, in most cases, unintentional, quite different from those deviations in tempo which are caused by deliberate exaggeration to obtain greater climaxes. (A famous conductor of a past generation deliberately took faster and faster tempos as he grew older, to prove to his hearers that his advancing age did not at all effect his vitality.) It is paradoxical that the ability to maintain a steady and undeviating tempo is beyond the powers of many. This faculty may be developed by studying such works as Ravel's *Bolero;* the second movement of Haydn's "Clock" Symphony; the second movement of Beethoven's Eighth Symphony, which immortalizes the metronome; Liadoff's *Musical Snuff Box;* and the *Perpetuum Mobile* by Johann Strauss, Jr.

A helpful exercise in this regard, though admittedly not a very exciting one, is to set the metronome at various speeds and beat various patterns, first with each hand separately and then with both hands. It will be found that it is often possible not only to beat various patterns for the same speed, but also to use main beats with and without subdivisions at the same speed.

It should be remembered that indications of tempo, shading, and phrasing vary according to the places in which they occur. They are as much matters of mood as of speed. Words like *larghissimo, largo, larghetto, andantino, andante, adagissimo, adagio, adagietto, lento, lentissimo, moderato, allegro, allegretto, con moto, vivo, vivace,* and *presto;* connecting words like *accelerando, stringendo,* and *affrettando;* and their antonyms, *ritardando, ritenuto, meno mosso, allargando,* etc., may be combined in any number of ways, not only with each other, but also with such qualifying terms as *ma non troppo, assai,* etc. These all vary with each individual, with each nation, with each epoch and composer, and above all, with the context of the term.

VERY SLOW AND VERY FAST TEMPOS

Let us compare patterns in very slow and in very fast tempos. Obviously, in fast tempos the patterns become shorter and cover distance in less time than in slow ones, and omit all possible curves, subdivisions, and extra motions. The faster the tempo, the shorter the rebound after the down beat. In very fast tempo this rebound practically disappears. The main accents of the pattern stand out while the weak beats tend more and more to become minor in strength and length. Weak second beats cease to jut out and tend to hug the center of the pattern. Furthermore, fast tempos limit the strokes to the wrist, with less and less arm movement. In broad tempos, on the contrary, weak beats assume more and more independence in length and strength, subdivisions reappear, and the arm shares the movement with the wrist.

It is odd—or is it?—that few young conductors seem able to vie with their older colleagues in beating very slow tempos with sustained elevation. This is a matter not simply of experience but rather of mellowness and spiritual serenity. The same statement applies to younger instrumental virtuosi. One of the tests of a conductor's maturity is indeed the playing of a slow movement by Brahms, Handel, Bach, Beethoven, or Gluck. Here technique counts for comparatively little, and the essence of the music must be inspired by the posture, attitude, and facial expression of the conductor.

To connect sections and movements of a work logically and smoothly requires taste and judgment. Schumann's Symphony No. 4, which should be played without pauses between movements, demands special skill and smoothness in going from the *scherzo* to the introduction of the last movement. The aim here is to make the transition of tempo and mood between the two movements imperceptible, from the *poco ritenuto* on the final sixteen measures of the *scherzo* to the start of the final movement.

Although it is difficult to translate tempo into written directions for baton motions, we might recommend for this passage the following succession of patterns. Beat one to the bar in the *scherzo,* but with two-measure grouping for measures 218–219 (beginning one bar before *poco ritenuto*) through the two-measure group 224–225. Note that the inhalations come on measures 217, 221, and 225. At measures 226–232, the pattern is more like three to the bar but so fluid that it suggests one to the bar. The mood and tempo abate so imperceptibly and gradually that by the time we reach the last measure of the *scherzo,* the quarter note metronomically equals the quarter note of the opening stroke of the new section—metronomically, that is; but the mood, in contrast to the brooding at the end of the *scherzo,* marked *langsam,* begins to stir mysteriously here; the atmosphere becomes quickened with anticipation; and when we reach the twelfth measure at the *stringendo,* quickened mood is added to quickened pace. When we reach the eighteenth measure, marked *lebhaft,* the tempo should be pretty nearly 126 for the quarter, as marked.

Often at a new section the composer has marked in the score a unit of the measure just left and its equivalent unit in time of the measure just reached. Thus, at the start of the *langsam* for the final movement, the marking might be "♩ = ♩". In interpreting such printed directions, one must remember that they are merely metronomic and mathematical symbols, and that the conductor must achieve the transition of mood in addition.

In the incomparable passacaglia in the last movement of Brahms's Symphony No. 4, we note that at the 97th measure (the flute variation) a quarter note equals a quarter note of the previous section. The connection in mood here between the variations as well as throughout this movement as a whole constitutes one of the great challenges to a conductor's architectural grasp of a composition. Instances of such transitions in mood might be multiplied at great length, among them, certain passages in Debussy's *L'Après-midi d'un faune*. Suffice it to say that whether or not a composer writes into the score the metronomic relation of sections or movements, one is always implied; otherwise a movement or section would rest in a vacuum, outside the orbit of the whole framework. Failure to achieve the correct transitions between sections and movements inevitably results in a wrench, not only in tempo, but what is worse, in mood. This statement does not apply, of course, to dramatic music, where abrupt changes are premeditated.

By using the proper patterns, one may easily beat changes in speed with fidelity to the outline, though change in mood can be neither described nor dissected. For patterns showing increase in speed, one may first beat six to the bar, using the regular pattern where each stroke is carefully articulated; then use a pattern with change in direction for each stroke; then beat two to the bar, first with subdivisions and finally without subdivisions. For decrease in speed, let us consider a case where we start with four subdivided. We may first omit the subdivisions and use a breath pause, then use a pattern which changes the direction of the strokes, and then beat two to the bar. The sequence naturally depends upon each passage. To detail representative cases would amount in effect to a résumé of practically all the patterns presented thus far.

Applying these patterns is a matter of art and not one of science. Here, we are at the extreme opposite of mannered and rigid measure-by-measure time-beating. If we are beating a retarding passage in six to the bar, we might first change to a pattern having a new direction for each stroke, and then add subdivisions. If we are beating in four to the bar a passage with twelve pulses a measure and accelerating tempo, we might first change to a pattern having a new direction for each pulse, then elide the middle subdivisions by observing breath pauses, and last elide both subdivisions and go into four to the bar.

In choosing patterns to delineate gradual changes in speed, you will note that one of the chief problems of the conductor is to beat *clearly* such places as are too fast for three to the bar and yet not quite slow enough for one to the bar, or too fast for six and too slow for two, and so on. Without some connecting patterns, the change often proves abrupt. Connecting such tempos requires skillful treatment so that the transition from one tempo to another is achieved with fluidity and conviction. One of the best means of doing this is to use for this connecting terrain patterns in which each stroke changes direction and yet in which the main stresses are clearly delineated. The procedure is somewhat akin to changing fingers in reiterated notes on the pianoforte keyboard. Two, three, and four to the bar offer no special difficulty; six- and eight-pulse patterns do.

CORRECTING PLAYERS WHO HURRY OR DRAG

One warning is worth repeating: guard against the tendency which some orchestras have to increase in speed with *crescendo* and to slow up with *decrescendo*. This is analagous to the tendency to increase in volume on ascending passages and to decrease in volume on descending passages. In a concert, where the conductor cannot speak, he still has technical devices for bringing erring forces into line. When the orchestra drags, he may bring the baton to the end of its strokes slightly ahead of the players and await them there. When they catch up, he may have the baton repeat this hint till the speed is right. He must make these motions, however, without wrenching. He may also shorten the strokes and elide all extra motions and subdivisions. This is a good place to recall once more that some brass and timpani players tend to be late on attacks and to hold back; consequently they may require special attention.

When players hurry, they may be held in check by adding breath pauses or quasi subdivisions. The baton may be dropped slightly at about the middle of the stroke, thus splitting the beat. It may then be raised to its proper place in the pattern by the end of the stroke. The left forefinger may be extended as a warning for extreme cases, but not too ostentatiously.

Some composers write their music in such a way that the metronomic change in pace is inescapable. But a change in mood still requires the conductor's suggestive powers. Two examples spring to mind. The first occurs in the last measures of Beethoven's *Coriolanus* Overture. Let us take it in two to the bar. Note the first violin and cello parts. At the nineteenth bar before the end, the first violins have a two-bar figure on middle *C* and the *B* natural below it. In the following bar the cellos have a figure of eight eighth notes. The violins then repeat the two-bar phrase, but the cellos vary their first figure to play six quarter notes in two triplet groups. The composer has written here *senza più piano* for the third time in the same number of measures. No diminution of power is needed. It is implied in the notes themselves, which grow longer in duration. The violins next play their figure over four instead of over two bars; the cello figure has dotted halves; and in the ninth measure before the end, the violins hold the *B* natural for four whole bars before relinquishing it to the *C* natural, while the cellos almost postpone their descent to the low *C*. Now comes a bar of Aeschylaen rest and three hushed murmurs *pizzicato*. By means so apparently simple as almost to defy description, the composer attains an effect of Olympian dissolution unique in the literature of music. It is scarcely necessary to observe the retard; the music breathes it.

A different kind of example occurs in Stravinsky's "Firebird" Suite (Kalmus score, 1919 version). The composer has indicated an *accelerando poco a poco* in the first bar of page 54. We are beating three brisk strokes to the bar. At no. 29, page 55, bar 5 (*più mosso*), we change to one to the bar, taking care that the previous single beat now equals a whole measure. The time-signatures have not changed. At no. 31, page 58, the time-signature becomes 2/2 and we continue in one to the bar. Actually we phrase two bars as one. At no. 33, page 60, bar 3, the 6/4 enters and we still continue one to the bar, phrasing two bars as one. At no. 37, page 63, the 3/4 enters; and here we definitely beat two bars as one to the end of the movement, which, for concert purposes, is on page 65.

While it is possible, even desirable, to increase the speed slightly and gradually until the end of the movement in the passage we have been discussing, the effect of increasing tempo has been practically achieved by the composer himself, who first gives us six eighth notes in three strokes, then six eighth notes in one stroke, then four eighths in four, then six quarters in one (or two as some take it); and who writes arpeggios in the wood winds and handfuls of *glissandos* in the harps in the last four bars of the movement. The result is an exciting musical "lift." A slight but appreciable *accelerando* is implied in the text, but it is hardly needed; the music itself suggests it in mood.

Chapter Eighteen

MEASURE GROUPINGS

AND RUBATO

MEASURE GROUPINGS

A distinguishing characteristic of maturity in interpretation is freedom and fluidity in phrasing. In even the simplest of compositions it is easy to mark the great difference between the comparatively stilted phrasing of the immature interpreter and the living pulsation of the artist. Except in those compositions premeditatively calling for rigidity and even monotony, communication of music's emotional content to an audience demands continuous change.

To achieve freedom and fluidity in musical interpretation, one must overcome subservience to technical patterns and to the bar line. One danger confronting the student who applies himself conscientiously to the mastery of baton technique is that he may tend to force the phrasing inherent in a musical work into the technical patterns he has been practicing assiduously. Remembering the old dictum that it is the function of art to conceal art, he must guard against this tendency at all times. He must absorb the spirit of a work so thoroughly that when he translates it into hand motions, his patterns will be governed by the music and not vice versa. He must also liberate himself from the tyranny of bar lines. These little strokes, placed at mathematically exact periods in measured music, are with rare exceptions meant by the composer merely as guide posts and only that. The music flows through them and is guided by them, as the walls on either side of a stream control its current as it flows at various speeds and in three dimensions.

The tendency of the amateur time-beater, already referred to in Chapter Eight, is to break down phrases into the smallest possible units.

Thus 4/4 becomes two 2/4's, while 6/8, 9/8, and 12/8 are split into successive 3/8's. Whoever has heard debut recitals by instrumentalists may have observed a similar tendency to shortness of measure groupings. The result, whether on an instrument or with an orchestra, sounds to the ear like musical snippets interlarded with clumsy breath pauses, a kind of musical hesitation, a stuttering, a stammering.

This effect is brought about not only by physical overstress of bar lines and minor accents but also by mental failure to grasp the fact that bars and phrases are single over-all units and part of larger units. The cure must be approached from both mental and physical angles. Any piece of music a conductor is called upon to interpret must be studied from the point of view of phrase groupings, until he can sing each part mentally. Not until he can do this will his baton cease beating each measure as if it had a fence around it, eliciting isolated, pedestrian formations instead of the smoothly flowing outlines of music.

Not the least reward of such study will be a wholly new understanding of the personal and individual melos which distinguishes every significant composer from every other. Even a little study of phrase groupings reveals surprising quirks and idiosyncrasies in composers often thought of as conservative. For contrast, study in pairs dissimilar composers: Tchaikovsky and Franck, Beethoven and Bach, Bruckner and Berlioz, Debussy and Mozart, Gluck and Richard Strauss. Note, as you study composers from this point of view, how inseparably phrase groups are bound up with each composer's manner of expressing himself, e.g., in his use of *legato* and *staccato,* volume, harmony, thematic interplay, architecture, and instrumental tone color.

Another reward of studying from the point of view of phrase groupings will be the special help it offers in memorization. It is obviously easier to grasp whole phrases than single bars considered as mosaics, dovetailed laboriously. Phrase grouping is of paramount importance at the beginning and ending of a work, for in these two places the auditors are most aware of the conductor, and a slip or a suggestion of less than complete authority at these crucial points may create an unfavorable reaction, conscious or subconscious, in the minds of the hearers.

Brahms's Second Symphony

Consider now, as a practical application, a part of Brahms's Symphony No. 2. The opening measure serves to introduce the basic motif. Bars 2 through 5 form a group with the horns carrying the main line. The next four bars form a group with the flutes, clarinets, and bassoons carrying the main line; the horn returns in the succeeding four bars;

then the wood winds again pick up the main melodic thread for six bars (really a four-bar group with two added measures, reaffirming the previous two). The next twelve bars form one large group, consisting of four-bar groups discernible but subordinate to it. The next three groups are of four measures each.

The illustration above is of phrase grouping from the cool mathematical point of view. Yet authorities disagree about the mathematics of musical phrasing just as they do about everything else. Some musical analysts feel that the timpano solos in the 32nd and 36th measures mark the end rather than the beginning of phrase groups. Each interpreter must decide such matters for himself and then fit his technical expression into what he feels the phrasing to be. Since even a short discussion of phrasing would carry us far beyond the limits of this volume, we must content ourselves here by pointing out that phrase groupings reveal themselves by such factors as melody, rhythm, thematic interplay, modulation, and instrumental coloring. Four-measure groups may be accepted as the norm of most classical and romantic works, though enough deviations certainly occur to make for interest. Frequently, however, seeming exceptions to this four-bar norm resolve themselves into four less one or four plus one, and so on.

In the Brahms excerpt under discussion, the opening measure in the cellos and basses obviously serves as a nuclear motif or "signal," as inspection of later measures will confirm. The full harmony in the next four measures, carried mainly by the bassoons and horns, causes them to stand out. We have another four-measure group at the start of the 6th measure, this time carried by the wood winds, which group serves as a contrast in tone coloring to the previous four measures. The next four bars return to the horn-bassoon coloring. Next, the flutes, clarinets, and bassoons take the main line for four bars, the last two of which are reaffirmed. On the 19th measure the first violins and violas steal in and take over, and carry the main line in octaves for twelve measures. At the 26th measure the first violins and cellos cut the twelve-bar group in half. Measures 20 through 23, as in previous groupings, are tied by a pedal point in the cello-bass part. The whole twelve-measure phrase is played ideally as if it were in one bow on one single instrument, gradually sinking in volume when the timpano roll in the 32nd measure (and also in the 36th) starts a new four-measure phrase. Not only does the instrumentation change but also the degree of *pianissimo*. At the 40th measure the timpano and contrabass in octaves (though practically in unison) start a four-measure group, and the first violin then enters to introduce the second part of the theme.

Let us see what happens to the movements and the patterns of the baton when they depict these measure groupings geometrically. Listen to a performance where the conductor beats each measure as if it had a fence around it. Instead of the smoothly flowing, ever forward, soaring and winging outlines of this music, we have isolated and pedestrian formations of measure for measure.

Think of the baton as a bow playing a stringed instrument. Beat the first measure quietly as an introduction, holding the baton at medium height. For the subsequent four-measure group, give a distinct preparation which brings the baton upward to about eye level. The hearer and watcher, even without being conscious of it, will feel that a distinct phrase has begun. For the last three measures of this four-measure group, use strokes slightly less broad than those of the first measure, and also drop the baton slightly. The over-all effect of the baton movements will be to show the grouping of these four measures as a one-phrase unit. In the last measure of this group, bring out slightly the basic motif in the cello and contrabass.

Observe similar procedure in the next two groups of four bars each. The group starting on the 14th measure follows the same interpretative pattern until the 17th measure, when a *crescendo* begins; here measures 18 and 19 reaffirm the two preceding measures. Cue in the last quarter note in the first violins and violas. From here until measure 33, use a neutral, serene beat with no break, as if the players were employing one bow for the whole twelve measures. The *decrescendo* starting at measure 27 calls for less length of stroke and slight dropping of the baton to signify lessening of melodic tension. Introduce the first measure of each of the next three four-bar groups by more distinct preparatory motions than you use for the surrounding measures, to achieve the effect of over-all unity. The use of the left hand to show contrast between the beginning of a phrase and the rest of the measure is of especial importance. This procedure may now be applied to the rest of the symphony, as well as to other classical and romantic works.

Berlioz' *Roman Carnival* Overture

Berlioz' *Roman Carnival* Overture offers us instructive examples of three-measure groupings, and merits close study. There are two places in the work where a careful analysis of phrase groups will prove of particular aid in obtaining a mental hold of the music. The first occurs at the 25th measure of the *allegro vivace*. The measure groups here follow a sort of repetitious arithmetic pattern: two-three, two-two. Knowing

MEASURE GROUPINGS AND RUBATO

this and memorizing the instrumental top lines help one to obtain an over-all grasp of the passage.

At the 114th measure after the *allegro vivace,* a passage occurs with an extended succession of two- and three-measure groupings. Sometimes these succeed each other; sometimes the triple and duple pulsations are combined. The conductor must carefully analyze these successions and combinations and indicate them in his movements.

Twenty-nine measures after the start of the 6/8 which follows the two measures in 2/4, the bassoon plays a six-measure group and then one of five measures. At this point it is necessary to choose a main thematic thread in the imitative orchestral web and to cue in such entrances. We choose the trombones, which now have a six-measure group, followed by one of five measures. But before they can play the last measure of the five-measure group, the flutes and oboes play a three-measure group in imitation. Next come the horns with a five-measure group. The trombones on the one hand, and the flutes and oboes on the other, continue their imitation. The trombones take the lead again with a seven-measure group, and we then return to groups mostly of four measures, sprinkled with some three-measure groups until the end. Phrasing this overture, using the eyes and left hand in addition to the baton, demands quick reflexes and a thorough command of the score.

For other three-measure groupings, see Dukas' *The Sorcerer's Apprentice* and, of course, the most famous example of all, the *ritmo di tre battute* in the second movement of Beethoven's Symphony No. 9.

RESTS AND SILENT BEATS

Before the student is ready to practice *rubato,* it is essential that he be able to show through his baton movements the difference between a stroke given for a living note and that for a silent beat on a rest, a "dead" or "empty" beat (as the latter is often termed). Our first exercise is to take various patterns in skeletal notation and to beat them out so unmistakably that the watcher can translate them into musical notation without the music. This conducting game has been practiced in Europe by conscientious students with great benefit. A little application will make for adeptness. The student should start in slow tempo, of course, and speed up very gradually. The measures in Example 169 may be varied ad infinitum by adding breath pauses, cut-offs, holds, end beats, rests, *staccato,* and *legato;* and by taking them in various combinations, time-signatures, and strokes. By this time the student should be able to evolve his own exercises, both by using skeletal notation and by finding

Ex. 169

Moderato to Adagio

examples from actual music—chorales, standard overtures, suites, tone poems, symphonies, etc.

Note carefully how the baton patterns change in these skeletal exercises. Again, note how much the baton proves like a bow in spirit; for example, in delineating four quarter notes; then a succession of dotted eighths, each with a sixteenth; then syncopation, and so on.

Note especially the difference between a stroke given for a living note and for a silent beat on a rest. The stroke on an actual note has body and weight; that on a silent beat is as short as possible, and has the nature of an inhalation-preparation. Indicating this difference is one of the greatest safeguards against wrong entrances at the disposal of a conductor. Proper consideration of rests, indeed, infuses music with the breath of life. Nothing is deadlier than beating rests and played notes the same way. Conducting without due regard to rests is like reading prose without punctuation marks.

Ex. 170.   Strauss: *Don Quixote* (Reprinted with the permission of the copyright owner, C. F. Peters Corporation, New York.)

Ex. 171.   Brahms: Symphony No. 1

There is, however, such a thing as overbeating rests, and this practice is fussy. Many of them are written in more to present the correct mathematical count than for actual musical observance. This is especially true at the beginnings and endings of movements and sections. Elide such rests in beating, when possible, or beat them as unobtrusively as you can.

In the excerpt from *Don Quixote* (Ex. 170), disregard the introductory rests. Cut off the hold to the left center, where the baton is ready to bring in the cello on the third beat to the right. In the excerpt from Brahms's Symphony No. 1 (Ex. 171), give a down end beat for the final chord and disregard the remaining rests. In the bars from Beethoven's Symphony No. 7 (Ex. 172), phrase two bars as one. Give the first and third bars with strong, long strokes, and the empty second and fourth bars with relaxed, short strokes near the top of the pattern. Treat the excerpt from the Ninth Symphony similarly (Ex. 173).

Ex. 172.   Beethoven: Symphony No. 7

Ex. 173.   Beethoven: Symphony No. 9

Ex. 174.   Sibelius: Symphony No. 5 (By permission of Wilhelm Hansen, Copenhagen, and of G. Schirmer, Inc., New York.)

The last nine bars of Sibelius' Symphony No. 5 (Ex. 174) offer us an illustration of treacherous alternation between played notes and rests, a situation which invites wrong entrances unless it is handled very carefully. The first thing to do is to get the phrasing clear in your mind. Treat each two-measure group as one phrase, with the following mental adjustments: the first two bars are a sort of preparation for the six main bars (the last six excluding the final bar), which form the nucleus of the passage; and the next-to-last chord has the characteristics of an inhalation–up beat, with the final chord like an exclamation point.

To beat out each stroke, even with careful differentiation between the explosive chords and the silent beats, may be logical enough in theory but is no protection against false entrances, even when the left hand moves only on the actual entrances. It is recommended here that you place quasi holds mentally on all the silent beats, and move the hands only for the preparation and entrance of each chord. The conductor may mentally count the rests.

This part of our discussion may aptly be brought to a close by recalling that Berlioz, in his *L'Enfance du Christ* (Ex. 175), directs that the conductor keep beating six bars of rests plus a fermata, and then proceed without pause to the next scene, "The Cradle of Bethlehem"! The conductor need not fear incurring a charge of irreverence here if he simply places a single long hold over the seven bars, gives a down beat, holds, and then proceeds.

Ex. 175.   Berlioz: L'Enfance du Christ

RUBATO

The dictionary definition of *rubato* is the shortening of some notes in a tempo so that others may be lengthened and vice versa. Such a definition, however, falls far short of translating into words a musical concept of this nature. With an artist *rubato* is liberty, always characterized by good taste and logic; with less than an artist, *rubato* is never far from license, lack of restraint, and exaggeration. With an artist, no matter how free the tempo becomes, the main thread of the musical outline is never lost sight of; with less than an artist, such an indulgence is always liable to becloud the main line. Was it not Liszt who once wrote that Chopin seemed able to take any sort of liberty with his right hand yet preserve strict tempo with his left?

Conducting *rubato* is one of the severest tests of a musician's good taste and rhythmic freedom. It calls into play every technical resource of the conductor. As practical applications of this kind of musical expression, two works will be considered in some detail. The first is the overture to Johann Strauss's *Die Fledermaus* (Breitkopf and Härtel edition).

Johann Strauss's *Die Fledermaus* Overture

The student should first place numbers at every ten bars to facilitate easy reference.

We start out beating two to the bar, conducting the violins; and noting the prevailing two-measure grouping in the first 12 bars, the *fz* in the 5th and 7th bars, the *subito p* in the last quarter of the 8th bar, and the *f* in the last quarter of the 9th bar. The whole mood is one of breathlessness. The quarter rest in the 12th bar should be held fairly long, to suggest the end of the introduction.

The *allegretto,* still in two, is slightly broader than the introduction and may be taken two quasi four to the bar. The two bars of "vamping" in the bassoons and violas are played with breath pauses between each note; they are also played *mp,* instead of the written *p,* which should become effective on the third bar with the entrance of the oboe solo. If the oboe soloist plays well, the conductor should let him take the lead and should follow him. The first violins at the 7th bar play a bit more broadly than the preceding oboe, and the *pizzicati* must be short and dry. In the 9th bar, the last dotted eighth and the sixteenth in the first violin section are taken up-bow, *scherzando,* and short. The first violins next imitate the preceding oboe solo, and like it, stress the notes but do not accent them. One should always remember that musical signs like accents ought to be adjusted to fit their context.

Bars 15–16: take the last two eighths up-bow *scherzando.* Start the two bars before the oncoming Tempo I.^{mo} *pp,* not simply *p* as printed; and proceed with a broad *allargando* and *crescendo* into the new tempo. Take the last bar before the Tempo I.^{mo} in two again, if you have taken the previous movement in two quasi four. The Tempo I.^{mo} must be immediately established and must be a return to the pace of the opening of the overture. The four bars before the *lento* are very broad and heavily stressed. The *C* sharp–*D* sharp in the third measure before the *lento,* and the next *E,* may be played by the outside stands an octave higher, returning to *loco* on the second quarter of the second measure before the *lento.* Cue in the trombones on the down beat *fp* and the glockenspiel on the up beat (we are still in two to the bar) so that it sounds with the flutes and oboe. See that the trombones observe the *pp* on the second bar of the *lento.* The mood of the *lento* is one of leisureliness.

The first four bars of the *allegretto* (bar 47) are merely "vamping" and should scarcely be heard. We are still in two to the bar. The *pizzicati* should be dry and short. Cue in the first violins on the top beat of the 50th bar; and watch the clarinet, oboe, bassoon, and flute as they corroborate the melodic outline. Note the *stringendo* in the 58th measure, and cue in the first horn. Increase the *stringendo* at the 68th measure.

Establish *at once* the new *allegretto* with broad, decisive strokes, still two to the bar. Characterize the first violins at the *meno mosso* (bar 75) by giving a slight swell leading up to the *B.* From bar 79 on the top beat until the 83rd bar, hold back the tempo, bringing it to a head at the two eighths on the up beat of the 82nd bar, which should be executed with up-bow thrown strokes and with breath pauses between them. Bars 83–86: repeat the procedure of bars 75–78. Bars 87–90: repeat the procedure of bars 79–82. Bar 101: start with a slight broadening, the violins and clarinet standing out. On bar 103 there is a slight hovering hairpin *crescendo* and *decrescendo,* and the tempo is at once retaken on the next four bars. A hovering hold occurs on the first quarter of bar 109, where the bassoons and horns enter and should be cued in.

Bar 110 resumes *a tempo* and *forte;* the notes in this bar and bar 112 are "sticky" in contrast to bars 111–113, which are light and airy. Start a *decrescendo* on bar 112, ending in the *p* at bar 114. Do bars 118–121 *calando,* with bar 121 quasi four to articulate the *pizzicati* in the cellos and basses.

At the *tempo di valse,* bar 122, beat one to the bar, phrasing mentally two bars as one, however. Bars 124–125: take *accelerando.* Observe a break on the double bar between bars 125–126, by bringing the baton down to the bottom of the stroke. After a wait of about one bar, bring the baton up as preparation for the attack on bar 126. Note the phrasing and measure-grouping at this point. Take bars 126–127 together, one to the bar. Bars 128–129 are broader than the two preceding bars; beat them quasi three to the bar with a sort of holding back, a hesitation. Continue this style: one to the bar in general, with quasi three on bars 131, 133, 136, 137, 139. Return to one to the bar with bar 139. Bars 147–149: retard and beat quasi three. Beat bar 150 in one again. Then resume the alternation of one to quasi three to the bar, with even more dash than before.

Bar 166: give a broad hold on the first quarter, a cut-off preparatory motion on the second quarter, and the last two eighths broad and subdivided. Bar 167: take *a tempo* and one to the bar again. Bar 181, page 15, *allegro:* beat two to the bar, *forte* but lightly with forward rushing movement. Bar 189: start *decrescendo,* to which join the retard at bar 197. Bar 197: cue in *pizzicati* in the cellos and basses. Bar 198: cue in bassoon. Bar 200: cue in bassoon again, on hold, *andante con moto,* three to the bar. Bar 201: observe swell and fade on bassoon solo; cue in the oboe and follow him if he plays well.

Bar 206: stress the first eighth of the flute-oboe solo. Bars 206–208: violins play on *G* string. Bar 207: bring out clarinet. Bar 208: bring out flute. Bars 210–213: bring out clarinet and cello, while violins and violas start down-bow on each measure, stressing the tied eighth notes, up-bow *scherzando.* Bar 214: stress the first eighth note in the clarinet, first violins, and cello. Bar 215: stress the last quarter note in the clarinet and first violins. Bar 217: bring out horn. Bars 218, 220: have oboe stress third eighth. Bars 219, 221: oboe plays sixteenths, *scherzando* in one breath. Bars 224–225: oboe and flute have breath pause before sixteenths, but without exaggeration.

Take the *allegro molto moderato* two to the bar. *Decrescendo* in the first two bars. Bar 228: take breath pause before last eighth. The next four bars are still slow. The *allegro* really starts at bar 237 and is prepared by an *accelerando,* starting at bar 233. Bar 237: cue in trumpet and keep it down to avoid anticlimax. Bars 241–243 are a three-measure phrase. Bar 244: give a strong preparation and down beat for *ff,* to bring to a close the three-bar grouping. Bar 251: start *mf;* slight *crescendo* in timpano. Bar 252: demarcate new bar group. Bars 258–259: timpano is *mf* and has a slight *crescendo.* Bars 260, 262: note *fp.* Bar 264: start *crescendo* to bar 272. Bar 272: cue in trombones. Bars 264–267: bring out cellos and basses.

The G.P. (Grand Pause) comes twice on page 23, in bars 275 and 277. To preclude a break-through by unwary players, hold up the left hand as a warning before each pause; also, give the end beat on the second stroke in each preceding measure, letting the baton rebound each time to the top and giving the down beat for the empty measure *immediately.* Keep the baton at the bottom of the stroke till you are ready to give the next up-beat preparation for the attacks on bars 276 and 278. Hold the silent measures longer than their surrounding measures. Note how the bars are grouped from bar 260 on: a four-bar group (two bars repeated), followed by two similar four-bar groups; at bar 272, three played bars with an empty bar making the normal four-bar group; then a played bar, an empty bar, and two bars for clarinets and bassoons, making another normal four-bar group. Grasp this grouping carefully to insure that there will be no accidents in silent measures. Take these bars, 260 to 280, at breakneck speed. Hesitation will betray lack of mental grasp of the phrasing in this passage.

From here until the end of the overture there is nothing which should occasion the student any trouble, if he has understood all that has been discussed thus far. It would be wise to note the four-bar grouping near the end, starting 17 bars before the end, with the last measure added as an exclamation point. Bars 6–7 before the end: conduct the horns. Next two bars: conduct the trombones. The last 5 bars: start the snare drum *p* and make a *crescendo* to the end.

Liszt's *Second Hungarian Rhapsody*

Our second example of *tempo rubato* in practice is Liszt's *Second Hungarian Rhapsody* in C Minor, as arranged for large orchestra by Karl Muller-Berghaus (Kalmus, small score). Place numbers at every ten measures for easy reference. Go through the score and get the main melodic lines in your mind before proceeding to the following analysis of technical procedures.

The eight introductory measures, beaten four to the bar (two quasi four), pose some problems calling for neat solutions.

First full bar: cue in the sixteenths in the bassoons, horns, cellos, and basses by giving the down stroke and forceful rebound immediately to the center of the pattern, there observing a quasi hold for the players to enter in imitation before giving the attack for the next sixteenth entrance. This gives a pattern of phrasing for the rest of the piece, wherever and whenever this characteristic figure occurs.

Bar 2 is a problem in subdivisions. The first three thirty-second notes (in the clarinets, violins, and violas) should come on the down beat; the sixteenth note on the rebound; the first eighth on stroke two; the second eighth on stroke three; the last five thirty-seconds on the fourth stroke, as follows: up, down, up, down, up. Bar 4: beat like bar 2, except that here we have six subdivisions on the last stroke of the bar; give a slight preparation and go out to the right as an extension of the main stroke; then beat up, down, up, down, up, bringing the baton in position for the next down beat. In giving these subdivisions back and forth, approach the top of the pattern steadily to avoid a last up-beat jerk.

Bar 8: cello, beat in four subdivided as twelve, with the subdivisions going back and forth (see Fig. 52). Give the releases for the hold and cut-off in one motion.

Beat the *andante mesto* two to the bar. Connect the two sections by making the eighth note of bar 8 equal to the quarter note of bar 9. Bars 12, 16, 20: bring out the seventh sixteenth note and elongate it to be a quasi hold, by dividing the second up stroke into two parts. Give the release in a leisurely manner by dropping the baton and allowing the players to catch it as it again ascends. Bar 24: give the second beat as an end beat to the right and let the clarinet play his cadenza *ad libitum*. Take charge again when he has played the last note before his hold, by giving a preparation on this note and reaching the hold with him. Bar 26 has a short hold. Bar 27ff: note that the figures here are sixteenth notes and not thirty-seconds as at the beginning. Bar 32: the seventh sixteenth note in the high wood winds should be slightly elongated.

Bar 35, *più mosso:* continue two to the bar. Bar 50: start the flute on the up beat and give an end beat, catching him later at the beginning of Tempo 1 (still beating in two). Follow his run but prepare for orchestral attack. Bar 61: give down beat and end beat, taking charge again on the last eighth of the flourish and using it as a preparation for the next attack.

Bar 62, *come prima:* beat in four as at beginning. For practice, observe a quasi hold on each beat, and give the ensuing attacks with the utmost precision. Bar 69: articulate carefully. Give the down stroke, and then the second stroke as "empty" preparation for the third stroke, which is to the right and upward. You are now ready for the next down beat, which is on a rest and must not be prepared or the players may be drawn into a false entrance. The left hand may give an upward fourth stroke to show the passing time, but the right hand must remain motionless at the top of the pattern to indicate the hold. After the hold, both hands descend on the rest, which serves as preparation for the entrance of the cellos and basses on the second eighth of bar 70.

Bar 71, *a tempo:* return to the speed of bar 27ff, again in two, though it is possible also in brisk four. Bar 82: divide the up stroke to bring out the eighths in the bassoons, cellos, and basses. Bar 83: give a down end beat. Raise the baton with the last four chromatic notes of the clarinet cadenza; bring in the cellos and basses with the high *D* ending the clarinet solo. Bar 85: continue in two; note that the accompanying figures are sixteenths, not thirty-seconds. Bars 92, 94: wait after the first stroke; cue in the strings.

Bar 109, *adagio:* beat in slow four; observe a tiny wait before the fourth stroke; cue in the cellos and basses. Bar 112: give the down stroke on the first three sixteenths and the second stroke on the first eighth; split the third stroke on the next two sixteenths; give a subdivision on each of the last sixteenths. Bar 113: give the first stroke on the first three sixteenths and the second stroke on the first half of the quarter note (cellos and basses); cue in the wood winds on the third stroke; subdivide the fourth stroke into two. Bar 116: give a down stroke for the hold and an up beat for cessation, followed by a down stroke (bar 117) as an end beat. Hold the baton low for the hold. Give the next up beat as preparation for the attack at *vivace.*

Bar 118, *vivace:* beat in two and not too fast, something like the tempo at the beginning, to allow for building up a climax. See that the violin grace notes are not skimped. Bar 142: cue in the horn solo and harp accompaniment. Bar 150: begin to pick up the tempo to reach a climax at bar 178 (*tempo giusto vivace marcato assai*). Some conductors observe a break between bars 177 and 178. Continue to beat in two. Bar 218: take *poco meno* to give contrast and to prepare for the next climax. Bars 227, 229: note the shift of accents to the ends of bars. Bar 234: tempo should be quite deliberate, almost holding back, and still in two. Bars 234–241, 242–249, 250–258: start a bit slowly and make a slight *accelerando* to the end of each phrase. Bars 260–269: maintain speed. Bar 270: start *poco ritardando.* Bar 273: beat in four. Note the two-measure groupings on the last few pages, especially in chromatic passages.

Bar 274: beat *a tempo* and in two again, but bring out the after-beats with split strokes. The following passage is in heavy march tempo, *pesante.* Bar 306: start picking up the tempo. Bars 344–359: note the two-measure groupings and the *sf's* on up beats. Bar 360: beat in four. Bar 361, *maestoso:* beat in two but with after-beats articulated. Bar 369: pick up speed.

Note *poco a poco dim. e riten.* from bar 393 until bar 409, when *ritenuto* returns again. Bar 409: still beat in two; the tempo almost drags. Bar 421: this is marked *prestissimo,* but do not start too fast, in order to allow for a climax. Note the two-measure groups till the end. Beat two measures as one till the last four measures. Bar 444: give a down stroke as an end beat, with a cut-off to the right. Hold till you are ready, and then give the up beat as preparation for the attack on bar 445. Bars 445–446: give each chord a quasi hold. Last two measures: take in three short whips, as fast as the orchestra can play them. Do not give three down beats here, but beat forward, back, and forward again.

The number of words necessary to describe approximately the deviations from the printed page in this composition reveals how difficult it is for a composer to convey even part of his wishes to a conductor. It is one thing for a single interpreter to play on a self-contained polyphonic instrument like the harpsichord, pianoforte, organ, or even the harp, and quite another for a conductor to improvise upon one hundred men. It requires indeed a high degree of both authority and technical control.

For further practice in this genre, study such works as Liszt's other *Hungarian Rhapsodies,* Brahms's *Hungarian Dances,* Dvořák's *Slavonic Dances,* Enesco's *Rumanian Rhapsodies,* and waltzes by Lehar, the Strauss family, etc.

Chapter Nineteen

ORCHESTRAL CADENZAS

AND ACCOMPANIMENT

ORCHESTRAL CADENZAS

In many instrumental concertos, brilliant displays aimed to reveal the technical virtuosity of the soloist and to develop the thematic material of the work are inserted into the codas of the first and last movements. They are usually announced by a hold over a dominant or 6/4 chord and they frequently end on a trill. Such cadenzas may be by the original composer, by the soloist, or by some other composer. In the case of standard concertos, the soloist often has a choice. It is not always possible for the conductor to inspect the cadenza before rehearsal time, and in such a case, he must keep his ears open for the approach of the dominant harmony, often accompanied by a suggestion of return to the main tempo of the movement. A glance at the start and end of the cadenza should be enough to give the conductor his bearings. The soloist should aid the conductor with a nod just before the cadenza ends. The conductor then takes charge again, waits for the eyes of the soloist and orchestral players to be focussed on his baton, and then proceeds.

The student should practice watching the fingers and bowings of stringed instrument players, the fingers and keyboard of pianists, and the breathing and phrasing of singers and of wind players. The more he can mentally feel himself in their places and play and sing with them, the better will be his accompaniment. He will find that even conductors of reputation are not necessarily good in accompaniment, and that conductors often accompany one kind of soloist better than other kinds. Each type of conducting has its special difficulties and problems. The conductor should memorize the first and last few measures of the cadenza, and he may even beat the last few with very small strokes, to bring the players back to the mood and tempo of the music. The left hand may

Ex. 176.   Strauss: *Till Eulenspiegel* (Reprinted with the permission of the copyright owner, C. F. Peters Corporation, New York.)

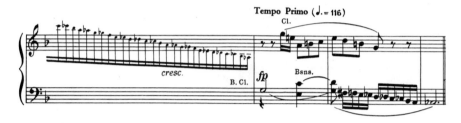

be held out unobtrusively as a warning during this preliminary beating, and then join the right hand in cuing in the whole orchestra at the proper time.

The subject of accompanying soloists will be discussed more later. At this time we shall consider purely orchestral passages which are quasi cadenzas. Thus, in Strauss's *Till Eulenspiegel* (Philharmonia edition, small score, page 31) (Ex. 176), the solo violin plays high *E* flat on a hold with the trombones and contra bassoons. The conductor holds as long as he wishes and then gives the release. The soloist then keeps the hold as long as *he* wishes and next proceeds to execute the descending chromatic *glissando*. It is the task of the conductor to see that the bass clarinet meets the soloist's open *G*. He should give one clear down beat during the violin solo and an up-beat preparation on the first few notes of the run, reaching the open *G* with the soloist and cuing in the bass clarinet. Then he should cue in the first clarinet and bassoons in rapid succession.

Rimsky-Korsakoff is a composer who indulged much in quasi cadenza passages in his orchestral compositions. Thus, in the 7th and 8th measures of his *Russian Easter* (Ex. 177), the solo violin has a cadenza to the accompaniment of clarinets and bassoons. For the 7th measure, it is necessary to give only two down strokes for the first whole note shared by the soloists and the accompanying instruments. The conductor is still in charge. Once he gives the third stroke to the right, the soloist plays *a piacere*. On, say, the last four sixteenths of the cadenza, the conductor gives the preparatory stroke for the next *a tempo*. This is a good

Ex. 177. Rimsky-Korsakoff: *Russian Easter* Overture

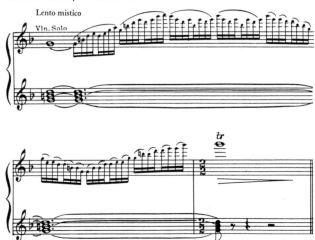

place to watch the violinist's fingers and to memorize the pentatonic chord outlined melodically. Twenty-two measures later the flute has a similar passage.

A quasi cadenza passage also occurs in this same composer's *Capriccio Espagnol,* at the start of the fourth section, *Scena e canto gitano,* for the horns and trumpets. Written as *allegretto,* with the quarter equalling 69 and the time signature in 6/8, this section is to be executed quite freely. The passage is prevailingly in two pulses between the dotted bar lines. The conductor brings in the drum on the down beat and holds. The up beat brings in the brass chord. The drum plays till the start of the next hold and fades just before the new bar line. The next four cadenzas are executed similarly, with quasi prose freedom but always in two-pulse beating.

Other quasi cadenzas in Rimsky-Korsakoff's works can be found in *Antar* (harp), *Le Coq d'or* (clarinet), and *Scheherezade* (violin, trombone, trumpet, and bassoon); they all offer further delightful instances. See also the flute cadenza in the last movement of Schumann's Symphony No. 1.

A most instructive example is found in Ravel's *Spanish Rhapsody* at no. 6, page 8, of the Durand et Fils small score (see Example 178). In this instance, the two clarinets play a *cadenza ad libitum,* an improvisatory passage which may be considered as containing five main groups. Each of the first two groups consists of six sixteenth notes plus a quarter note. The third group consists of eight thirty-second notes and a quarter note; while the fourth group consists of nine units: four quintuple and five

ORCHESTRAL CADENZAS AND ACCOMPANIMENT

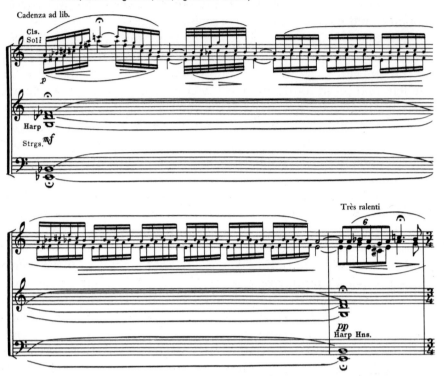

quadruple. The fifth and last group or unit is the half note just before the bar line with an implied hold.

In this interpretation, the long measure containing the *cadenza ad libitum* may be beaten five to the bar with various subdivisions. The conductor may aid himself by counting silently something like the following verbal and numerical aids: one "and"; two "and"; three "and"; four (one, two, three, four, five, six, seven, eight, nine); five (hold) "and."

The first group, containing six sixteenths, is given a full down stroke with rebound; the quarter-note hold is indicated by another down stroke with rebound, this time half-length as if it were a subdivision, and the baton is brought back once more to the center of the pattern. The second group also has two parts. The first stroke to the *right* takes care of the six sixteenths, and a second stroke, again to the right, takes care of the quarter note. The third group with its eight thirty-second notes and quarter note is beaten similarly to the left as two subdivisions. The hand is now in the correct position to beat the third group. Note at this point the ties connecting each of the quarter notes to the following notes in the first three groups. If the ties were not there and the pitch of the notes after the quarter notes changed, an extra cessation-preparatory motion would have to be given for each release.

The fourth group must be so beaten that after moving nine times, the hand will come out at the extreme right of the pattern to be ready for the up beat. Give the first "subdivision" to the right, the second to the left, and so on until nine have been given. Each short stroke will bring the hand more and more to the right during this procedure.

For the implied hold on the half note, give the stroke upward to the top of the pattern. Release by giving the down stroke as a combined cessation-preparatory motion, since there is a tie to a following note on the same pitch.

In the first group of the next bar, there are six eighth notes. Give the down beat to release the hold and return to the center of the pattern; give the second "subdivision" to the left, the next to the right, and so on until you have indicated the six eighth notes. The hand is now ready to give a stroke to the right. Change the hold mentally on the dotted quarter to a hold on the first quarter. Give it a full-length stroke to the right. To release, split the up beat so that the first half, a quasi end beat with a flick to suggest a tiny breath pause, indicates the eighth represented by the dot; the second half of the stroke indicates the final eighth of the bar. To repeat and to summarize: the method we have used in beating this cadenza amounts in practice to five to the bar with subdivisions.

The cadenza is reaffirmed at no. 8, page 10, this time with two bassoons; and we hereby leave it for the student to work out for himself (see Example 179).

ACCOMPANIMENT

Accompaniment is an art in which not all conductors are at their best. This qualification might even be applied to some well-known names. It would seem that pianists, who often accompany at some time in their careers, should generally be better accompanists than conductors who play other instruments, but this has not always proved to be the case. Conductors who have studied concertos by playing them themselves would again seem to have an advantage, but again this has not always proved true. Some conductors with established authority take their own tempos and force all but the most famous and hence most independent soloists to conform to them; and occasionally this policy leads to violent disagreements, both personal and artistic. Sometimes the result is one set of tempos for the *tutti* passages and another for the accompanied solo

Ex. 179.   Ravel: *Spanish Rhapsody* (Permission for reprint granted by Durand et Cie, Paris, copyright owners; Elkan-Vogel Co., Inc., agents for U.S.A.)

passages. Ideally, there should be no conflict. And it may be stated parenthetically that usually the more mature the soloist, the easier he is to accompany.

The first task the conductor-accompanist has before him is to learn the solo part so well that he can watch the soloist and not the score. He must play the solo part mentally—breathing, bowing, or fingering, as the occasion demands, simultaneously with the soloist. A real accompanist does not follow the soloist; he literally *accompanies* him. Some conductors "play safe" by waiting until an important entrance is upon them and then bringing in the orchestra a split second later. This procedure is irritating to sensitive ears and is justifiable only when the soloist is erratic or when rehearsals have been inadequate.

The most common fault occurs when a conductor follows the soloist's line with the baton instead of conducting the accompaniment. In such cases, the accompaniment in the orchestra has one kind of phrasing and style, the soloist another. The players, who hear the soloist, realize that the baton is outlining his lines instead of the accompaniment, which they must therefore improvise. The result is a feeling of insecurity. There is always present the temptation for the conductor to outline the solo part, but he must not succumb to it. He must follow the solo part mentally but conduct the orchestral background.

An example in orchestral music of a place where some conductors are tempted to follow the main line occurs at the start of the second movement of Tchaikovsky's Symphony No. 4. The *pizzicato* accompaniment of the oboe solo will suffer if the baton gives the oboe line. *Pizzicati* must be precisely brought in, and the players will not be able to give neat entrances if the baton gives the *legato* outline of the solo oboe. Except, then, for the first bar, where the oboe is cued in and the phrasing pattern established, the baton must pay particular attention to the string background. The conductor's head can and does follow the *legato,* and the baton may also do so when the strings have rests between the *pizzicati.* Another place similar in this regard occurs in the *fugato* of the slow movement of Beethoven's Seventh Symphony, which will be detailed in a later chapter.

The moral again to be drawn from such illustrations is that there is such a thing as conducting an orchestra too much. The conductor must know when to allow his players freedom and when to divide his authority with them. In long passages with little or no change in tempo, the conductor should let the players proceed on their own momentum, just keeping his hand lightly upon them, so to speak. An excerpt which may be cited in this connection occurs in Berlioz' "Fantastic" Symphony, on page 60, small score, the last two bars, and the first two bars of the next page. The conductor may very well follow the two harpists on the last two bars of page 60 and with them, the flutes, oboe, and clarinets in the next two. He should concern himself mainly with the string background. It is difficult to give any rules in this regard, but a little experience will show a conductor when to take complete command and when to share it with players. The ability to differentiate thus is one sign of maturity.

The solo part must be allowed to dominate the ensemble only when it has the main line and must be subordinated when its part becomes secondary, as is often the case. Immature and egocentric soloists sometimes attempt to dominate the music throughout their stay on the platform, and the result is anything but art. There must be give and take between soloist and orchestra.

When it is difficult to hear a soloist because of acoustical conditions, balance may often be obtained by having the orchestra play softer. When the brass tends to obtrude in such cases, discreet editings of *forte-pianos* may help, especially in sustained chords. In concertos like Mozart's, written for smaller orchestras than are usual nowadays, some of the strings may be dispensed with. The conductor might arrange to listen to the orchestra from a balcony or from the rear of the ground floor while the concertmaster takes over. Various sections of the orchestra may be asked whether they hear the soloist at all times. Extreme care should always be taken that the soloist's part comes through the orchestral web.

A technical safeguard is always to keep the baton moving, however slowly, especially in retards, so that the players have something to hold to. If the baton has stopped and the tempo is then suddenly changed by a burst of speed on the part of the soloist, a jerk in the baton will result in an ugly wrench.

Another recommendation is to keep some of the length of the baton motion in reserve for a preparation as warning for a sudden change in tempo, particularly on the last stroke of the bar. For if the baton is brought to the end of the stroke too soon with no leeway, the hand is in an awkward place if the soloist makes a sudden retard. In that case the baton must be pushed high above the usual pattern, too high for comfort and good appearance, in order to give a preparatory stroke for the coming attack. Some conductors, while accompanying soloists, let the baton hover and dart a bit forward in spurts, while approaching the next entrance. They then catch the next pulse of the erratic and elusive soloist with a lightning-like thrust. This requires neat manipulation and acts as a safety device. But one must have no little experience for its successful employment.

In accompanying complicated melodic figuration in the right hand of a pianist, the conductor will find it helpful to watch the pianist's left hand, which often has chordal formations outlining the harmony and rhythm. In the case of string soloists, a change in bowing often shows a change in phrase. When a singer has coloratura passages, one should watch his breathing and lips.

To repeat: the most important preparation a conductor can have in providing a good accompaniment is to know the solo part so well that he can keep his eyes on the soloist. And he must really conduct the accompaniment, not outline the solo.

Mozart's Pianoforte Concerto in A Major (K.288)

Let us now consider a few examples from standard concertos which sometimes cause concern in the minds of student conductors. The Mozart Piano Concerto in A Major (K.288) is a good example with which to start. References in this discussion will be to the Broude Brothers edition, in which numbers are placed at the top of each staff and in which each movement starts with number one. The orchestra is conducted four to the bar in its opening measures, like any symphonic work. The pianist starts on the 67th measure, where he should wait for the conductor's nod. The general tempos should have been previously agreed upon so that the pianist's pace will be something like that of the conductor's introduction, since the same theme starts both the solo and the orchestral introduction. More than a reasonable difference in mood, phrasing, and tempo between conductor and soloist will cause an aural dichotomy.

The conductor nods to the pianist, who, it will be noted, plays a normal four-measure phrase alone. Beat these four unaccompanied bars with as short and as quiet strokes as possible, or simply with one down beat a measure. Bar 71: prepare and cue in the cello and bass with a clear "empty" beat; do *not* give a preparation for the rest on the first beat of the string entrance. Show that the actual entrance is on the second stroke. Bars 73–74: it is best to beat here in detail, though unobtrusively. Bar 74: cue in the violins on the third beat of the measure. Make the distinction between silent beats (on rests) and living beats (on actual notes) unmistakable. Bar 82: cue in the *tutti* with both hands for the *F,* remembering that this is Mozart and not Tchaikovsky or Wagner. Bars 95–98: follow the pianist's left hand and keep the wood winds with it, giving very precise strokes. Bring out antiphony and imitation between solo and orchestra in bars 114, 115, and 116, and between violins and flute-clarinet in bars 127 and 128.

Bar 126ff: watch soloist's left hand, as is recommended whenever his right has ornate figuration. Bar 137: cue in wood winds and horns, and do so whenever they have more than a few bars' rest, not because they cannot count but for a unified attack. Bar 143ff: *meno.* Bar 149ff: give one down beat a measure with the other strokes very short and light. Bars 156, 157, 160, 161: cue in each wood-wind entrance here and in similar places. Bars 162–163: watch soloist's left hand and keep strings with it. Bar 161ff: the soloist yields to the conductor. Bars 164–165: bring out clarinet and flute. Bar 194: cut off strings; give down stroke as end beat. The next three bars need only down beats, with perhaps just the suggestion of the other strokes, though the down beat alone usually suffices. Bar 198: give a clear preparation for *tutti* re-entrance. From here until the cadenza, the procedure is like that for passages already discussed. Prepare for the cadenza 16 bars before the end of the movement on page 21, by observing a very broad down stroke and a second stroke as an end beat, followed by a break. On the trill announcing the ending of the cadenza, bring the baton up to warn the players. When the soloist's left hand strikes the dominant seventh hold, give a short preparatory stroke to the right, then take charge by giving a half upward and inward hook to the left. When the eyes of the soloist and the players are on your baton, start the *tutti.*

In the *andante,* do not beat until bar 11. Bar 11: give only "empty" beats to establish the mood. The beat is six to the bar. Bar 12: bring out the clarinet and violin. Bar 13: bring out the bassoon. Bar 14: bring out the flute. Bar 15: emphasize the violin and flute. Bar 16: emphasize the violin and clarinet. Bar 20: give a down stroke as an end beat. Bars 20–24: give empty and very short strokes, intended more to hold a lofty mood than to beat time. Bar 25: cue in the strings. Bar 31: do not exaggerate the *forte piano* in the strings. The harmony suggests a gentle elongation and stress, not an accent. Bar 35: flute and clarinet should be together on the thirty-second notes. Bars 46–47: cue in the flute and the bassoon carefully with a precise fourth stroke. Bar 80f: see that the bassoon echo imitates the solo. Bar 85ff, *colla parte:* follow the solo here but do not outline its phrases with the baton; give precise strokes for *pizzicato,* which needs exact demarcation in such accompaniments. Watch for a possible *calando* in the solo toward the end of the movement.

Beat the *presto* in two. The solo has eight bars with *tutti* repeating in outline. Agree on the mood and speed with the soloist in advance, and guard against overwhelming the soloist in this movement. Get the entrance of the violins on the 32nd bar clear in your mind. A down stroke is enough to bring them in. Bar 62ff: a down beat a measure is enough. Bars 70–71: cue in clarinet and horns. Bar 97ff: down beats only are enough. Watch pianist's left hand. Bar 106: take this *poco meno* and singing style; it must prepare for piano soloist's repetition of the same melodic outline. Bar 125: watch chromatics and *animato* here in soloist. Bar 151ff: watch soloist's left hand. Bar 163: keep strings and soloist together.

Bar 176ff: exaggerate the precision of your strokes to get clean and neat *pizzicato* entrances. Bar 187ff: watch soloist's left hand. There is an *allargando* at bar 195, with *a tempo* at bar 202 and *meno mosso* at bar 238. Bar 245: give a strong down beat to bring in the strings. Bar 262: take the clarinets *cantante* and *soavamente;* here the pianist yields, at bar 270 regains command, yields again at bar 278, and regains command at bar 286. Bar 300 is *animato.* Note bars 304–310: a seven-measure phrase with clarinet and bassoons enters on the last half of bar 307. Bar 312: pianist may make a slight *accelerando.* Bar 320 is *meno mosso;* bar 337, *a tempo.* Bar 347ff: bring out the imitation between the wood winds and the soloist. Bar 359: watch for the soloist's *animato,* which continues to the end of the work. Bar 375: keep strings and solo together. Bar 385ff: keep strings with soloist's left hand. Bar 395: keep strings with soloist's left hand. Bar 401 is *a tempo.* Watch for soloist's left hand. Bar 418: clarinet and bassoon enter here one bar *after* cellos and basses; guard against a premature entrance. Bar 423: watch soloist's left hand. Bar 438: watch chromatics for slight *allargando.* Bar 441 is *a tempo.* Bar 472: watch for the entrance of the violins; cue in with down beat only. Bar 489: cue in the wood winds. Bar 496: cue in the first violins. Bar 502: note *p.* Bar 508: note *f.* Bar 514: watch soloist's left hand.

Beethoven's Violin Concerto

The student will find many challenges to neat accompaniment in Beethoven's Violin Concerto. Here, repeatedly, he will find illustration of the wisdom of holding some of the length of the baton in reserve for unexpected liberties by the soloist, in both sudden *accelerandi* and *ritardandi,* and especially on the last stroke of a measure. Thus, in the first movement, at bar 330 (page 34, Philharmonia edition), the three sixteenths rounding out the soloist's trill are often taken broadly. Here the baton should give the last quarter note to the horns and still have enough space left to go upward with the soloist. Watch his bow arm and bring in the down beat at the change of bowing. In accompanying a string soloist, follow his left hand with your ear and his bow arm with your eye.

The second movement of the concerto presents a severe test of the conductor's ability to sustain a very slow tempo. Though the beat is four to the bar in the main, it will often be found that the baton has to be stopped near the ends of strokes for waits, and that the next stroke has to be prepared. With some soloists, quasi eight will best fit mood and pace. The conductor-accompanist must be prepared to shift from one pattern to the other at any time throughout the movement. The only recommendation which can be made is that the conductor so identify himself with the solo part that he can feel instinctively what the latter is about to do. It is not easy to follow a soloist in the numerous scale passages, especially if he establishes his initial tempo and then does not abide by his own decision. Again, a change in the bow arm serves as a beacon.

The last movement (*rondo*) offers an unusual opportunity for neat and precise accompaniment. The entrance of the cello on the second eighth of the first full bar supplies a characteristic figure repeated frequently throughout the movement. The baton is held high to suggest an ensuing down beat. An up stroke must *not* be given under any circumstances! The fact that a rest starts the measure may inveigle some unwary player to break through. The moment the conductor hears the soloist's high *D* in the up beat, he brings down his baton to coincide with the first note of the next full bar, the *A*. The players use the down beat as the preparation (on the rest) and catch the rebound of the baton for their entrance. It is hardly necessary for the conductor to watch the soloist in these places. He should wait for the tonic in the solo, and bring down the baton to coincide with the soloist's next note, the dominant.

At bar 92 there are two successive holds in the solo part. The conductor should hold the oboes and bassoons through the second hold, with an up beat. The moment the soloist's left hand starts to descend, the conductor should flick the baton upward for a combined cut-off and preparatory motion, while the soloist plays the low *D;* then the baton descends for the next attack as usual. The whole movement points up the difference between outlining the solo part and conducting the accompaniment.

The last four measures of the concerto require the closest attention of the conductor, and his eyes should not leave the soloist. The third and fourth bars before the end should be given in two to the bar. The next-to-last bar should be given with a down beat; but the up beat is divided into three parts, each part going in a different direction, so that the players will have something to hold to in the two final smash chords. The subdivided up beat should be given up, down, and up again, since three stabs in the same direction would go too fast for the players' eyes and be awkward in execution. The second subdivision must be in the nature of a preparation for the third subdivision, which cues in the second last chord. To follow a soloist here and in similar rapid chord successions in other finales requires very neat timing.

The *Allegro Vivace* from Schumann's Pianoforte Concerto in A Minor

The famous passage from the third movement (the *allegro vivace*) of Schumann's Pianoforte Concerto in A Minor may be considered at this point. The orchestra and soloist play together at the start of the movement. The soloist then plays alone for eight measures. When the orchestra rejoins the soloist at the 213th measure, it maintains a triple pulse with phrasing which covers two measures for a unit; so that each two-measure group might be thought of as one 6/4 instead of two 3/4's. This rhythm conflicts with the soloist's right hand, which is playing two-measure phrases, each composed of three two-pulse figures. In other words, the orchestra suggests two times three (especially since rests start even measures) and the piano suggests three times two (especially because of the ties over each set of four notes). Without too much trouble, we can see here another example of a kind of four against six, if we think of each two measures as one unit in 6/4.

For the first measure of this passage, give the down beat divided, so that its last third acts as a long rebound slightly to the right and back to the top of the stroke. For the second measure, give another down stroke, with a rebound on the last third of the stroke back to the original starting point of the baton for the first written measure. In other words, beat two bars as one, but with the down strokes so close together that the players are unaware of what you are doing and think you are giving the usual one to the bar.

Since measures 2, 4, 6, etc., of this passage start on a rest, be especially careful to give clear down beats for the players so they can catch them for their entrances. The orchestra here must be so dominated by the conductor that it will not listen to and attempt to follow the soloist. The conductor must follow the soloist *mentally,* but his beat must be directed at the players. The slightest attempt to outline the solo part will immediately cause confusion. Since this passage has acquired a somewhat alarming reputation, the attitude and beat of the conductor should be nonchalant, with an implied suggestion that nothing unusual is happening.

Chapter Twenty

RECITATIVE

ORCHESTRAL RECITATIVE

Recitative may be defined as music freed from the ordinary rules of rhythm, so that the outlines of its phrases more nearly approach the changes and pitch of natural speech and elevated prose. Accompaniment of this sort of declamatory musical utterance presupposes knowing the soloist's part so intimately that the printed page need be consulted not at all or, at most, only occasionally.

Various sorts of quasi free musical speech occur in purely orchestral music, and these frequently approach vocal recitative both in outline and design. Accompanying such passages calls for close collaboration between conductor and soloist. Often composers insert phrases like *a piacere* (at pleasure), *ad libitum* (at will), *colla voce* (with the voice, i.e., take the tempo from the singer), *colle parti* (with the principal parts, i.e., take the tempo from the instruments), etc., to show that they wish the soloist to be given full freedom.

Strauss's *Till Eulenspiegel*

A good example for the student approaching the study of instrumental recitative (good because it requires very little direction from the conductor yet is often "overconducted") is the first horn solo of *Till Eulenspiegel*. Though apparently written in strict time, it is almost always played with a slight *accelerando* during its six measures. The passage is difficult enough for horn players to play well without the extra burden of slavishly following a baton. Moreover, horn players everywhere practice this passage as a warming-up exercise, so they have their own conception of it. The conductor, of course, may sing or hum the solo in the rehearsal to give the horn player an idea of the phrasing he wants, but he should then permit him the liberty of a soloist.

It is enough to give a down beat on the first measure of the 6/8 (6th measure from the start); beat one down beat a measure with short wrist motions for the unchanging accompaniment in the violins, during the six measures of the solo; and then give a longer down beat when the horn reaches the written low *C,* sounding *F* a fourth above (first space below bass clef). This slightly longer down beat will cue in the violins. Treat this passage as a solo and follow the horn player. To hold him in check smacks of officiousness. Formerly, a horn player accustomed to low notes would take over the solo on the last three notes; nowadays one hornist almost always plays the whole solo.

Beethoven's *Leonora* Overture No. 3

The trumpet solo behind stage in Beethoven's *Leonora* Overture No. 3 (at measures 272 and 294, almost exactly in the middle of the composition) need only be started. It is hardly necessary even to give one down beat a measure in the unchanging string background. Consider the six measures one hold. When the trumpet reaches measures 277 and 299, the conductor takes charge again and brings in the other players.

Rimsky-Korsakoff's *Scheherezade*

The opening measures of the second part of Rimsky-Korsakoff's *Scheherezade* offer us another example. Start the violin solo with a preparation and down beat with rebound to the center of the pattern, and hold the baton there as long as you wish. Use the second stroke to the left as preparation for the entrance of the harp arpeggio on the third beat. Make this third stroke swerve upwards so as to have the baton in position to give the next down beat. Give no fourth stroke for the first measure. Hold the baton motionless while the violinist plays his solo *ad libitum,* which he starts only after the harp chord.

For the second measure, do not give a preparation, since a rest starts it. Give the down beat with the violinist; give the second stroke to the right and up for the second harp chord; there the baton waits for the third measure. Prepare the harp's third entrance on the fourth beat. After cuing in the harp, keep the baton motionless until the violinist reaches high *C,* marked *"ten."* (abbreviation for *tenuto,* held or sustained), at which point you take charge.

At the *molto moderato* (3/2), four measures after "D," the composer has actually written *"recit."* and *"ad lib."* Give the down beat and hold as long as desired at the bottom of the stroke. When you are ready, use the rebound as preparation for the second stroke, on which the trombone is cued in. When the trombonist reaches his last note, take charge again with a short preparatory motion to the right and a half hook upward and inward. He yields here as you give the next down beat. This time the baton rebounds to the center, where it is ready to hold and then to cue in the trumpet. Take charge again when the trumpeter reaches his last note with the hold.

At the *moderato assai* (4/4), letter "F," the composer again has written *recit., ad lib.,* and *colla parte.* For three measures the clarinetist executes roulades against a strummed accompaniment, obviously connoting exotic Oriental instrumentation. The clarinetist starts his solo just after the baton has given the third stroke to the right. The baton remains motionless during the rest of the measure until after the final three sixteenths, when it follows them in an up-beat preparation for the down beat in the second measure. It now takes charge again until the third stroke and repeats the procedure of the first measure. In the third measure a quasi hold is observed on the second last note, the *G,* first space above the staff. It is marked "*ten.*"

Further instances occur at measure 138 in the third movement of the same work, at the 8th and 28th measures of the fourth movement, and also at the 25th and 6th measures before the end. Rimsky-Korsakoff's *Sadko* offers equally fascinating instances of quasi improvised musical speech.

In Richard Strauss's *Ein Heldenleben,* where the violin solo tells us of the hero's beloved (just before no. 23 in the Eulenburg small score), and in the same composer's *Don Quixote,* where the solo violoncello paints for us the unforgettable picture of the death of the immortal tilter at windmills, we have two great examples of orchestral instruments assuming the role of the operatic singer. In each work, the extreme technical and musical demands are such that it is unthinkable that less than first-rate interpreters would ever be entrusted with responsibility for executing the solos. Such being the case, the conductor should treat these soloists as colleagues and allow them the fullest possible liberty in these passages. The interpretation should, of course, be discussed in detail and agreed upon before the general rehearsal. The conductor should follow these soloists when they have the main line and then take charge when the soloists retreat into the ensemble. Accompanying instruments should be cued in with special care in these passages. There should be constant give and take, the conductor and soloists all yielding at the proper time. Only in this manner can the intention of the composer to obtain complete musical freedom be fully realized.

The supreme instance of orchestral recitative, is, of course, to be found in Beethoven's Ninth Symphony.

VOCAL RECITATIVE

We turn now to vocal recitative, where, in standard works from the lyric repertory, tradition plays a great part in interpretation and delivery. While this tradition must usually be obtained firsthand in the opera house, recordings and broadcasts make available to students of today means of comparison of different performances, rarely possible to their predecessors. The matter of what language the singer uses should give the student conductor no concern. If he knows the vocal line he should be able to conduct the score regardless of what language or translation the singer may use.

In conducting orchestral accompaniment to vocal recitative, one has a choice of two possible procedures. The first is to follow slavishly every note in the vocal line, and to beat out every note and rest in the orchestral part. This method is preëminently safe but often becomes very fussy and labored. The other extreme is to ignore all rests and waits and to cue in only notes which are actually played. Under less than ideal conditions, this method should be reserved for the virtuoso conductor. It is dangerous with less than first-rank organizations. Between these two extremes lies a compromise method, followed by most conductors, which minimizes danger of wrong entrance and avoids overbeating.

Though conductors may seem to conduct vocal recitative differently, closer study reveals that their underlying principles are pretty much the same. The differences lie in detail and are usually dictated by the special circumstances under which each conductor meets his musical forces. He must adapt his technique to the circumstances in which he finds himself. Thus, if one comes as a guest with only a few rehearsals, it may prove best to beat out every detail, especially if the orchestra is less than first-rank and the music is not well known to most of the players and singers. If, on the other hand, the conductor directs the same forces week after week, if they are first-rank, if they have rehearsed together long enough to know each other's musical styles well, and if the music is part of the standard repertory, details are hardly necessary, and only general indications of mood, tempo, and entrance are needed.

Whatever adaptations of technique the conductor makes, the players will want to know, above all, where the start of the measure comes. Where the whole measure is silent, one down beat is enough. Where there are notes in a measure (with or without rests), a clear down beat (not necessarily a strong and long down beat) should be given. The actual entrance of the players should be noted and must be unmistakably differentiated from the surrounding rests by the preparation and strong stroke. The rests in the measure must be differentiated from the played notes by being given as silent beats, that is, beats which are light and short and which have a suggestion of inertia. The strokes cuing in actually played notes, on the other hand, are characterized by their weight, force, and body, which at once set them apart from the silent beats. This, then, is one of the secrets of good recitative conducting: the baton shows the players in the orchestra which parts of the measure are rests and which are played. The left hand and facial expressions naturally aid in this.

This procedure applies especially to measures which start with rests. Where rests end a measure, it is usually possible and desirable to ignore them. If the conductor feels he *must* beat these final rests, let him do so as unobtrusively as possible. It is here recommended that these final rests be ignored, and that the last stroke for notes actually played in a measure be executed to the right, where the baton is ready to give the attack for the next measure's down beat. This next attack may be of two kinds: first, a down beat which brings in notes played at the start of the stroke and which should be preceded by an up-beat preparation; or, second, a down beat which brings in a rest, and which does *not* have an up-beat preparation, the down beat itself assuming that function. If a preparation is given for a measure starting on a rest, some unwary player may be inveigled into a premature entrance. This principle must be reiterated, for it concerns one of the most dangerous and treacherous aspects of conducting recitative.

The only general recommendation which can be made about vocal recitative (it applies to orchestral recitative as well) is that players should usually have a down beat for every measure. This permits them to count, especially in long waits, and to make entrances on time. Even then the conductor should indicate the exact point of entrance, not because the player cannot count (as has already been stated), but to give an over-all unified interpretation. There are exceptions to this one-down-beat-a-measure procedure, especially at places where players have very long waits. Its general purpose is to preclude accidents when singers hurry, drag, repeat, or skip. Incidentally, the conductor need not give the down beats for each measure exactly with the singer when the players are silent. He may beat them out quickly, hold the baton poised until the singer catches up to him, and then cue in the players.

The principles concerned with bringing in orchestral attacks as background for vocal lines are very much like those governing attacks in general. These have already been discussed in some detail in Chapter Ten and may be profitably reviewed at this point. It may be added here that rests at the start of the measure are indicated by empty beats up to the stroke before the actual orchestral entrance, at which point the preparation and attack are given as if the music were starting for the first time. Implied in this statement is the absolute requirement that the conductor know at all times what is coming in the next measure, especially at its start. Only thus will he know where his baton must be directed after the last played note of the measure he is conducting, so that he will be ready and in the correct position to give the proper motion for the ensuing attack.

The next implication is that the conductor must *not* delineate the vocal line; this he must follow mentally. The motions of his baton should have no visual relation to the line sung on the stage; they should clearly indicate the orchestral background. Conduct the orchestra, not the singer, though this does not preclude the giving of cues and all sorts of assistance to the singer when necessary.

To sum up: give a clear down beat for every silent measure and for measures having sustained chords, holds, and tremolos. Successions of measures like these need not be followed note for note in the vocal line; they may be beaten in rapid succession ahead of the singer, and the baton may then wait for the singer to reach the point where the preparation for the next attack is to be given. Ignore rests at the ends of measures or beat them as unobtrusively as possible. Indicate rests at the start of measure with silent beats; use the pulse before the actual entrance as a preparation; and execute the stroke on the last played note toward the right, so that it will be ready for the next down-beat attack. It is possible, when the stroke in such cases normally goes to the left, to give it so and then immediately to give a stroke to the right, though this is finicky. When the next measure starts on the beat, give a preparation; when it starts on or within a rest, use the down beat for this purpose and do *not* give an up-beat preparatory motion or you may drag some player into a premature attack. When the harmony changes in a measure, or when special rhythmic or melodic figures emerge in the text, show these with the baton.

Verdi's *Il Trovatore*

Let us now see what happens in actual practice. The simplest sort of recitative occurs when the orchestral background consists of unchanging chords or tremolo. These may be considered holds whether so marked or not.

The passage quoted in Example 180, from Verdi's *Il Trovatore* (brace 2, page 81, Ditson edition), starts with Manrico's words, "In no-stra

Ex. 180. Verdi: *Il Trovatore*

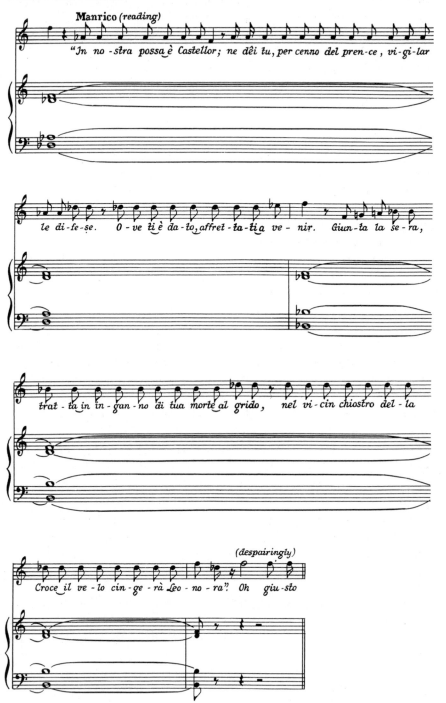

Manrico (reading)

"In no-stra possa è Castellor; ne dêi tu, per cenno del pren-ce, vi-gi-lar

le di-fe-se. O-ve ti è da-to, affret-ta-ti a ve-nir. Giun-ta la se-ra,

trat-ta in in-gan-no di tua morte al grido, nel vi-cin chiostro del-la

(despairingly)

Croce il ve-lo cin-ge-rà Leo-no-ra". Oh giu-sto

pos-sa è Castellor." A messenger has just brought him a letter. Many tenors have traditionally made it a special point of professional pride and honor to rush through the letter at the utmost possible speed.

Simply give a down beat on the *D* flat chord and hold until the change in harmony. Repeat this procedure for the next long bar and then give an end beat upward for the tied eighth-note chord which starts the measure before the ensuing *allegro agitato mosso.* At the end of each long hold, give the up beat as preparation for the next attack. The baton now remains motionless until the preparation on the last beat of this measure for the singer's attack on the high *A* flat, which starts the *allegro agitato mosso.*

In the following comments upon passages containing operatic recitative, we shall not use direct musical quotation, because of the availability of the vocal-piano scores of Bizet's *Carmen,* Massenet's *Manon,* Gounod's *Faust,* and Verdi's *Aida.*

Bizet's *Carmen*

In Bizet's *Carmen* at no. 3-bis, where Zuñiga addresses Don José with the words, "C'est bien là, n'est-pas, dans ce grand bâtiment que travaillent les cigarières?" directly after the "broomstick" chorus of street boys, we have examples of a rest on the first stroke of the bar (bars 1 and 5), silent bars (bars 3, 4, 6, and 7), rests filling out a measure after played notes and rests (bars 2 and 8), and an attack within the second stroke (bar 9).

In bars 1 and 5, give the empty down beats as preparation. In bars 3, 4, 6, and 7, give one down beat each. In bars 2 and 8, the second stroke goes to the right top and waits there until the singer reaches the next measure, when the baton gives the down beat. Ignore the final rests in these measures. In bar 8, the baton goes to the right top on the third stroke and descends *at once* as an empty beat on the first stroke of the next measure, with the singer's first quarter note, the second line *G.* The baton moves with the *F* sharp eighth and brings in the orchestral players. There is no preparation otherwise, the second stroke serving as such, as if the orchestra were entering for the first time in any similar attack.

Massenet's *Manon*

In Massenet's *Manon,* on page 209 of the Novello vocal score, where Des Grieux begins a recitative with the words, "Manon, dearest Manon," we find a passage containing harmonic changes which must be indicated by the baton. The surrounding text is to be minimized.

Bar 1: give a down beat; the up beat cues in the singer. Bar 2: give a down beat only, or give the other beats in the measure unobtrusively. Bar 3: give the down beat as the preparation for the second stroke, since the first quarter is tied to the previous bar. Bar 4: take as you did bar 2. Bar 5: make the first beat unobtrusive; give the second beat as preparation for the third beat; make the fourth beat unobtrusive. Bar 6: make the first three strokes unobtrusive; the fourth stroke prepares the next down beat. Bar 7: give the down beat *sf;* the rest of the measure is unobtrusive. Bar 8: keep this unobtrusive, since it is tied to the previous bar; give the third stroke to the right top. Bar 9: give a down beat with an immediate rebound to the top, to be in position to give the empty down beat of bar 10 as preparation for the entrance on the second stroke, marked *allegro agitato.*

The really bothersome places in directing recitative come where the accompaniment is choppy, entering and stopping on any part of the measure. In such places, it is absolutely necessary to indicate with the utmost clarity the differences in rests, preparations, and entrances. Not only the baton, but also one's facial expressions must preclude ambiguity. Recall that a clear down beat does not necessarily mean a strong or long one, especially on a rest. The left hand must assist the right when there is any danger of wrong entrances. Success in conducting recitative depends much upon preparation and cuing in.

"Jewel Song" from Gounod's *Faust*

At this point, let us consider Marguerite's "Jewel Song" in Act III of Gounod's *Faust,* "Je ris de me voir si belle" (*allegretto*). Number the measures in your score to facilitate reference.

First note how the measures group themselves into phrases. Conduct the music by phrase-units instead of by single measures; thus you will obtain a better musical line and memorize the music much more readily. The first eight measures of orchestral introduction form one phrase, taken one to the bar in two-measure units. This phrase, therefore, consists of four groups of two measures each. The trill phrase, covering four measures, is done one to the bar; and the baton then awaits the lady's pleasure on the 12th bar, where a breath pause usually announces the trill's end. The baton darts upward with the ascending run and catches the singer's high *G* sharp on the next down beat. Continue in one to the bar until bar 23, when a *meno mosso* calls for three to the bar. Bar 30: beat again one to the bar. Bar 46: return to three to the bar. Bars 49, 55, 59: hold back. Bar 60: beat again one to the bar. Bar 67: give only the down beat. Bars 68–72: beat three to the bar. Bar 73:

again, beat in one. Bars 91–96: beat in three. Bars 96–106: beat in one. Bar 97: again beat one to the bar. Bars 107–110: these are a repetition of the opening bars, with a slight holding back. Beat one to the bar until bar 125; then beat in three again until bar 132. The singer often holds the *G* in bar 131 through the third beat. Bars 132–139: beat in one. Bars 140–144: beat in three. At bar 144, the half note *B* is often held. Bars 145–146: beat in one. At bar 156, the high *A* is often held.

From here until the end, beat one to the bar. The trill bars 161–163 are often taken *very* rapidly. The quarter-note chord for the orchestra in bar 164 is often held for a whole measure during the singer's high *B*, proceeding directly to bar 165 without a break. From here until the end, go as rapidly as possible. Applause usually makes this section almost inaudible in any event.

The ability to switch with suppleness from one to the bar to fluid three to the bar at almost any time, and the ability to make any beat coalesce with any other, are the main factors in a good accompaniment to this aria.

Verdi's "Celeste Aida"

Our attention is next to be directed to Verdi's *Aida,* specifically to Rhadamès' romance, "Celeste Aida," which is sung a few minutes after the curtain rises. Again, number the measures in your copy for easy reference.

We start with the words, "Se quel guerrier io fossi!" Bars 1–3: give one down beat a measure. (With a routined orchestra, even this would be pedagogic and can be omitted.) Bars 4–5: beat four to the bar. Bar 6: give the second stroke to the right top; do not beat the final rests. Bar 7: hold the down beat at bottom till you are ready to give the preparation for the next bar, on the tenor's last eighth note. Bars 8–10: do as you did bars 4, 5, and 6. Bar 10: give the second stroke to right top; ignore the rests; give a preparation on the tenor's sixteenth note. Bar 11: beat in four. Bar 12: give the second stroke to right center; give a preparation for the next down beat on the tenor's last quarter note. Bar 13: do as you did bar 10. Bars 14–15: beat in four. Bar 16: give a down beat with rebound to right center, ready for the preparation on the tenor's last eighth note. Bar 17: make the first and third strokes strong and the others very light, thus bringing out the change in harmony. Bars 18–20: make the down strokes here empty and inhaling, the second strokes strong and exhaling. Give all the beats, both played and silent, in order to keep strict tempo. Show the players each definite entering place by making a thrust on the second stroke, and nod to the singer at his entrances. Bar 20: beat out the final rests, to keep strict tempo, but make them empty beats. During this bar, your eyes (or mind if you are using no score) should already be at the start of the next bar. Bar 21: give two empty beats quickly to indicate rests, and give the third stroke on the singer's quarter-note *A* flat as preparation for the strong attack on the last quarter. Bars 22–23: take four to the bar. Bars 24–26 contain quasi holds. Cue in the singer at the start of the *andantino* 6/8.

From the *andantino* on, beat six to the bar with the utmost fluidity and suppleness, to give the singer complete freedom of movement. Note that conductor and tenor must each yield to the other at points, the orchestra coming through in the singer's held notes. Bar 42: cue in the singer. Bar 50: give four strokes rapidly and leave the singer alone on his high *B* flat and short cadenza; note that the last sixteenth of the measure, *E* natural, is held. Bar 51 is a good place at which to bring out the orchestra. The measures following must be conducted with neatness, precision, and interplay between soloist and conductor. Cue in the singer at the start of each phrase and then follow him until he has the long note during which the orchestra details the lace-work background. Bar 70: watch the singer's lips and breathing. Bar 74: stress the third eighth. Bar 75: beat in two, with a quasi hold. Bars 76–77: beat in six, though again applause usually drowns out these bars. On the last eighth, give an end beat.

SUMMARY

From the foregoing remarks concerning the accompaniment for these arias from *Faust* and *Aida,* it is obvious that printed notes convey only approximately what the composer wants. In standard operas the music has acquired traditional tempos and other conventions. These can be learned only by hearing authoritative performances first hand, though recordings and discussions with singers who have the traditions do help. But one must always be careful to distinguish between stylization and genuine tradition.

An attitude of conviction and ease on the conductor's part should instill a feeling of security into the players and singers. Artistic results depend, first, upon the conductor's intimate friendship with the singer's parts, and second, upon a baton technique which allows of no ambiguity in indicating rests, preparations, and entrances. The conductor must *not* follow the vocal line with his baton, but with his mind, and he must accompany by directing the orchestra. He must accustom himself to shifting his gaze from the stage to any section of the pit back and forth suddenly, and he must be able to cue in any participant not only with his baton but also with his eyes and head. The spectacle of a conductor gazing into far distances and giving cues, however mathematically correct they may be, conveys the impression of science rather than art. There should be a feeling of personal contact between the conductor and his fellow artists at all times.

Chapter Twenty-One

STUDYING AND ANALYZING

AN ORCHESTRAL SCORE

In any work of art the whole is greater than the sum of its parts. Dissecting it, no matter how minutely, does not necessarily mean entering into its spirit. Did not Henri Bergson in his essay on "Genius" once say that the man of talent sees an infinite number of closely placed dots but that the genius sees the connected line? In music, the final synthesis depends upon each interpreter, and no amount of study of infinitesimally detailed and microscopic minutiae will take the place of inner compulsion. At the risk of stressing the obvious, it must be repeated here that each work of art is *sui generis* and presents its own technical and spiritual problems.

The student of conducting should approach his study of an orchestral score knowing that the apperception and understanding of its spiritual message is so peculiarly individual and personal that each man is literally for himself, and must hew out his own road through experiment and trial and error. An important part of that hewing-out process is the minute analysis of a score into its technical components. There is no single "best" way of making this analysis. Each student must develop his own methods and learn through his own experience. Yet valuable help may come to him from the experiences of others. All a teacher can do for him is to present the results of his own and others' experiences in studying scores and let the student adapt all this to his own individuality.

There are various methods by which score analysis may be approached. Some conductors prefer to obtain a perspective of the whole work and then get down to details; others approach the work as a succession of mosaics and then bring them together into a whole; some seem to use these two approaches simultaneously. Some go directly to the score with no intermediary steps; some learn the score at a piano; some enlist the aid of a pianist or two; some use recordings or follow the score over the air or at public rehearsals or performances. Some conductors have been known to learn a score during their own orchestral rehearsals, but this luxury is rarely granted to ordinary mortals. Each individual must use the means at hand and fit them into his own mental and artistic processes.

One warning must be given. Avoid the practice which many students follow, of reading about a composer and his works from biographical, historical, and esthetic points of view *before* they have studied the score they are approaching. This is not to disparage what can be learned from musical connotation; it is merely to emphasize the fact that extra-musical study should follow and not precede a conscientious examination of the music itself.

With these thoughts in mind, here is a suggested procedure for studying an orchestral score.

(1) Inspect the list of instruments, the clefs, the transpositions, and the foreign and technical terms.

(2) Sing through *every* part in succession horizontally, as it actually sounds.

(3) Sing through the parts up and down, first starting on the lowest staff in each section (wood wind, brass, string), and then starting at the bottom of the staff on each page, until you can sing, hum, or solfège any chord or line across or up or down the page.

Note: this does not mean that one must have a good or even a decent voice. An octave suffices, and when the part goes too high or low, the student can ignore the extreme ranges and bring the part within his one octave. His solfège should include sounds which can follow each other in rapid succession, much like those used in double and triple tonguing on certain wind instruments. "Bee" and "Dee" are good alternates for duple effects, while "Bee," "Dee," and "Kay" serve for triple. Conductors' voices are notorious and the student need not be self-conscious in this regard. The only professional singer to become conductor of a large orchestra whom this writer recalls offhand was Sir George Henschel. Singing lyric passages presents no special difficulty; but often coloratura excerpts in the violins, flutes, and even clarinets demand no little vocal, lingual, and maxillary agility. Facility in this skill, which might be termed conductor's solfège, serves not only the purpose of giving the student an insight into the details of the score, but also a further purpose at rehearsal, in enabling the conductor to show the players quickly what he wants and how he wants it.

(4) Analyze the music architecturally so that you have a bird's eye view of the main outlines in your mind. Pay special attention to transitions and development sections.

(5) Analyze the rhythmic figures, periods, and phrases of the work.

(6) Analyze the harmony, the modulations, the counterpoint, and the thematic interplay.

(7) Analyze the changes in instrumental coloring, and note places which you think might prove troublesome for the instrumentalists to play.

(8) Analyze the changes in volume horizontally to determine where the climaxes are, and vertically to determine problems of tone balance. In doing this, remember that some instruments have more penetrating tones than others and that dynamic signs do not always tell the whole story.

(9) Now combine the previous categories in your mind and note how phrasing, dynamics, volume, and instrumental coloring are often inextricably intertwined.

(10) Consider the tempo and mood of each section and movement individually and in relation to the other parts of the work.

(11) Beat through the work and note places requiring special attention, which may be troublesome for players or singers to follow. Do not say simply: this section requires so many strokes to the bar. It is rare music indeed that does not call for constant and subtle change in delineation of baton patterns. Question yourself constantly whether your motions and demeanor are interpreting the music, not only in tempo, but also in volume, tone, balance, style, mood, and the other facets which have been discussed in this volume.

(12) When you have done all this, and when you feel you have a good command of the score technically and apperceive its spiritual content, the time has come to read what those who speak authoritatively have written about the score. A list of such works is found in the Bibliography.

Finally, do not be discouraged if progress has been slow. After conscientious examination of a few scores, you will find that the time needed for getting at the essentials of a score will become shorter and shorter. There is no royal road to learning an orchestral score, and you will save time by facing this fact at once.

SOME NOTES ON BEETHOVEN'S SEVENTH SYMPHONY

Let us now consider Beethoven's Seventh Symphony from the point of view of the student conductor, to suggest ways of aiding him in the solution of some conducting problems. References made here are to the Breitkopf and Härtel edition of the full score. If this edition is not available for home use, bring your small score to the music library and copy into it the lettering and pagination of the Breitkopf and Härtel score, for easy reference while reading the following lines.

After the student has studied the symphony according to the procedure just outlined in this chapter, he is ready for a consideration of the main line, by which is meant the chief musical idea at any given time. It may be rhythmic, melodic, harmonic, or contrapuntal, and is often, in a purely orchestral work, inextricably associated with the instrumental tone coloring with which the composer has clothed the passage. The Seventh Symphony, even more than other symphonies by Beethoven, contains striking examples of this association, e.g., the second movement, where the main line, architecture, and instrumental coloring *seem* to have been born in the composer's brain simultaneously.

One of the best methods of viewing the main lines of a symphony is to make a piano arrangement of it, without too much regard for the playable possibilities and pianistic idiom, which are not what we are after here. Remember that a pianist is bound by ten fingers; a conductor is not. Such a chore will yield gratifying results in rehearsal, for it should help the conductor to be able to pick out any passage instantly. Having set the main lines of the whole symphony in his mind, the student should now hum or solfège them until he is able to carry them through the symphony from beginning to end, changing from one instrument to another and dovetailing instrumental solos into a single line, as they will really sound after transpositions have been made.

In singing through the single main line, consider this score from the point of view of tone balance, which meets us almost at the very start. The main line is carried successively for two measures each by the oboe, the clarinets, the horns, and the bassoons. The single oboe, after the smashing *tutti* chord, sounds thin. The bassoons in the 7th and 8th measures do not come through the orchestral textures so easily as do the clarinets in the 3rd and 4th measures and the horns in the 5th and 6th measures. Nor do the low horns sound with enough body in the 9th measure. All this must be adjusted if the auditor is to be enabled to follow the main line with clarity. Another problem arises at the 5th bar of the *finale,* where, unless great care is taken, the trumpet blares out against the musical texture. The trumpeter's *sf* must be played *mezzo;* he should immediately diminish to let the violins come through; and he must be urged to give a mellow tone instead of a bugle call. Many other passages in the symphony present similar problems in tone balance.

An exhaustive consideration of this single point of view would obviously transcend the limits of the present volume. The student is referred for an authoritative discussion of tone balance to Weingartner's *On the Performance of Beethoven's Symphonies.*

In analyzing the harmonic fabric of the score, learn to get at the core of the chords, i.e., disregard at the start extraneous matters like passing notes, retardations, suspensions, and all notes we may for our purposes call arabesques. A student conductor should approach the harmony of a score to get the chief outlines, not to analyze chords in the spirit of the etymologist. Once he has grasped aurally the block formations and modulations stripped of all ornaments, the details will give him no trouble. Further, what is on the printed page means nothing unless he has translated it into sound. He should study the harmony by learning whole phrases, the longer the better. He should test himself by listening to recordings, a pianist, or actual performances and seeing whether he can really name the chords and modulations. Such training is excellent for preparing for the rigors of initial rehearsals, where the orchestral web coming from all directions often sounds jumbled to the self-conscious apprentice conductor, beset by many simultaneous problems.

Our next step is to analyze the phrases so that we may be able to indicate the rise and fall of stresses by movements and planes in the baton. The beginning of a phrase obviously has more stress than the rest of it, and the end of a phrase has the suggestion of an end beat. Consider the normal phrase as consisting of four measures and mark each group with a cross or caret at the bottom of the staff. Note where phrases are other than four-measure, and where they are really four-less-one or four-plus-one or -two. Remember that phrases need not start on the bar line; they may start anywhere within a measure. Moreover, a phrase may have been telescoped by ending in one instrument and starting in another, simultaneously.

Observe the *fugato* in the second movement, starting on page 40. It is preceded by an extra measure, a kind of underlining by the composer of the last measure of the previous four-bar phrase. Unless one has analyzed this place (and other similar places), the baton sometimes betrays a desire to go on. Since the conductor has had the extra measure in mind as the reaffirmed end of a phrase, he may then cue in the first violins at the start of the *fugato* clearly, though *pp,* starting a new section with an unmistakably etched stroke.

Solfèging this *fugato* is an excellent exercise. Count the measures which are accorded to the motif each time it is sounded, and note which instruments enunciate it. Note where the group consists of four, two, or some other number of measures. Thus, on page 40 the following instruments each have the motif for four measures: the first violins at brace I, bar 7; then the second violins; then, starting on the last two bars and going to the next page, the cellos and basses; and finally, the violas. Next the motif, cut into snippets, is given for a single measure to the cellos and basses, to the violas, and to the cellos and basses again. Then the first violins, the second violins, and the cellos and basses all have it successively for two measures each. Next come the violas for two measures, with the oboe and bassoon on the second measure; then the flute and clarinet together have it for three measures, to which is joined the fourth closing measure of the group. The motif now becomes a paean chanted and intoned by the horns, trumpets, timpani, and strings against the figuration of the wood winds. Note the mosaic-like snippets and the unique use of changes in instrumental tone color for contrast in the final section of the movement. Analysis like the foregoing is invaluable for getting the main line and the phrasing and for memorizing.

The third movement has some tricky places, and an analysis will be of great aid in pure time-beating. The rhythmic pattern is four measures long and starts on bar 3, page 45. The first two bars on the page inhale and are merely introductory. The long stroke for the main phrase, therefore, comes on the third bar. The main phrase might be said to consist of two four-bar groups, making one unit of eight bars. On page 47 starting on the last beat of bar 10, the oboe and bassoon have a two-bar group, tacked onto the three-bar group of the strings which started at bar 7. This arrangement results in an extra measure for the strings before the characteristic figure of the movement is taken up in the oboe. The long down stroke for the oboe comes on the 13th bar of page 47. On page 48, starting at bar 2, the cellos and basses, the violas, and the second violins each start a measure apart, but the first violins enter *two* measures after the second violins. This is a place to watch, for the first violins sometimes imitate the other instruments and try to come in a bar ahead. These "extra" measures must be recognized, especially in the music of Beethoven, who has a way of writing with Jovian whimsicality. For detailed consideration of phrasing in Beethoven's symphonies, the student is referred to the works by Goetschius and Evans listed in the Bibliography.

Now the student should make an analysis of the architecture of the whole symphony. The special approach at this time should be to see how the composer has so intertwined the instrumental coloring and the form that they seem to be artistically inseparable. A full understanding of this symphony is impossible without a mental perspective of its form in relation to its instrumentation.

One of the most striking examples of this relation occurs in the second movement, which has characteristics of both rondo and variation forms. At the beginning, the rhythmic phrase is given out *p* in the three lower strings for two balanced eight-measure groups and is answered in echo by another eight-measure group, a formal device which Beethoven repeats in the last movement of the Ninth Symphony. The second violins take the burden in a higher octave, then the first violins still another octave higher, then the horn gives it in climactic form, followed by a *diminuendo*. Note how strings and woods are contrasted in the sections. The last page of the movement, page 44, stands out especially in this matter of tone-color contrast. Note the balance of the opening and closing bars of the movement, with the horn on the dominant at the bottom of the 6/4 chord, imparting a mood of unrest.

Form should be studied from the point of view of modulation also. The modulations connecting the sections of each movement must be firmly fixed in the ear of the student. Orchestras have been known to go back deliberately to the exposition when they were supposed to have proceeded to the recapitulation, leaving the unsuspecting conductor nonplused. It is a clever trick and not likely to leave a conductor happy. If he catches the orchestra trying it, he should never again have trouble with *that* orchestra. Tenseness and climax and their reverse hinge, too, upon form. Note where these occur in the score, a procedure which should help you to arrange dynamic and tempo climaxes logically and without repeated exaggerations.

It surely will not escape the attention of the student that each movement of this work is characterized by a rhythmic figure so striking and individual that you can quite easily recognize it by merely hearing it tapped on a board. Wagner called the Seventh the "apotheosis of the dance," as is well known.

What the mood of each movement should be is one of the most difficult problems a conductor has to face. By the time the student has made his repeated analytical tours of the score, he should have his own ideas in this regard. The decision need not be forced or hurried, however, for given time and thought, a solution will crystallize sooner or later. Once the technical questions have been analyzed conscientiously, the student is justified in consulting men who have established their right to speak on the matter. But, concerning the mood and spirit of a work, the counsel of no authority is to be accepted unless it is in harmony with the student's own inner conception.

Let us start again at the beginning of the score. Take the introduction four to the bar. Indicate the first chord by a sweep of the baton suggesting powerful down bows; then direct your attention immediately to the oboe, outlining its half notes.

The measures containing the sixteenth notes (page 4, measures 1, 3, and 5 through page 5, measure 3) must be given with precise, short strokes of the baton, each of which is the length of *one* sixteenth. Only four strokes to the measure, however, are to be given. If the baton beats full strokes, each long enough for four sixteenths, as is the temptation, the players will have little to hold to while the baton is moving; whereas if the baton enunciates crisply only the *first* sixteenth of every four and then waits until the first sixteenth of the next set is reached, the players will imitate and keep together, as they often fail to do otherwise.

On page 4, make the alternating bars for the sixteenths and those for the half notes quite distinct. At bar 6, note that the second violins and *not* the firsts begin the half-note motif. Do not allow the players to use too much bow, or a *diminuendo* will result. The lower half is enough.

Vivace

The *vivace,* marked in the score as starting with the 6/8, really enters at full tilt four measures later and is, of course, taken two to the bar. It is preceded by a tiny breath pause in the winds to separate the *crescendo* from the *subito p*. On page 9, bar 18, the hold is long and proceeds *without* a break.

Page 15, brace 1: beat the rests with empty strokes; and note that they consist of two measures after normal four-measure groups before the repeat, but are part of the four-measure group after the repeat. Page 15, bar 16: note the ten-measure group consisting of two-measure units, enunciated successively by the cello and bass, the first violins, the second violins, the violas, and the oboe and flute. Stress the first note of each entrance. See that the lyric imitations are played as one man by the five colorists. Page 17, bar 2: give a tiny breath pause before the next bar to point up the *p*. Page 23, bar 4: do not make the hold too long or it will hurt the effect of the hold in the next measure. Cut off with a sweep to allow the baton full play to bring in the wood-wind chord attack on the sixteenth note. This place, very much like the opening measures of the overture to Mozart's *Marriage of Figaro,* invites frayed edges unless the greatest possible care is taken. Give the preparation as if you were playing the sixteenth note with the orchestra. Wait at the top of the pattern for the players to imitate your motion. Then descend together, with the attack on the hold. The preparatory motion must be unhurried and positive. Bar 5: there is no break after this hold; proceed *pp* without a cut-off to the oboe. Page 27, bar 12: take a tiny breath pause before the *pp* implied Neapolitan sixth.

Allegretto

The first two bars are quasi holds; then beat two to the bar. Page 33, bar 14: keep the second violins on the *D* string for eight measures. Bar 22: keep the first and second violins on the *A* string until bar 12, page 34, then on the *E* string. Page 36, bar 2: still beat in two, *legato*. Page 43, bars 18–21: let the tone float mystically, to prepare for final outburst of tone in the movement. Page 44, last played bar: keep the first violins on the *A* string. Last two played bars: keep the second violins on the *G* string.

Presto

Page 45: beat one to the bar, phrasing two bars as one. Page 46, bars 19–20: note when the sudden dynamic changes are *ff* and when they are *pp*. A *fortissimo* motion in the wrong place is likely to look silly.

Assai Meno Presto

On page 50 is one of the famous tempo question marks. Continue to beat one to the bar but square the speed with your musical conscience. Page 53, bars 23–24: observe a tiny breath pause just before *ppp,* and hold back on these two measures to prepare the ear for the noble harmonic change. Beat these two bars in three, with a slight hold on the second stroke of measure 24 to give the entrance on the up beat for the return of the *presto*. Page 63, bars 5–6: follow similar procedure. Page 64, bar 9: hold back a bit to give the wood winds a chance to play this difficult place cleanly (do the same on page 79, brace 2, bar 5, which is awkward for the flute to play). Page 68, bar 6: the last quarter note in the basses may be articulated by the baton if it does not come through precisely enough. The final *presto* should be slightly broader than the movement as a whole, like five exclamation points.

Allegro Con Brio

At page 69, adopt the tempo for the whole movement at the start and do not let up once; do not start one tempo and speed up till the outline becomes indistinct, or start a tempo which the players cannot maintain. Premeditatively rigid tempo is very effective. Note that the first four bars are introductory and that the silent measures (2 and 4) have empty beats and are quasi holds. Avoid anticlimaxes.

For a reading and reference list on Beethoven's symphonies, see the Bibliography.

Chapter Twenty-Two

MARKING, CORRECTING, AND

EDITING SCORES

Most conductors have personal methods of marking scores in ways which call attention to important places. There are conductors who assert that they never, *never* have marked their scores and that they carry everything in their heads. Of some of these it has been said that, though the scores they exhibit are new copies with freshly cut leaves, those they have used for study look like war maps. Certainly most conductors, even those who conduct public performances without a score, still mark their scores for study purposes. Memories vary, but even a good one should not be burdened unnecessarily.

There is such a thing as cluttering up a score with so many markings that the over-all picture runs into the danger of being swamped by details. Markings on a score may be likened to fingerings for instrumentalists, and methods for making them may well be studied. Fortunately for the student of conducting, orchestral scores which have been marked up by experienced conductors have reached our public libraries, where they may be consulted. Two points should interest those inspecting such scores: what was considered of enough consequence to mark and how the markings were made.

Some conductors use one color to denote music for the stage and another to show music for the pit, or different colors for different sections of the orchestra. This sort of color scheme can be easily overdone. Some use a death's-head, an exclamation point, or an arrow to warn of places of extreme danger, for example when a quick turn of the page is called for, followed by an important cue or change in tempo. The traditional "v.s." (*volta subito,* which means turn immediately) is frequently employed for such spots.

Some conductors have ideographs for instrumental cues, for example, an outline of the timpano, a Δ for the triangle, a large "O" to suggest the bell of the horn, intertwined circles for cymbals, an "H" for the harp, a comb to suggest a keyboard, "I" for first violins, "II" for second violins, and obvious abbreviations like vla, trb, cl, flt, ob, bsn, vlc, etc. Showing sudden changes of time-signature and dynamics in color often proves of aid. Circling an accent or important note is a common practice. A line increasing in thickness or the reverse has often been used to show change in volume.

Where single notes in a measure are to be articulated, a single vertical line over each note will call attention to it. This device is of special aid in recitative and retards. When a whole passage or a group of measures is to be taken in the same number of beats to a measure, the first measure may be marked with the same number of short vertical lines, circled and followed by an arrow pointing to the right.

Dangerous cues and sudden changes at the start of a page may be noted on the preceding page, on the staff to be affected. Similarly, the direction and kind of stroke on a page may be noted on the page before, as may a change in the number of strokes, in signature, or in transposition.

In marking cuts, be careful to enclose the exact places to be elided. Use thick vertical lines to catch the eye. Perhaps because the eye muscles follow a curve more easily than a straight line, it will usually be found that a cut marked as in Figure 116 reads more comfortably than one marked as in Figure 117.

When there is more than one page to a cut, clip the pages affected so that they will turn as one. It is also a good plan to mark at the start of the cut what is coming at its end, e.g., "to bottom page so-and-so," "horn," "in three," etc. Pasting blank pages over elided passages is not wise since the cut may vary at another time.

See that consecutive numbers or letters, or both, are placed at about every ten measures, at every important change in time-signature and tempo, and at other strategic points. These will prove invaluable aids in starting, stopping, and finding one's place easily. See that these indications agree in your score and in the players' parts. Remember that editions vary in this regard and that much time and patience in rehearsal may be lost if the indications do not tally. If worst comes to worst and they do vary, you should know your score well enough to be able to say to your orchestra: "Start at such and such a solo or change in tempo or time-signature and tell me whether I am to give an up or down beat and how many beats to the bar. And sing a few notes to me." After a note or two you should be able to tell exactly where the place is. Orchestral players like this sort of team work.

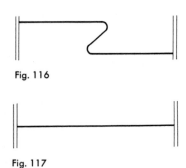

Fig. 116

Fig. 117

MARKING, CORRECTING, AND EDITING SCORES

Have all bowings, special fingerings and strings, breathings, phrasings, and other indications of style marked in the parts plainly *before* the rehearsal. No management should waste money or time (synonymous today in orchestral rehearsals) for matters which can be attended to at the copyist's desk. You will, of course, have consulted section leaders and the concertmaster when instruments are to play passages of thematic imitation which require similar phrasing. They probably know their instruments better than you do.

To repeat: do not overmark. This habit is a kind of subconscious attempt to shift responsibility to the printed page; it impels one sort of conductor to belabor his scores with innumerable doodlings. When you make a mark, be sure it is justified; memorize that mark as if it were part of the music itself; but do not lose sight of the forest for the trees.

The task of correcting scores is one which understandably causes young conductors no little concern. New scores have their quota of errors, and even many standard works have occasional misprints and possible variations. Works in manuscript have more than their share, and the prospect of detecting errors on the spot in rehearsal may cause the conductor of limited experience to become flustered and nervous.

Such errors are likely to fall into a few definite categories. The first is wrong accidentals. Copyists work for a living, and they have been known to speed up towards the end of their tasks much as did the tailor in the "Peer Gynt" Suite. Some, like Rossini's favorite, have an inordinate fondness for sharps and flats as artistic devices. When accidentals disagree, an analysis of the string, harp, or trombone parts, which often outline the complete harmony, gives the correct answer quickly. Thus, in the 18th measure of Berlioz' "Fantastic" Symphony (Eulenburg edition), the cello part has a misprinted *A* flat, whereas the other instruments play the triad *F-A-C.* In the 27th measure of Strauss's *Don Juan* (Kalmus edition), the second violins have the half notes on the first line *E* and the third space *C* sharp; these notes should read a third above, i.e., second line *G* sharp and fourth space *E,* as an inspection of the *E major* chord in the other parts will show. Many other standard works will reveal similar copyists' or proofreaders' errors.

In Stravinsky's "Firebird" Suite (1919 version, Kalmus edition), we meet a series of errors in various categories. These obvious errors, difficult to understand in the case of a living composer, will serve to show the categories into which such deviations often divide themselves.

In the 16th measure from the start, the last note of the first violins should read second line *G* and not the printed *F* sharp on the first space. The following note *F* should be *F* sharp. In the 18th measure, the first violins should have a natural before the sixth eighth note.

In the "Variation de l'Oiseau de feu et sa danse," at no. 11, measures 9 and 10: cancel the *jeté* (thrown bow) in the violins. This is solo bowing and impracticable for a whole section. (Berlioz commits a similar error by directing *spiccato* at the tip of the bow [*à la pointe*]. This looks good on paper but just does not come off in actual performance.) Two measures before no. 13: the clarinet part should (but doesn't) read *A* sharp throughout the measure. The second note in the harp part should be *F* sharp. Three measures after no. 17, add a natural sign before the first violin *A* harmonic, for safety.

Going back to the introduction, one measure after no. 3, the strings play a *glissando* of natural harmonics. The composer or his editor should have marked in the bowing. The first violins may start down-bow and give eight notes to a bow, with the last four thirty-seconds up-bow. The second violins and violas start up-bow, eight notes to the bow. Cellos start down-bow and take ten notes to a bow. Do not try to get mathematical exactitude; the effect is impressionistic and the bowing suggestions are meant only to help the players follow the baton and come out right at the next bar.

In the "Variation de l'Oiseau de feu," at no. 9: violins, first triplet, down-bow; next two triplets up-bow and *simile* for all strings.

In the "Ronde des princesses," at the second measure after no. 6, the third eighth note should be *A* sharp, a semitone below the printed third line *B*.

In the "Danse infernale du Roi Kastcheï," the xylophone solo heard in the third measure before no. 4 should be repeated in the bar preceding no. 4, i.e., two measures later. Two measures before no. 16, the viola part should be in the treble clef, changing back to the alto clef at no. 16.

In the "Berceuse," the bassoon part in the third bar preceding no. 7, and the harp part in the two measures before no. 10 need correction, which is left to the student as an exercise.

In the "Finale," at the third measure after no. 12, fill in the harp part so it will remain in unison with the clarinet part for the four-measure passage beginning at no. 12. At no. 16, the violas should be in the alto clef; and they should change to the treble clef at no. 17. The tuba part in the sixth measure before no. 19 should duplicate the third measure before no. 19, i.e., start both measures with an eighth *E* below the staff.

Here, then, are a few representative typographical errors in a score by a living composer, errors in melody, harmony, clefs, accidentals, and omission of notes. They should suggest methods of correction in similar cases in other scores.

The problems of correcting errors which have crept into works even in the standard repertory, not to speak of recent and contemporary scores, have occupied distinguished writers of the past. Some of these errors are discussed in books by Robert Schumann, Sir Donald Francis Tovey, and Felix Weingartner, listed in the Bibliography. Schumann's comment in the introductory paragraph of his essay "On Certain Probably Corrupted Passages in the Works of Bach, Mozart, and Beethoven" should be taken to heart by every conductor:

. . . if earthly tones penetrate beyond the grave, I think the masters must often smile when they hear errors that custom, tradition, and even reverence, have permitted to continue in their works. It has long been my intention to refer to a few in some of the better known works of the masters mentioned above, with the request that all artists and connoisseurs test them, whenever possible, by comparisons with the original manuscripts. Even these themselves are sometimes incorrect. No composer would dare to swear with certainty that any manuscript of his is entirely free from errors. It is quite natural that among the thousand skipping dots that he writes in an incredibly short space of time, a dozen or so should be jotted down too high or too low; indeed, composers oftentimes set down the maddest harmonies.

The matter of editing scores is one which the conductor must face from time to time, especially in older works. Some editing tasks are the substitution of present-day instruments for obsolete or archaic ones when the latter are not available or desired; the addition of notes in extreme ranges for French horns and trumpets, which have been perfected since the score was written; and the translation of old ornamentation and clefs into contemporary usages.

Another type of editing facing the young conductor arises from the need to obtain proper tone balance in music by such classic composers as Haydn and Mozart, who wrote originally for orchestras differing in size and proportions from those of today. Some places in Beethoven's orchestral music, for various reasons, including the constitution of the orchestra, the technical limitations of the instruments of his time, and his deafness, need *reverent* adjustment in getting proper tone balance. Doubling the woods may solve one problem; cutting down the strings another; changing dynamics a third.

Still another type of problem in securing proper tone balance is met in the music of more recent composers such as Bruckner, Schumann, and Chopin, who were not at their best as orchestrators, and in the music of Brahms himself, who envied Bizet in this respect. Before a young conductor, however, attempts to trust his own judgment in such matters, let him first consult authorities and try such expedients as adjusting volume and doubling or diminishing instrumental sections. The solution of these problems is largely a matter of experience. Until the time comes when he has sufficient experience, he should go to authorities for procedure.

Composers themselves, Vaughan Williams and Debussy, for example, have made variants of some of their works, a situation which offers yet another problem for the young conductor. The following reactions to the two versions of Mozart's G Minor Symphony, by two of the most distinguished authorities of the past generation, should serve to point up the difficulties here.

Donald Francis Tovey writes, "In the G Minor Symphony he [Mozart] at first did without clarinets, and most editions of his score give only his original version; but he afterwards rewrote the oboe parts, giving all their softer and less rustic utterances to the clarinets, and it is a great mistake not to accept this revision." (*Essays in Musical Analysis*, Oxford.)

While Felix Weingartner says, "I exhort, at the very outset, that the clarinets, allegedly added later [to Mozart's G Minor Symphony], be renounced. They thicken up the timbre and rob this symphony of the indescribably delicate charm with which the very absence of clarinets invests it." (*On the Performance of the Classical Symphonies*, vol. II, Breitkopf.)

In view of these sincere differences between two such distinguished authorities, the need for humility of soul in the young conductor facing similar problems is obvious. He has only his good taste and his conscience as his guides.

Chapter Twenty-Three

PREPARING FOR THE REHEARSAL

The time comes in the life of the apprentice or student conductor when he faces his first rehearsal. The orchestra at his command will be a far cry from the orchestras he will face later if he achieves success as a conductor. It may seem to the student that suggestions in this and the following chapter, which discuss some of the procedures which have been found effective for making rehearsals smooth and efficient, are impractical in view of the limitations of the players and facilities with which he will have to work. If he, as a young student of the flute, violin, or piano had had only a poor and musically limited instrument upon which to learn and practice, however, he would want to approach it in the way most likely to make him efficient when he might later be able to have a far better instrument. He should approach his first rehearsals in the same spirit.

Some of the suggestions which follow may not be practical for the inadequate conditions the student conductor will meet when he first practices his art. In some instances his very first position, especially if it is connected with an educational institution, may give him opportunity for one big program at the end of the year, for which he may have many rehearsals. When conditions are not favorable for the kind of work he would like to do and he is forced to bend to necessity, he should bend only temporarily, never losing sight of the goal he hopes to reach later. If he knows the best procedures, he may be able to follow them oftener than seems possible at first.

Some aspects of the work, approached in earlier chapters from the student's point of view, will now be reviewed from the point of view of the man preparing to rehearse an orchestra. The suggestions which follow will, if conscientiously carried out, go far toward making initial meetings with performers a minimum trial and insuring a logical and well-ordered series of rehearsals. The student is reminded again that, as was noted in the Foreword, some of the problems he will meet in rehearsals are not discussed here, especially those having to do with subtleties of tone balance and technical knowledge of orchestral instruments, information which is easily available in clear detail in such works as Forsyth's *Orchestration* and Scherchen's *Handbook on Conducting*.

LEARNING THE SCORE

When the conductor prepares for a rehearsal he has a definite program in mind. Whether the music to be played is Smetana's *My Country*, a Bach chorale, or Schubert's "Unfinished," his first task is to master the score. He must know it so well that he has his own interpretation of it clearly in mind and the ways in which, from every page of the music, he intends to elicit that interpretation from players and instruments. He needs to hear in his mind, before a single note has been played, what the critic demands after all the rehearsals have ended and the final result is being judged.

As the painter visualizes first in his mind's eye the tones and colors he sees on the blank canvas on his easel, the conductor must achieve an inner audition, as he masters the score in front of him, of accurate and clean playing of the notes, of good pitch, warm tonal quality, knife-edged attacks and releases, musical phrasing, proper balance of tone, proper distribution of dynamic climaxes, *fortissimo* which is not feathery as a poor orchestra makes it, and *pianissimo* which is full. He must be able to hear clearly the main line of the music, which may be rhythmic, harmonic, contrapuntal, or melodic. He must have a plan in mind which relegates main and subordinate parts to their proper places; a plan, also, which places dynamic climaxes in their proper proportions and not as a series of anticlimaxes.

As he prepares to rehearse a score, he must achieve a unified and individual concept of the music as a whole and hear in his mind's ear how it will sound eventually under the direction of his baton. If, in the final performance, he does not reach his ideal, he can console himself with the knowledge that this difference between projected and actual performance has plagued even the greatest conductors. Rarely indeed has it been granted to an interpreter to be wholly satisfied with his performance in all respects.

As a first step in preparing to rehearse a score, the conductor should study and analyze it by some such procedure as that suggested in Chapter Twenty-One. He may next be able to get hold of the composer or of a recording under the composer's direction or by an authoritative interpreter. This procedure is usually wise but it should be undertaken with the knowledge that listening to recordings is apt to take away the conductor's own individuality, especially in new works, unless he is very careful. From these sources the conductor may learn correct tempos, phrasing, balance, and other important matters. If the composer is not living, or if he is not available in person or through correspondence, the conductor should endeavor to obtain technical studies about his compositions and his epoch. The conductor is then ready to decide whether the score needs correcting, adjusting, and editing, and to mark it according to methods suggested in Chapter Twenty-Two.

As he is preparing to rehearse his score, the conductor should obtain an accurate idea of the time required to play through it and through the entire program. This means the time which will be consumed when the music is played in his own tempos, not those of some one else, which may easily be ascertained from recordings, broadcasts, other conductor's performances, or from books mentioned in the Bibliography. The only safe method is to go through the works oneself, taking into account time for intermissions, pauses between movements, choral groups going on and off stage, the seating of late comers in the audience, and even applause.

STUDYING AND ANALYZING THE INDIVIDUAL PARTS

A good idea, one which if carried through may lessen the self-consciousness and nervousness which often assail comparatively inexperienced conductors at rehearsals, is to take home the individual parts of a score and go over them with the full score. Players often read notes incorrectly at rehearsals, and the conductor has armed himself well if he has gone over microscopically, in advance, the harmonic bases of the score section by section.

Study of the individual parts of a score will reveal that errors are apt to creep into the parts of transposing instruments like the clarinets, French horns, trumpets, and English horns. Misprints in clefs are apt to be found in the parts of violas, cellos, bassoons, and trombones. Other advantages, in addition to checking possible errors, accrue from this type of score study. It will acquaint the conductor with notational idioms peculiar to each instrument, which by their very concentration may confuse the inexperienced conductor when handed to him suddenly for inspection during a rehearsal. Familiarity with these idioms enables him to talk to the instrumentalist in the idiom peculiar to his instrument.

When he has his own full score in front of him, containing his own markings, comparison of that with the individual parts will call his attention to instruments with long waits, and he may note on his own score where to cue them in. Better still, he may also write in his full score a few bars of the main line which immediately precedes such entrances. He can make note of passages where low notes in the flute are easily overpowered; passages where notes in the oboe's middle range may obtrude too pungently; and passages where extremes in range and rapid shifts in pulse and tempo will form danger spots for him when he faces his men at rehearsal.

Especially when the apprentice becomes a guest conductor will he be grateful for this full and detailed study transcribed with care to his own individually-owned score. Otherwise he may be faced with a score that has been marked and re-marked in various colored pencils, making it extremely confusing for him to read. He will have enough to do without that added burden, for he will doubtless be facing men who have to forget what they have been directed to do previously, in order to adopt another style for him.

TIMING AND SCHEDULING REHEARSALS

Performing forces should rarely be called upon to rehearse for more than an hour and a half at one stretch. After this period of concentrated attention, the returns are diminishing to both conductor and conducted. Periodic rests should be scheduled to allow minds, voices, and fingers to relax, and to let people smoke and stretch their legs. It is an established fact that workers can accomplish better work with rest periods than without them, because mental concentration flags after a comparatively short period. Performers should be made to understand, however, that a fifteen-minute rest period means just that, and that they are to be back and ready for work *tuned up* within these fifteen minutes, just as they are expected to be in their seats with instruments warmed up when rehearsals are called. If this is not insisted upon at the start, many precious minutes will be lost and the amount of loss will stealthily increase.

The question of the number of rehearsals to be held is often one whose answer is dictated by circumstances. One of the best means of getting a better and better ensemble is to have the orchestra or choir rehearse often, until tone balance is felt by each member and until the organization as a unit develops a personality of its own.

Leave time at the end of each rehearsal, especially at the final rehearsal preceding a performance, for polishing, tonal adjustments, and an over-all review of the high lights and danger spots, so that the performers retain a feeling of the whole as an art work and not as a series of fences.

The conductor will of course arrange sectional rehearsals for complicated works. It is preferable that he take these himself, although the task can be delegated to the leaders of the several sections. In that case the conductor must himself check later and perhaps modify instructions somewhat. But he will have missed valuable aural experience. Preliminary consultations with sectional leaders before rehearsing starts should by all means be held. If there are conflicts the conductor must resolve them and he should do so in time for his full score, with his markings, letterings, and numberings at strategic points, to be given to the copyist for transference to the individual parts before the first rehearsal. The conductor need not fear that experienced players feel it beneath their dignity to take their parts home to look over, even when the work is in the standard repertory. Some of the best players do this religiously, even in top-flight orchestras.

The young conductor in the act of timing his rehearsals is warned against thinking that certain "war horses" and shorter compositions may be allotted more limited rehearsal time than newer or longer works. The truth of the matter is that some of the classics need time to freshen up; they are difficult to keep alive because they are overplayed and may degenerate into stylized performances unless great care is exercised; while some of the shorter works often demand more rehearsal time than longer works.

In timing rehearsals, the conductor should take care to avoid the resentment and irritation felt by performers who are forced to wait around during periods while others rehearse, or who are called for a short period, left waiting for a long period, and then recalled for another short stint. Each singer and instrumentalist should be apportioned his fair share of time, in an order that will keep him in the rehearsal room for the shortest possible length of time. It is often possible to arrange for certain of the less frequently played instruments, like the bass trombone, the bass clarinet, the English horn, and the harp, to be rehearsed at the start or end of sessions. This arrangement can sometimes be extended to whole sections.

Instrumental and vocal soloists should be rehearsed with the piano before the general rehearsal, to assure that the starts and ends of cadenzas are clearly understood on both sides, and that moot questions of tempo, phrasing, and tone balance are ironed out. In appointing rehearsal time for vocal soloists, even the conductor who has not studied the techniques of singing should be aware that very early morning rehearsals are not conducive to the best results, that voices do not sound the same in the early morning as later in the day, and that for these good reasons singers should be called as late as possible for morning rehearsals. The difficulties which Chaliapin is known to have made for all concerned when he was scheduled to rehearse before noon were not simply due to artistic temperament, but were based on sound physiological reasons.

REHEARSAL HALLS

The conductor will, of course, see to it that the best available quarters are at the disposal of the performers. This precaution is not alone for altruistic and humanitarian reasons. Good lighting, adequate ventilation, and healthful temperature have a definite influence upon performance. They make for better tempers and temperaments. Rooms with high ceilings are desirable for better acoustics; rooms with echoes should be avoided. Chilly or overheated rooms work havoc upon organ tuning and have equally whimsical effects upon winds and strings, making some high and some low, so that even after a quarter hour the divergence may become acute and painful. Proper dynamics and tone balance are difficult enough to achieve without these handicaps. The players' efficiency is seriously impaired by extremes in temperature. Some of these sheerly physical matters may be more a problem for an engineer than for the conductor. If so, get his expert advice.

In the matter of rehearsal halls, it is wise to insist upon having available for the last rehearsal the same hall where the concert takes place. Music sounds different not only in different halls but in the same hall when it is empty and when an audience fills it. It takes experience to judge these differences, but a rehearsal in the concert hall or the conductor's attendance at another concert in that hall will give him some sort of gage. Failing these aids, he should listen intently at the start of his concert and have trusted assistants report to him, after they have tested various parts of the hall, as early as possible in the program.

SEATING PLANS

Prepare all seating plans so that there is no doubt in any performer's mind about just where he is to sit or stand. There are various effective methods of arranging performers, but traditional usages should be followed until a conductor has had enough experience to know what he wants and to be sure that he can get it only by deviating from established arrangements. Theater pits and broadcasting stations present special problems. Sometimes the work itself suggests that certain sections sit near each other, but this matter can easily be overdone and should be reserved for special occasions. Changes in choral seating may be dictated by weakness or strength in one section, the weaker ones being placed in front.

One characteristic of a good seating arrangement is that every performer has a direct line of vision to the conductor's baton and face and that the conductor can see the instrument and face of every performer. Whatever the seating arrangement, straining to see on the part of conductor or performers should be avoided at all costs.

GETTING THE PLAYERS' POINT OF VIEW

The conductor preparing for a rehearsal envisions what he expects and plans to get from his men. If he is facing a professional group, his men also envision, from the moment he steps before them, what they expect of him, and it is a great aid for him to know something about the players' point of view. This is especially valuable for those conductors who have never played as members of an orchestra. Even for those who have been orchestral players, a fresh recollection of themselves as they sat under the baton of another should be good for the sense of balance.

As he looks forward to meeting his men, the student conductor should realize that the first and foremost source of irritation experienced by orchestral players in relation to conductors is pretension, affectation, and their concomitants: posing; attitudinizing; premeditated gyrations, contortions, and gesticulations; and aping of famous conductors by placing hand over heart, hand on hip, both hands in the air as if evoking Olympian thunder, and by other histrionics. Oddly enough, the conductor need not fear that, at the concert, the player will usually resent sincere histrionics, which he feels are a matter between conductor and audience. The rehearsal, however, the player feels is a matter between the conductor and the orchestra. As he puts the matter bluntly and racily, he has seen and played under so many of the best and worst conductors and has taken so many of them in his stride that he views histrionics at the rehearsal with a grain of cynicism.

The player will want to know what the conductor wants without long abstractions, exegesis, and lectures. He will not want to be practiced on. He has spent years acquiring a competent technique and expects no less from the man who presumes to lead him.

The player will demand a clear baton technique. This means above everything else a clear down beat. It means neither overbeating so that the watcher's eye is confused by the excess of motion, nor underbeating so that there is nothing to hold to between "clicks." The player will want to know at all times what the baton is delineating: the tempo, time-signatures, phrasing, pulsations, subdivisions, measure groupings, and dynamics. He will not want useless motion from the conductor, indulged in for its own sake and effect. He will want the conductor to look at the performers with a face that constantly reveals the mood of the music. He will want the main line kept always in evidence, and the music which is secondary in importance in the tonal web held in abeyance, that is, he wants musical balance. He will want the conductor to cue every significant change *in good time:* attacks, releases, pauses, and holds. In short, the player will demand that the man with the baton *conduct,* and project his own interpretation.

Though instrumentalists have never been very articulate in writing about these things, they have been both voluble and biting in speaking of them on propitious occasions. Excluding a certain bitterness in those of the inevitable minority who feel they would have been conductors themselves except for a quirk of fate, there remains much that is just, objective, and germane in their comments. Two works of great interest in giving the player's point of view are Bernard Shore's *The Orchestra Speaks* and *Sixteen Symphonies.* Mr. Shore writes with keenness, charm, and mature judgment about the many years he has played as solo violist with the B.B.C. Symphony Orchestra, under many of the world's chief conductors. In the same category, though regrettably not available in English, are Nikolas Lambinon's *Der Orchestermusiker* (The Orchestra Player) and Hans Diestel's *Ein Orchestermusiker über das Dirigieren* (An Orchestra Player on Conducting), with a foreword by Richard Strauss. The young conductor will find much of value about rehearsing in these four volumes and learn much about what the player rightly demands of the conductor. He may well take to heart, as he attempts to see himself at face value through the eyes of the players he must first face at rehearsal, some words written by Herr Strauss in his foreword to the Diestel book: *

Don't be too proud of your three curtain calls after the third Leonora overture. Down there in the orchestra amongst the first violins, in the back amongst the horns or even at the other end at the timpani there are argus-eyed observers, who note each of your crochets or quavers with critical regard,

*This translation is that of L. J. Lawrence in *Recollections and Reflections,* and is used by permission of Atlantis Verlag, Zurich, and Boosey and Hawkes, New York.

who groan if you wave your baton furiously in their faces conducting *Tristan* "alla breves" in four, or when you celebrate the movement "By the Brook" or the second variation in the adagio movement of the "Ninth" by beating twelve complete quavers. They even revolt if you constantly shout "ssh" and "piano, gentlemen" at them during the performance, whilst your right hand constantly conducts forte. They wink if you say at the beginning of a rehearsal "the woodwind is out of tune" but cannot indicate which instrument is playing too high or too low. The conductor up there may imagine that they follow reverently each movement of his baton, but in reality they go on playing without looking at him when he loses his beat and they blame his "individualist interpretation" for every false tempo when he is, let us say, conducting a symphony for the first time which they have played a hundred times before under better conductors.

In short the stories of how conductors have been caught out by members of the orchestra would fill volumes. And yet this malicious mob, who plod their weary way in a chronic *mezzoforte,* who cannot be flattered into accompanying *pp* or into playing chords in a recitative precisely unless the right man happens to be at the rostrum, with what enthusiasm do they not play— tortured though they be by blunderers with no idea of rehearsing, tired out as they are by giving lessons—with what self-sacrifice do they not rehearse if they know that their conductor will not worry them unnecessarily, how readily will they not obey his slightest gesture on the evening of the performance (especially if he has let them off a rehearsal), when his right hand, fully mastering the high art of conducting conveys to them his exact intentions; when his eye surveys their playing severely yet benevolently, when his left hand does not form a fist in *ff* passages and does not unnecessarily restrain them in *p* passages.

Chapter Twenty-Four

THE REHEARSAL

More and more I have come to think that what decides the worth of conducting is the degree of suggestive power that the conductor can exercise over the performers. At the rehearsal he is mostly nothing more than a workman who schools the men under him so conscientiously and precisely that each of them knows his place and what he has to do there; he first becomes an artist when the moment arrives for the production of the work. Not even the most assiduous rehearsing, so necessary a prerequisite as this is, can so stimulate the capacities of the players as the force of the imagination of the conductor. It is not the transference of his personal will, but the mysterious act of creation that called the work itself into being, which takes place again and again in him, and, transcending the narrow limits of reproduction, he becomes a new-creator, a self-creator. The more, however, his personality disappears so as to get behind the personality that created the work—and to identify itself, indeed, with this—the greater will his performance be.

Felix Weingartner: *On Conducting*

A well-ordered, smoothly functioning rehearsal is of the utmost importance and no pains should be spared to insure its achievement. If preparations have been conscientiously made, the conductor should have enough confidence in himself, during the rehearsal period, to be quite free to make last-minute adjustments and even to extemporize a bit. He will have passed through the stage of the critic, where he imagined an ideal performance, and that of the explorer, where he went over the ground and prepared to lead his party over it through the easiest, most interesting, and most revealing roads. Now, as he faces his forces, he becomes a teacher and guide who will show them the best methods of traversing the country.

The rehearsal is not primarily for him but for the performers. The goal he has for them is that they resemble a good string quartet, every member of which is, in a real sense, an equal partner who understands the style of every other member and feels instinctively when to come to the fore and when to yield. While the conductor knows in his heart that the large orchestra cannot, except perhaps in very rare instances, reach the ideal tonal balance of a string quartet, he will aim at his organization's greater elasticity, homogeneity, and tonal balance, and he will attempt to help each player develop as an individual instead of as simply one cog in a large machine.

GAGING THE CALIBER OF THE ORCHESTRA

Rehearsal procedures depend to no small extent upon the kind of group one faces, its standards, and the position in which the conductor finds himself in relation to it. A guest conductor interpreting standard works with a first-rank group does not rehearse in the same way as a resident conductor with a smaller and less professional group. In the former case, the men have played the works many times before under all sorts of conductors and they only want to run through the main points to ascertain this conductor's wishes. Explanations which would be proper for less experienced groups would be resented by members of a professional orchestra.

When the apprentice conductor faces experienced groups as their guest, if he frankly accepts his situation and tacitly suggests that he is happy to learn, the players will usually be put in a frame of mind where they are ready to assist him cordially. Members of good orchestras possess an *esprit de corps* which prevents them from permitting performances by their group to drop below certain standards. Also, they are pretty well aware that even experienced choral conductors, organists, and composers are not, as a general rule, routined orchestrally; and conversely, that orchestrally routined conductors are not always equally conversant with problems related to organ playing and choral singing.

Educational and amateur organizations present special problems which require patience, understanding, tact, and good humor. Matters of fingering, breathing, and bowing, taken for granted in professional groups, must here be detailed and drilled in. The necessarily protracted rehearsals usual with such amateur organizations make it difficult to get away from rigidity, and the conductor is faced with the task of achieving some sort of elasticity during the final sessions. The most troublesome aspect of working with nonprofessional groups (and sometimes even with professional ones) is obtaining good intonation. Regardless of all else, this simply *must* be present, for without good pitch the results can hardly be called music in any real sense.

Whether dealing with an amateur group, a famous orchestra or choir, or with an ensemble of various grades between these two extremes, the conductor should quickly grasp the personality of the group he faces and adapt his methods and procedures to its needs. He will find that some groups are phlegmatic and tend to drag tempos and be late on attacks, while others are tense and tend to rush and anticipate attacks. He will find that the tone of some verges on the thinnish side, while that of others is thick. Any number of differences in groups will soon become apparent, and the conductor must cast about and find ways of correcting their defects and approximations. With one group he will hold back, with another he will take slightly faster tempos to instil vitality, and so on. These differences in group personalities are matters of previous training, traditions, geographical location, and national temperaments, and he must learn to sense them quickly and adapt himself to them.

PANTOMIMIC SIGNS

It should be axiomatic that the student conductor possess a good command of physical techniques by the time he meets his forces in rehearsal, and that all his gestures relating to the music to be played have been practiced until they have become automatic. These techniques should at the rehearsal be supplemented with certain pantomimic signs that have been found useful in avoiding confusion between performers and conductor.

Extending the left forefinger as a warning to a singer or player to prepare for a sudden or important entrance goes back to primitive times. Holding up one finger for a first ending and two for a second ending may be used as a reminder, but this system must be understood on both sides, for some conductors have used the same signals to mean exactly the opposite, i.e., one finger to mean once only (second ending) and two fingers to repeat (first ending). If one finger means once only (take second ending and go ahead), follow it with a motion to the right (to go ahead); if two fingers mean repeat, motion backward.

The left hand may be brought up to show that some one is flat and should come up; the hand may be brought down to mean someone is sharp and should come down.

To show an orchestra how many beats a measure are to be given for a passage (perhaps because a singer changes his mind in performance, or because rehearsals have been inadequate), hold up the required number of fingers in the left hand while continuing to beat with the right. It is not so easy as might be thought to separate fingers in one's hand suddenly so that some stand out prominently. Awkwardness in this regard during a performance will not prove amusing. For one, try the forefinger; for two, the forefinger and middle finger; for three, the third, fourth, and fifth fingers; for four, all but thumb; for six, three fingers shown twice, and so on. Practice a bit shifting quickly from one set of fingers to another.

REHEARSAL PROCEDURES IN GENERAL

Obviously, one procedure for all types of orchestras and choirs cannot be suggested, but a few general suggestions for economical and effective rehearsals can be made.

(1) Works should first be played through as a whole, then their details stressed, and then they should be played through as a whole again. Running completely through familiar works to get warmed up is often a good procedure.

(2) Weather and atmospheric conditions have definite effects upon throats, and conductors should be considerate with singers under adverse conditions.

(3) It is hardly wise for a conductor to allow the orchestral web to overbalance singers, or to take passages with extreme ranges repeatedly and thus wear out their throats. The same consideration should be extended to players of instruments like the oboe and French horn. Take the desired vocal passages at half voice by keeping the other parts down most of the time, so that the soloist may save himself for the concert.

(4) For unfamiliar and difficult works start with an over-all picture. Give the prevailing tempo and your choice of beat; stress solo passages requiring special attention; and explain the general mood of the piece. Play as much as you can without stopping. When comparatively small errors occur in the first reading, make a mental note of them. It is better to stop once to correct several places at the same time than to stop many times for detailed treatment of single places.

(5) Another suggestion to be almost universally applied is do not overtalk. The conductor's privilege of talking during rehearsal is often abused. Some conductors, even famous ones, have distorted this privilege into the license to lecture orchestras on various abstractions for long periods. This addiction may have its origin in inability to express oneself adequately with the baton alone. Never explain in prose what can be shown your players with solfège or your baton.

(6) Starting and stopping in rehearsal are facilitated by the letters or numbers which have already been placed every ten bars or so in the score, depending upon where important changes in the musical sense occur. A start may be made at any spot by directing the players to "five bars before 'M'" or "six bars after 'L'." Do not start at awkward places but at the beginning of a musical phrase. It is bad psychology to give a player a wrench by stopping abruptly in the midst of a phrase; let him complete it. If the exact spot you want in the score is not easily found by the players, it is simple to say something like this: "The strings (or the oboe), two to the bar with upbeat"; or "Where the phrase starts like this," and then you proceed to solfège the main line. Much time and patience may be conserved by the use of such practical parlance.

(7) If you wish to take a difficult rapid passage slowly in order to iron out the notes or intonation, remember that some passages are actually more difficult, in a different way, when taken slowly than when taken at correct tempo. Thus, a very rapid string *spiccato* taken *largo,* with bows hugging the strings, may come out cleanly enough, but doing this does not rehearse *spiccato.* Take the passage as slowly as possible in the tempo necessary for *spiccato.* Similar procedure should be followed in double and triple tonguing. Start before the disputed passage in order to give the players a feeling of continuity and context. Taking a group of players measure by measure through a difficult passage often smacks of the schoolroom and arouses the suspicion that the conductor is rehearsing himself. Again, the general principle is to start with an over-all picture, go on to more and more detail as needed, and end with another over-all reading for unification.

(8) Tempos at the rehearsal may be slower or faster than at the performance, but it is a good plan to take at least one portion of each item at correct tempo. The players must then listen to each other and "sing," and the conductor must not talk.

(9) Do not take the edge off by over-rehearsing. Weingartner has observed that he once conducted the "Ninth" twice on the same day, as indeed von Bulow and others had done before him. After one such spiritually exhausting experience, Weingartner vowed never to repeat this stunt. Over-rehearsing has much the same effect and often results in an anticlimax.

HANDLING PLAYERS' ERRORS

It is much easier to detect errors in a first-rank group than in an amateur group. The reason is simple. In a really good orchestra an error stands out against a clear background and calls attention to itself, whereas in an amateur group errors are likely to abound simultaneously. Some of the more common faults of amateur organizations are poor enunciation of clipped notes, especially on the up beat; fuzzy attacks and releases; and slovenly reiterated notes.

The ability to detect deviations in a complicated tonal web varies greatly with different conductors. One sort of detection may be termed stylistic recognition. For example, a man may have studied the music of Handel or Ravel so closely that he feels the composer's harmonic vocabulary instinctively. If he hears a chord or progression which, although it sounds pleasing, is not one which Ravel or Handel could possibly have used, he knows forthwith that it must be wrong. He could call out wrong notes this way in a score he has never conducted or one he is reading by sight in a rehearsal. The student conductor's ability to detect wrong notes will increase enormously not only as he becomes more familiar with various composers' styles but also as his ears become more and more accustomed to apperceiving details of single and combined tone colors within the mass of sound reaching his podium.

Usually a player knows almost as soon as does the conductor that he has played a wrong note (which is often caused by a misprint). Almost invariably the inside desk man will pencil in the correction, and in any event, the player will usually not repeat the error. A smile in the player's direction is enough to show him that you both recognize the error, and thus a bond of understanding is established. If the conductor feels that the player cannot or will not play the correct notes (especially in the forest of strings), he might look the other way. There is such a thing as seeing and hearing too much. With wood winds, the deviation cannot be passed over diplomatically in the same way. But singling out a string player for solo playing as a punishment should be used rarely.

Once in a great while an orchestral player will try tricks and will play wrong notes maliciously. If the conductor knows the instruments well enough, he can often detect such defections visually even if he cannot hear them, by noting that the player is on the wrong string or in the wrong position. Unless one is very sure, however, discretion is the better part of valor. It goes without saying that at the concert nothing in the conductor's demeanor should reveal any knowledge of such antics. Of course the matter may be taken up later, man-to-man.

The conductor's solfège should be facile enough and his knowledge of the score intimate enough to enable him at a moment's notice to sing a chord up and down or down and up, in order to correct a wrong note. Tell the players you are singing "concert" pitch, that is, the notes as they actually sound, and then tell them what notes should be in their parts after the notes have been transposed for their instruments. Use orchestral parlance, not literary verbiage.

Preawareness of some common orchestral dodges in rehearsal should assist the young conductor in spotting them. Players of transposing instruments such as clarinets, horns, and trumpets sometimes use instruments of a size other than that called for in the score. Hornists may stop notes with mutes instead of by hand as some scores direct; the brass, especially the trumpet, must be warned against blaring. Percussion players on occasion arrange the snare drums and cymbals so that one man can play them, a solecism borrowed from jazz; the percussion sometimes tries to set the tempo; the triangle and bells must be struck in the right places and in the correct manner to produce their best effects; the brass and percussion must be watched for late attacks, especially on repeated notes. Strings tend to execute tremolos lazily and to produce *pizzicato* which is dry and late in attack; string vibrato is often too slow and lifeless; string players are prone to let the concertmaster count long rests and to watch him for re-entrances. Contrabasses have been known to transpose extremes of range up or down an octave or to simplify figurations; flutes may drop an octave.

A most serious musical fault occurs when a player fingers, bows, or tongues his phrases to suit his instrument's idiom, and thus defeats the composer's intentions. In thematic imitation, such divergences may well bring about lack of musical unity.

When, instead of actual errors, frayed and false entrances and other approximations occur, blame yourself inwardly; as often as not the fault will be yours and not the players'. The next time you come to the place, make your baton indications and facial expressions so unmistakably clear that a break-through is practically impossible. These frayed and false entrances, as well as blurred harmonies, mean that some players begin too soon or too late. Listen intently to discover who they are.

ATTITUDE OF THE CONDUCTOR TOWARD PLAYERS

Various technical aspects of the attitude of the conductor toward his players have been considered. A human relationship beyond those sheerly technical aspects exists between conductor and players, also, and is of great importance to the young conductor. As he establishes his own relationship with his men, he should recognize that orchestral players feel with no little justice that much of the burden of labor falls upon them, but that most of the honor falls upon him. In every possible way he should strive to deserve this honor.

Several common attitudes which young conductors often assume toward their forces are to be avoided. The first is that of the humble apprentice trying to ingratiate himself with players by being flattering and even apologetic, by acceding to "suggestions," by shortening or cancelling rehearsal time to promote good will, by permitting laxity of attention, conversation, and smoking. This attitude invariably leads to gradual lowering of standards and discipline, and eventual loss of control. Its inevitable result is loss of respect.

Another attitude, possible to conductors of great reputation or to those who can engage and dismiss players, but to be avoided by the young conductor, is the magisterial pose which implies omniscience. Part of this pose is to imply that the player is guilty till proved innocent. Of course, if the young conductor thinks he can carry through this attitude technically and musically, he may be able to force his will against the players' resentment, but such occasions are simply negligible. Many instrumentalists are veterans at showing up the slightest pretension and know enough dodges to test any but the most resourceful, experienced, and coolest of conductors.

Still another pitfall to be avoided springs from the inexperienced conductor's psychological fear of orchestral players whose experience far exceeds his. He attempts to bolster his own insecurity by taking a very difficult work through at breakneck speed, which he hopes will keep the attention of the seasoned players upon the work instead of upon him. This procedure is full of peril, unless the conductor possesses an inordinately keen ear and can detect instantaneously minute deviations from the score.

Finally, do not fall into the tendency to nag and to indulge in paternalism.

A reasonable attitude for the young conductor to assume toward his players is that they are colleagues and fellow workers dedicated to the interpretation of music, each having his appointed task which he performs to the best of his ability and to which he brings his varied experience in differing measure. In assuming this attitude the conductor need be neither humble apprentice nor *grand seigneur*. He has made adequate preparations for this moment and has a sincere concept of the interpretation of the music. He knows he has a right to demand that the forces he is rehearsing give him the same coöperation, both in letter and spirit, they would give to a more experienced leader. The young conductor may be assured that if he really does know the score and if he approaches the music with dedication, orchestral players will immediately recognize it, respect it, and work wholeheartedly with him.

This reasonable attitude, lying between that of the humble apprentice and *grand seigneur,* can and should be maintained with dignity.

The employment of humor and anecdotes to enlist the players' interest is risky, for it tends to break down the necessary barrier between the conductor and those conducted. A conductor of reputation may unbend on occasion, but his professional stature protects him from undue familiarity, whereas the procedure might be fatal to a lesser figure. It is better to hold the players' interest by purely musical means, such as the keenness of one's reactions to the playing, and by efficient rehearsing.

Lightness of touch may sometimes be used, however, without loss of dignity, if it concerns itself with purely musical matters and is used to illustrate the music being rehearsed. One story which has been told and retold with many variations and in many locales concerns a conductor who found that numerous repetitions of a reiterated figure for trumpets, horns, and trombones in "The Ride of the Valkyries," consisting of a dotted eighth, a sixteenth, and an eighth, did not prevent the players from sounding it as an eighth and two sixteenths. He finally succeeded in obtaining what he wanted by asking the men to think "Amsterdam, Amsterdam," or "Washington, Washington." Another story tells about Arturo Toscanini's letting a silk handkerchief float gently through the air to the floor to dramatize the kind of tonal quality he wanted. A strained atmosphere and frayed nerves may sometimes be relieved by such methods, but they should not be resorted to too often.

A conductor must be a pretty fair psychologist during a rehearsal, adjusting himself rapidly and instinctively to human reactions under constantly changing conditions. Nikisch used to assert that orchestral players demand different treatment according to the instruments they play. Toward oboe and horn players he counselled deference; toward viola and large brass players, calm and good humor, and so on. One does not address a well-known soloist as one addresses the run-of-the-mill executant. Coloraturas differ in temperament from lyric and dramatic sopranos, as do tenors from baritones and bassos. In any event, courtesy and friendliness yield dividends, and a conductor soon learns lessons in diplomacy.

THE DIFFERENCE BETWEEN THE REHEARSAL AND THE CONCERT

The statement has been made sometimes that the conductor's principal task is to rehearse his forces, and that with this task done thoroughly, his presence at the concert is merely to remind the performers of what has been ironed out at the rehearsal. Nothing could be farther from the truth or more indicative of a lack of comprehension of the conductor's true function. This misconception ignores the basic distinction that at the rehearsal the conductor is essentially a pedagogue; at the concert he is, or should be, an inspired interpreter.

It ignores, too, the basic distinction between the rehearsal and the concert. At its best, the conductor's aim at the rehearsal is to achieve an excellent technical rendering of the notes; at the concert his aim is to re-create a work of art. The rehearsal is the aggregate of all the technical parts inherent in the music; the concert is all this and something more. At the concert the conductor ceases being the pedagogue; he lays aside his prerogatives of teaching, of starting and stopping, of talking and explaining, and even of singing aloud, despite the fact that some eminent conductors do sing aloud. He has only his hands, his bodily attitudes, and his facial expressions to translate his inner conception to his forces and to his audience.

An old theatrical tradition has it that a poor rehearsal means a good performance. A sound substratum of truth exists beneath this seeming bit of superstition, the truth that once the rehearsals are over and the conductor and his forces perform before an audience, each man may somehow rise above himself. This is a phenomenon known to every conductor and organization. It results from the warm and glowing feeling of artistic coöperation brought about by working toward a common goal and re-creating music together. Under the proper conditions, such *rapprochement* kindles and rekindles each side. It is a phenomenon which psychologists might well investigate. If the performers tell the conductor after the concert that the smoothness of the ensemble seemed to have been inevitable, calling for no conscious effort, this is the highest and most sincere compliment the conductor can ever hope to receive.

The proper audience, too, has its definite part in the making of such music. When performers, conductor, and audience are *en rapport,* the performance can reach heights which no one would have suspected lay within the powers of those interpreting the music. This silent transference of an inner conception of a musical work by an interpreter to a group of performers, and through them to an audience, involves nothing less than mass hypnosis. No teacher, no book, can tell the student conductor how to achieve it.

Certain gifts must lie within the young conductor if he is to bridge successfully the gap between rehearsal and concert. Much indeed has been written about the interpretative aspect of conducting. Admittedly this sort of writing has often been of literary interest and of undoubted value to the concert-goer and the critic; but in the final analysis, it has been of no real value to the conductor as interpreter where he must prove to himself and to others that he is a unique musical personality. For once on the platform about to interpret a musical work, the conductor is alone with no one to look to for aid but himself. He is on his own.

The long and tedious preparations are over. The technical training, the poring over scores, the diplomatic and pedagogic bouts at rehearsal, the research about the composer and the music—all have been merely means to an end. His is now the task of evoking the composer's vision from the performers facing him and projecting it to the auditors behind him. How he succeeds in transmuting the lifeless symbols on the printed page into living music will now tell whether he is merely another talented time-beater or an interpreter—a conductor.

APPENDICES

WORKING REPERTORY OF CLASSICAL AND ROMANTIC SYMPHONIES
ANALYZED ACCORDING TO THE NUMBER OF STROKES TO THE BAR

At this point in his study, the student should practice much sight-reading and faithfully apportion a certain amount of time daily to this end. The rules of the game should be that there are to be NO stops for any reason whatever. The aim should be uninterrupted and instantaneous solution of the usual technical problems. If a mistake occurs, do NOT stop; go on. For introductory practice, any good collection of piano music, dance music, hymns, folk songs, or chorales offers excellent material. Almost every leading publisher issues such. After this initial practice, which should soon result in clear and graceful beating of whole movements which usually have no change in time-signature, the next step should be to apply the same procedure to overtures, suites, operettas, and potpourris of national songs and operas. A pianist or small ensemble will greatly aid here, though it is also good to conduct mentally from the music to develop the ability to hear through the eye.

The ensuing tables of symphonies, with skeletal suggestions as to time-beating, are not to be taken too literally. These suggestions are not meant to preclude personal adjustments and qualifications. They are merely introductory mapping, to be filled in by the student as he gets to know the music better and better, and as his judgment, taste, critical faculties, and technique develop and mature.

Many decisions will necessarily be subjective, and the tempos adopted will determine the models. Differences of eight to the bar, four subdivided, four quasi eight, and occasional eight in four to the bar, for example, are far too subtle for objective description. The same interpreter may even beat the same passage differently at different times.

Composition	Movement	Time-Signature	Strokes to the Bar
BEETHOVEN			
Symphony No. 1	1. Adagio molto	4/4	4 subdivided (or 8)
	Allegro con brio	¢	2
	2. Andante cantabile con moto	3/8	3
	3. Allegro molto vivace	3/4	1
	4. Adagio	2/4	2 subdivided (or 4)
	Allegro molto e vivace	2/4	2
Symphony No. 2	1. Adagio molto	3/4	3 subdivided
	Allegro con brio	C	2
	2. Larghetto	3/8	3
	3. Allegro	3/4	1
	4. Allegro molto	C	2
Symphony No. 3	1. Allegro con brio	3/4	1 (occasionally 3)
	2. Adagio assai	2/4	2 subdivided
	3. Allegro vivace	3/4	1
	4. Allegro molto	2/4	2
Symphony No. 4	1. Adagio	C	4
	Allegro vivace	¢	2
	2. Adagio	3/4	3 subdivided
	3. Allegro vivace	3/4	1
	4. Allegro, ma non troppo	2/4	2
Symphony No. 5	1. Allegro con brio	2/4	1 (2 bars as one)
	2. Andante con moto		
	Più mosso	3/8	3
	3. Allegro	3/4	1
	4. Allegro	C	2 (quasi subdivided)
Symphony No. 6	1. Allegro, ma non troppo	2/4	2
	2. Andante molto mosso	12/8	4 (often subdivided)
	3. Allegro	3/4	1
	A tempo, allegro	2/4	2
	4. Allegro	C	2
	5. Allegretto	6/8	2
Symphony No. 7	1. Poco sostenuto	C	4
	Vivace	6/8	2
	2. Allegretto	2/4	2
	3. Presto	3/4	1
	4. Allegro con brio	2/4	2

Composition	Movement	Time-Signature	Strokes to the Bar
Symphony No. 8	1. Allegro vivace e con brio	3/4	3 (often 1)
	2. Allegretto scherzando	2/4	4
	3. Tempo di Menuetto	3/4	3
	4. Allegro vivace	¢	2 (even 1 possible)
Symphony No. 9	1. Allegro, ma non troppo, un poco maestoso	2/4	2
	2. Molto vivace	3/4	1
	Presto	¢	2 (1 also possible)
	3. Adagio molto e cantabile	C	4 (occasional subdivisions)
	Andante moderato	3/4	3
	4. Presto	3/4	1 (quasi 3)
	Allegro assai	C	2
	Allegro assai vivace	6/8	2
	Andante maestoso	3/2	3
	Allegro energico, sempre ben marcato	6/4	2
	Allegro ma non troppo	¢	2
BERLIOZ "Fantastic" Symphony	1. Largo	C	4 (occasional subdivisions)
	Allegro agitato e appassionata assai	C	2
	2. Valse allegro non troppo	3/8	1
	3. Adagio	6/8	6
	4. Allegretto non troppo	C	2
	5. Allegro	6/8	2
BORODIN Symphony No. 2	1. Allegro	¢	2
	Poco meno mosso	3/2	3
	2. Prestissimo	1/1	1
	Allegretto	6/4	2
	3. Andante	C and 3/4	4 and 3
	Poco più animato	3/4	3
	4. Allegro	3/4 and 2/4	3 and 2

Composition	Movement	Time-Signature	Strokes to the Bar
BRAHMS			
Symphony No. 1	1. Un poco sostenuto	6/8	6
	Allegro	6/8	2
	2. Andante sostenuto	3/4	3
	3. Un poco allegretto e grazioso	2/4– 6/8	2
	4. Adagio	C	4
	Più andante	C	4
	Allegro non troppo, ma con brio	C	2
Symphony No. 2	1. Allegro non troppo	3/4	3 (sometimes 1)
	Quasi ritenuto	3/4	3
	2. Adagio non troppo	C	4 (often subdivided)
	l'istesso tempo, ma grazioso	12/8	4 (often subdivided)
	3. Allegretto grazioso (quasi andantino)	3/4	3
	Presto, ma non assai	2/4	1
	Presto, ma non assai	3/8	1
	4. Allegro con spirito	¢	2
Symphony No. 3	1. Allegro con brio	6/4	2
		9/4	3
		6/4	2
	2. Andante	C	4
	3. Poco allegretto	3/8	3
	4. Allegro	¢	2
Symphony No. 4	1. Allegro non troppo	¢	2
	2. Andante moderato	6/8	6
	3. Allegro giacoso	2/4	2
	4. Allegro energico e appassionata	3/4	3 (occasionally quasi 1)
		3/2	3
DVOŘÁK			
Symphony No. 5, "From the New World"	1. Adagio	4/8	4
	Allegro molto	2/4	2
	2. Largo	C	4
	3. Molto vivace	3/4	1
	4. Allegro con fuoco	C	4 (occasionally 2)
FRANCK			
Symphony in D Minor	1. Lento	C	4
	Allegro ma non troppo	¢	2
	2. Allegretto	3/4	3
	3. Allegro non troppo	¢	2

Composition	Movement	Time-Signature	Strokes to the Bar
HAYDN			
Symphony in F Sharp Minor (Breitkopf and Härtel 18), "Candle" or "Farewell"	1. Allegro assai	3/4	3
	2. Adagio	3/8	3
	3. Menuetto-Allegretto	3/4	3
	4. Presto	¢	2 (even 1 possible)
	5. Adagio	3/8	3
Symphony in D Major (B. & H. 86)	1. Adagio	3/4	3 (or subdivided)
	Allegro spiritoso	C	2 (or subdivided)
	2. Largo	3/4	3
	3. Menuetto-Allegretto	3/4	3
	4. Allegro con spirito	C	2 (quasi subdivided)
Symphony in D Major (B. & H. 93)	1. Adagio	3/4	3 (quasi subdivided)
	Allegro assai	3/4	3
	2. Largo cantabile	C	4
	3. Menuetto-Allegretto	3/4	3
	4. Presto ma non troppo	2/4	2
Symphony in G Major (B. & H. 94), "Surprise"	1. Adagio cantabile	3/4	3 (occasionally sub-divided)
	Vivace assai	6/8	2
	2. Andante	2/4	4 (or 2 subdivided)
	3. Allegro molto	3/4	3
	4. Allegro di molto	2/4	2
Symphony in C Minor (B. & H. 95)	1. Allegro moderato	C	4
	2. Andante cantabile	6/8	6
	3. Menuetto	3/4	3
	4. Vivace	¢	2
Symphony in C Major (B. & H. 97)	1. Adagio	3/4	3 (or subdivided)
	Vivace	3/4	3
	2. Adagio ma non troppo	C	4
	3. Menuetto-Allegretto	3/4	3
	4. Presto assai	2/4	2
Symphony in B Flat Major (B. & H. 98)	1. Adagio	C	4
	Allegro	¢	2
	2. Adagio cantabile	3/4	3
	3. Menuetto allegro	3/4	3
	4. Presto	6/8	2

Composition	Movement	Time-Signature	Strokes to the Bar
Symphony in E Flat Major (B. & H. 99)	1. Adagio	C	4 (or subdivided)
	Vivace assai	C	2 (occasional subdivisions)
	2. Adagio	3/4	3 subdivided
	3. Menuetto-Allegretto	3/4	3
	4. Vivace	2/4	2
Symphony in G Major (B. & H. 100), "Military"	1. Adagio	C	4
	Allegro	¢	2
	2. Allegretto	¢	2 (or subdivided)
	3. Menuetto moderato	3/4	3
	4. Presto	6/8	2
Symphony in D Major (B. & H. 101), "Clock"	1. Adagio	3/4	3
	Presto	6/8	2
	2. Andante	2/4	2 (subdivided or in 4)
	3. Allegretto	3/4	3
	4. Vivace	¢	2
Symphony in B Flat Major (B. & H. 102)	1. Largo	C	4
	Allegro vivace	¢	2
	2. Adagio	3/4	3 subdivided
	3. Allegro	3/4	3
	4. Presto	2/4	2
Symphony in E Flat Major (B. & H. 103), "Drum Roll"	1. Adagio	3/4	3
	Allegro con spirito	6/8	2
	2. Andante	2/4	2 (or subdivided)
	3. Menuetto	3/4	3
	4. Allegro con spirito	¢	2
Symphony in D Major (B. & H. 104)	1. Adagio	C	4
	Allegro	¢	2
	2. Andante	2/4	4
	3. Menuetto-Allegro	3/4	3
	Trio		1 (quasi)
	4. Allegro spiritoso	¢	2
MENDELSSOHN Symphony No. 3 in A Minor, "Scotch"	1. Andante con moto	3/4	3
	Allegro un poco agitato	6/8	2
	2. Vivace non troppo	2/4	2
	3. Adagio	2/4	4
	4. Allegro vivacissimo	¢	2
	Allegro maestoso assai	6/8	2

Composition	Movement	Time-Signature	Strokes to the Bar	
Symphony	1. Allegro vivace	6/8	2	
No. 4	2. Andante con moto	C	4	
in A Major,	3. Con moto moderato	3/4	3	
"Italian"	4. Presto	C	4	
Symphony	1. Andante	C	2	
No. 5	Allegro con fuoco	¢	2	
in D Major,	2. Allegro vivace	3/4	3 (occasionally 1)	
"Reformation"	3. Andante	2/4	2	
	Andante con moto	C	4	

MOZART

Composition	Movement	Time-Signature	Strokes to the Bar	
Symphony	1. Allegro con spirito	¢	2	
No. 35	2. Andante	2/4	2 subdivided	
in D Major	3. Menuetto	3/4	3	
(K. 385),	4. Presto	¢	2	
"Haffner"				
Symphony	1. Adagio	3/4	3 quasi 6	
No. 36	Allegro spiritoso	C	4	
in C Major	2. Poco adagio	6/8	6	
(K. 425),	3. Menuetto	3/4	3	
"Linz"	4. Presto	2/4	2	
Symphony	1. Adagio	C	4	
No. 38	Allegro	C	2 (or subdivided)	
in D Major	2. Andante	6/8	2 (quasi 6)	
(K. 504),	3. Presto	2/4	2	
"Prague" or				
"Without				
Minuet"				
Symphony	1. Adagio	C	4 (often quasi 8)	
No. 39	Allegro	3/4	3 (often quasi 1)	
in E Flat	2. Andante con moto	2/4	2 (quasi 4)	
Major (K. 543)	3. Menuetto	3/4	3	
	4. Allegro	2/4	2	
Symphony	1. Allegro molto	¢	2	
No. 40	2. Andante	6/8	6	
in G Minor	3. Menuetto-Allegretto	3/4	3	
(K. 550)	4. Allegro assai	¢	2	
Symphony	1. Allegro vivace	C	2	
No. 41	2. Andante cantabile	3/4	3 (occasional	
in C Major			subdivisions)	
(K. 551),	3. Allegretto	3/4	3	
"Jupiter"	4. Allegro molto	¢	2	

Composition	Movement	Time-Signature	Strokes to the Bar
SCHUBERT			
Symphony	1. Andante	C	4
No. 7	Allegro ma non troppo	¢	2
in C Major,	2. Andante con moto	2/4	2 (or subdivided)
"Great"	3. Allegro vivace	3/4	1
	4. Allegro vivace	2/4	2 (quasi 1)
Symphony	1. Allegro moderato	3/4	3
No. 8	2. Andante con moto	3/8	3
in B Minor,			
"Unfinished"			
SCHUMANN			
Symphony	1. Andante un poco	C	4
No. 1	maestoso		
in B Major,	Allegro molto vivace	2/4	2
"Spring"	2. Larghetto	3/8	3
	3. Molto vivace	3/4	1
	Molto più vivace	2/4	1
	4. Allegro animato e	¢	2
	grazioso		
Symphony	1. Sostenuto assai	6/4	6
No. 2	Allegro ma non troppo	3/4	3
in C Major	2. Scherzo allegro	2/4	2
	vivace		
	3. Adagio espressivo	2/4	2 subdivided
	4. Allegro molto vivace	¢	2
Symphony	1. Lebhaft	3/4	3 quasi 1
No. 3	2. Scherzo-Sehr	3/4	3
in E Flat,	Mässig		
"Rhenish"	3. Nicht Schnell	C	4
	4. Feierlich	C	4
	5. Lebhaft	¢	2
Symphony	1. Ziemlich langsam	3/4	3 (or subdivided)
No. 4	Stringendo	2/4	2
in D Minor	Lebhaft	2/4	2
	2. Romanze	3/4	3
	Ziemlich langsam	3/4	1 (2 bars as 1)
	3. Scherzo-Lebhaft	3/4	1 (2 bars as 1)
	4. Langsam; Lebhaft	C	4
	Schneller	¢	2

Composition	Movement	Time-Signature	Strokes to the Bar
SIBELIUS			
Symphony No. 1 in E Minor	1. Andante ma non troppo	¢	2
	Allegro energico	6/4	2
	2. Andante ma non troppo lento	C and 6/4	2
	3. Scherzo-Allegro	3/4	1
	4. Allegro molto	2/4	2
Symphony No. 2 in D Major	1. Allegretto	6/4	2
	2. Tempo andante, ma rubato	3/8	1
	Lugubre	C	4
	3. Vivacissimo	6/8	2 (or 2 bars as 1)
	Lento e suave	12/4	4 quasi 12
	4. Allegro moderato	3/2	3
Symphony No. 5 in E Flat Major	1. Tempo molto moderato	12/8	4
	Allegro moderato (ma poco a poco stretto)	3/4	1 (or 2 bars as 1)
	2. Andante mosso quasi allegretto	3/2	3
	3. Allegro molto	2/4	2
	Un pochettino larga-mente	3/2	3
TCHAIKOVSKY			
Symphony No. 4 in F Minor	1. Andante sostenuto	3/4	3
	Moderato con anima	9/8	3
	2. Andantino in modo di canzone	2/4	2
	3. Allegro	2/4	2
	4. Allegro con fuoco	C	4
Symphony No. 5 in E Minor	1. Andante	C	4
	Allegro con anima	6/8	2
	2. Andante cantabile con alcuna licenza	12/8	4
	Moderato con anima	C	4
	3. Allegro moderato	3/4	3
	4. Andante maestoso	C	4
	Allegro vivace (alla breve)	¢	2

Composition	*Movement*	*Time-Signature*	*Strokes to the Bar*
Symphony No. 6 in B Minor, "Pathétique"	1. Adagio	**C**	4
	2. Allegro con grazia (cf. Figs. 86 and 87)	5/4	Quasi 2
	3. Allegro molto vivace	12/8 and **C**	4
	4. Adagio lamentoso	3/4	3

REFERENCE TABLE OF TIME-SIGNATURES

The student should now apply his own exercises by practicing passages and movements in the following works from the point of view not of time-signatures, but of the number of strokes to the bar. At the start, five, seven, and eleven patterns may be omitted, and then taken up later. Enough examples have been cited to make it probable that most libraries will possess representative items in their collections of full scores. Where a rare though possible time-signature has been omitted, it is because no orchestral work has been found to illustrate it. This is no reason, however, why some composer somewhere sometime may not suddenly decide to write such theoretically possible pulses. In any event, the student can easily fill in the missing time-signatures in skeletal notation.

It is to be stressed again that the choice of patterns and the number of strokes to the bar are often matters of individual preference and are largely the result of the tempos adopted. Thus, it is possible to beat a given passage in one or two for duple and three for triple pulses, in two or four, in three or six, and with or without subdivisions. The determining factors are speed, accents, context, and style. A given passage, indeed, may be taken in half a dozen different ways, each logical, clear, artistic.

It is the final and inescapable responsibility of each interpreter to choose his own tempos and *then* to fit his patterns into these tempos, not the other way about. Many students fit tempos and phrasing into their technical capabilities, and thus do grave injustice to the music. Choose patterns which will keep the pulses of the music flowing and yet give the players something to hold to at all times, patterns which will not pass before the eyes of the watchers too rapidly to follow easily, and which delineate the phrasing. A final reflection: time-signatures are, in essence, only general indications of the composer's intentions.

1/1	Borodin: Symphony No. 2, Movement 2
	Elgar: "Enigma" Variations
	Variations for Orchestra, No. 7
	Rimsky-Korsakoff: Symphony No. 2
2/1	Rimsky-Korsakoff: *Russian Easter*
3/1	Rimsky-Korsakoff: *Russian Easter*
	Saint-Saëns: Symphony in C Major and C Minor
1/2	Copland: *Appalachian Spring*
	Elgar: "English" Symphony No. 1, Movement 2
	Strauss, Richard: *Death and Transfiguration*
	Weiner, Leo: *Csongor és Tunde*
	Williams, Vaughan: "London" Symphony
2/2	Debussy: *La Mer,* Part 3
	Delius: *Appalachia*
	Elgar: Variations for Orchestra, No. 11
	Symphony No. 1, Movement 1, after Introduction; Movement 4, after Introduction
	Glazunoff: Symphony No. 5, Movement 4
	Hindemith: *Mathis der Maler*
	Mahler: Symphony No. 3, Movement 4
	Symphony No. 5, Movement 1, Movement 2 (*Molto Cantando*)
	Mussorgsky: *Night on the Bald Mountain*
	Prokofieff: "Classical" Symphony, Movements 1 and 4
	Lieutenant Kije, No. 3
	Respighi: *Fountains of Rome*
	Rimsky-Korsakoff: *Antar,* Movement 2
	Russian Easter
	Scheherezade, at start
	Saint-Saëns: *Carnival of Animals,* "Fossils"
	Scriabin: *Poem of Ecstasy*
	Sibelius: *Finlandia*
	Pelléas and Mélisande, Part 1
	Symphony No. 6, Movement 1
	Stravinsky: *Chant du Rossignol*
	"Firebird" Suite
	Le Sacre du Printemps
	Wagner: *Huldingungsmarsch*
	Williams, Vaughan: "London" Symphony, Movement 1
	Symphony in F Minor, Movement 4
Alla Breve in the Modern Sense of ¢	Auber: *The Bronze Horse* Overture
	Beethoven: Overtures: *Fidelio; Leonora* I; *Prometheus,* after Introduction
	Symphony No. 1, Movement 1
	Symphony No. 2, Movement 4
	Symphony No. 4, after Introduction
	Symphony No. 8, Movement 4
	Symphony No. 9, Movement 2 (*Presto*), Movement 4 (*Allegro ma non troppo*)

Berlioz: *Benvenuto Cellini* Overture
Borodin: Symphony No. 2, Movement 1
Brahms: Symphony No. 2, Movement 4
  Symphony No. 3, Movement 4
  Symphony No. 4, Movement 1
  Tragic Overture
  Variations on a Theme of Haydn's, Finale
Bruckner: Symphony No. 4, Movement 1; Movement 4, after
    Introduction
  Symphony No. 7, Movements 1 and 4
  Symphony No. 9, Introduction
Chausson: Symphony in B Flat, Movement 3
Franck: Symphony in D Minor, Movement 1, after Introduction;
    Movement 3
Glinka: *Russlan and Ludmilla* Overture
Gluck: *Alceste* Overture
Goldmark: *Rustic Wedding,* "Serenade," "Final Dance"
Haydn: "Clock" Symphony (Breitkopf and Härtel 101), Movement 4
  "Drum Roll" Symphony (B. & H. 103), Movement 4
  Symphony No. 2 (B. & H. 104), Movement 4
  Symphony No. 12 (B. & H. 102), Movement 1 (*Allegro vivace*)
Honegger: *Pacific 231*
  "Symphony for Orchestra," Movement 1
Mahler: Symphony No. 5, Movements 2 and 5
Mendelssohn: Overtures: *Midsummer Night's Dream; Ruy Blas*
  Symphony No. 3, Movement 4
Mozart: Overtures: *Abduction from the Seraglio; Cosi Fan Tutte; Don
    Giovanni; Magic Flute; Marriage of Figaro*
  Symphony No. 12 (Koechel Catalogue 110), Movement 2
  Symphony No. 35 (K. 385), "Haffner," Movements 1 and 4
  Symphony No. 40 (K. 550), Movements 1 and 4
  Symphony No. 41 (K. 551), "Jupiter," Movement 4
Rachmaninoff: Symphony No. 2, Movement 1, after Introduction;
    Movements 2 and 4
Saint-Saëns: Symphony No. 3, Movement 2 at *Allegro*
Schubert: Symphony No. 4, "Tragic," Movement 2
  Symphony No. 5, Movement 1
  Symphony No. 7, "Great," Movement 1, after Introduction
Schumann: Symphony No. 1, "Spring," Movement 4
  Symphony No. 2, Movement 4
  Symphony No. 3, "Rhenish," Movement 5
Sibelius: Symphony No. 1, at start of Movements 1 and 2
  Symphony No. 2, Movement 1, Sections 2 and 3
  Symphony No. 4, Movement 4
Smetana: *Bartered Bride* Overture
Strauss: "Alpine" Symphony
  Don Juan
Tchaikovsky: Symphony No. 5, Movement 4, after Introduction
Wagner: *Lohengrin,* Prelude to Act III

3/2	Bach: Prelude No. 8, Book I in *The Forty-Eight*
	Beethoven: *Egmont* Overture (3/2, 3/4, C)
	Symphony No. 9, Movement 4 (*And. maestoso*)
	Borodin: *Polovetzian Dances*
	Symphony No. 2, Movement 1, at *Poco meno mosso*
	Brahms: Symphony No. 4, Movement 4, Variations 12, 13, 14, 15
	Debussy: *Martyrdom of St. Sebastian,* Parts 1 and 4
	Delius: *Briggs Fair*
	d'Indy: "Istar" Symphonic Variations
	Symphony No. 2, Parts 1 and 4
	Elgar: Variations for Orchestra, No. 6
	Handel: *Water Music* (arr. Harty)
	Hindemith: *Mathis der Maler*
	Kalinnikoff: Symphony No. 1, Last Movement, at *Maestoso*
	Rimsky-Korsakoff: *Russian Easter*
	Scheherezade
	Saint-Saëns: Symphony in C Major and C Minor
	Scriabin: *Divine Poem*
	Sibelius: Symphony No. 2, Movement 4
	Symphony No. 5, Movement 2; Movement 3, last section
	Symphony No. 7, from start to E flat tonality, and final *Largamente*
	Strauss: *Don Quixote*
	Stravinsky: "Firebird" Suite
	Le Sacre du Printemps
	Williams, Vaughan: "London" Symphony, Movement 1, at start;
	Introduction to Movement 4
	Symphony in F Minor, Movement 1, at *Meno mosso*
4/2	Barber: *Second Essay for Orchestra*
	Copland: *Appalachian Spring*
	Debussy: *Martyrdom of St. Sebastian,* Part 2
	Koechlin: *Five Chorales in Middle Age Modes*
	Rimsky-Korsakoff: *Russian Easter*
	Schoenberg: *Von Heute auf Morgen*
	Wetzler: *Assisi*
5/2	Barber: *Second Essay for Orchestra*
	Holst: *The Planets*
	Koechlin: *Five Chorales in Middle Age Modes*
	Rimsky-Korsakoff: *Russian Easter* (then ¢)
	Snow Maiden
	Tsar Saltan
6/2	Steffani: *Reginam Nostram*
7/2	Borodin: Symphony No. 2, Movement 1, *Animato assai*
	(3/2 2/2 2/2 = 7/2)
1/4	Copland: Symphony No. 1
	Hindemith: *Mathis der Maler,* "Grablegung"

Holst: *The Perfect Fool* (ballet music)
Ravel: *Miroirs,* "Une barque sur l'océan," Part 3 (for pianoforte)
Stravinsky: *Petrouchka*

2/4   Beethoven: *King Stephen* Overture
    Symphony No. 1, Movement 3
    Symphony No. 3, Movements 2 and 4
    Symphony No. 4, Movement 4
    Symphony No. 5, Movement 1
    Symphony No. 6, Movement 1
    Symphony No. 7, Movements 2 and 4
    Symphony No. 8, Movement 2
    Symphony No. 9, Movement 1
Bizet: Prelude to Act 1, *Carmen*
Brahms: Symphony No. 1, Movement 3
    Symphony No. 2, Movement 1
    Symphony No. 4, Movement 3
    Variations on a Theme of Haydn's, Nos. 1, 2, 3, 6
Bruckner: Symphony No. 4, Movement 3
d'Indy: Symphony No. 2, Movement 3, at start; Movement 4
Dvořák: Symphony No. 5, Movement 1, after Introduction
Glinka: *Life for the Czar* Overture
Haydn: Symphony No. 7 (B. & H. 97), Movement 4
    Symphony No. 12 (B. & H. 102), Movement 4
Liszt: *Hungarian Rhapsody* II
Mahler: Symphony No. 3, Movement 3, first section
Mendelssohn: Symphony No. 3, Movements 2 and 3
    Symphony No. 5, Movement 3, first section
Mozart: Symphony No. 1 (K. 16), Movement 2
    Symphony No. 12 (K. 110), Movement 4
    Symphony No. 35, "Haffner" (K. 385), Movement 2
    Symphony No. 36, "Linz" (K. 425), Movement 4
    Symphony No. 37 (K. 444), Movement 2
    Symphony No. 38, "Prague," "Without Minuet" (K. 504),
      Movement 3
    Symphony No. 39 (K. 543), Movements 2 and 4
Schubert: Symphony No. 4, "Tragic," Movement 2
    Symphony No. 5, Movement 4
    Symphony No. 7, "Great," Movements 2 and 4
Schumann: Symphony No. 1, "Spring," Movement 1, after Introduc-
    tion
    Symphony No. 2, Movements 2 and 3
    Symphony No. 4, Movement 1, after Introduction
Shostakovitch: Symphony No. 1, last section
Sibelius: Symphony No. 1, Movement 4, at start
    Symphony No. 4, Movement 2, section 3
    Symphony No. 5, Movement 3
Strauss: *Aus Italien,* Movement 4
    Sinfonia Domestica, first section

2/4   Tchaikovsky: Symphony No. 3, Movement 4
(*Cont.*)   Symphony No. 4, Movements 2 and 3
          Weber: *Abu Hassan* Overture
          Williams, Vaughan: "London" Symphony, Movement 3, final section

3/4   Auber: *The Black Domino* Overture
          Beethoven: Overtures: *Egmont* (*Allegro*); *Leonora* II (then ¢); *Leonora*
             III (then ¢); *Prometheus*
           Symphony No. 1, Movement 3
           Symphony No. 2, Introduction to Movement 3
           Symphony No. 3, Movements 1 and 3
           Symphony No. 4, Movements 2 and 3
           Symphony No. 5, Movement 3
           Symphony No. 6, Movement 3
           Symphony No. 7, Movement 3
           Symphony No. 8, Movements 1 and 3
           Symphony No. 9, Movement 2 (*Molto vivace*); Movement 3 (*And.*
             mod.); Movement 4, at start
          Berlioz: *Waverley* Overture (then ¢)
          Borodin: Symphony No. 2, Movement 3 (*Poco più animato*),
             Movement 4
          Brahms: Symphony No. 1, Movement 2
           Symphony No. 2, Movement 3
           Symphony No. 4, Movement 4, "Ground Theme Variations,"
             Nos. 4, 8
           Variations on a Theme of Haydn's, No. 8
          Bruckner: Symphony No. 7, Movement 3
          Chausson: Symphony in B Flat, Movement 1, after Introduction
          d'Indy: Symphony No. 2, Movements 3 and 4
          Dvořák: Symphony No. 5, Movement 3
          Elgar: Symphony No. 1, Movement 4
          Flotow: Overtures: *Alessandro Stradella* (then ¢); *Martha*
          Franck: Symphony in D Minor, Movement 2
          Glazunoff: Symphony No. 5, Movement 1, after Introduction
          Goldmark: *Rustic Wedding,* "Bridal Song"
          Haydn: "Clock" Symphony (B. & H. 101), Movement 1, after
             Introduction; Movement 3
           "Drum Roll" Symphony (B. & H. 103), Introductions to
             Movements 1 and 3
           "London" Symphony No. 4 (B. & H. 98), Movements 2 and 3
           "London" Symphony No. 5 (B. & H. 95), Movement 3
           "Military" Symphony (B. & H. 100), Movement 3
           "Surprise" Symphony (B. & H. 94), Introductions to Movements
             1 and 3
           Symphony No. 2 (B. & H. 104), Movement 3
           Symphony No. 3 (B. & H. 99), Movements 1 and 3
           Symphony No. 5 (B. & H. 93), Movements 1 and 3
           Symphony No. 7 (B. & H. 97), Movements 1 and 3

Symphony No. 10 (B. & H. 86), Introductions to Movements 1 and 3; Movement 3

Symphony No. 12 (B. & H. 102), Movement 2

Symphony No. 45, "Candle" or "Farewell" (B. & H. 18), Movements 1 and 3

Mahler: Symphony No. 3, Movement 2

Symphony No. 4, Movement 3 (*Andante*)

Symphony No. 5, Movement 3

Mendelssohn: Symphony No. 3, Introduction

Symphony No. 4, Movement 3

Symphony No. 5, Movement 2

Mozart: Symphony No. 12 (K. 110), Movements 1 and 3

Symphony No. 35 (K. 385), Movement 3

Symphony No. 36 (K. 425), "Linz," Introduction, Movement 3

Symphony No. 37 (K. 444), Introduction

Symphony No. 39 (K. 543), Movements 1 and 3

Symphony No. 40 (K. 550), Movement 3

Symphony No. 41 (K. 551), "Jupiter," Movements 2 and 3

Prokofieff: "Classical" Symphony, Movement 2

Ravel: *Bolero*

Spanish Rhapsody, Parts 1 and 2

Rossini: *William Tell* Overture (then **C**)

Saint-Saëns: *Danse Macabre*

Schubert: *Rosamunde* Overture (then **¢**)

Symphony No. 4, "Tragic Introduction" and Movement 3

Symphony No. 5, Movement 3

Symphony No. 7, "Great," Movement 3

Symphony No. 8, "Unfinished," Movement 1

Schumann: Symphony No. 1, "Spring," Movement 3

Symphony No. 2, Movement 1, after Introduction

Symphony No. 3, "Rhenish," Movements 1 and 2

Symphony No. 4, Introduction, Movements 2 and 3

Shostakovich: Symphony No. 1, Movement 1, last section

Sibelius: Symphony No. 1, Movement 3

Symphony No. 4, Movement 2

Symphony No. 5, Movement 1, Sections 3 and 4

Symphony No. 6, Movement 2

Strauss: "Alpine" Symphony, "Apparition"

Ein Heldenleben (from No. 41 in Eulenberg Miniature Score)

Tchaikovsky: *Marche Slav*

Symphony No. 3, Movements 2, 3, and 5

Symphony No. 4, Movement 1, at start

Symphony No. 5, Movement 3

Symphony No. 6, Movement 4

1812 Overture

Weber: Overtures: *Jubel; Preciosa*

Wagner: *Tannhäuser* Overture

Williams, Vaughan: "London" Symphony, Movement 1 (*Poco più mosso*), Movements 2 and 3

<u>3 1/2</u>   Schmitt, Florent: *La Tragédie de Salomé,* "Danse des éclairs"
4   Varese: *Intégrales*

4/4   Auber: Overtures: *Fra Diavolo; La Muette de Portici*
    Bax: Symphony No. 3, Movement 2
    Beethoven: Overtures: *Coriolan; Consecration of the House; Leonora* I
        (then ¢, 3/4); *Namensfeier*
      Symphony No. 1, Introduction to Movement 1
      Symphony No. 2, Movement 1
      Symphony No. 4, Introduction to Movement 1
      Symphony No. 5, Movement 4
      Symphony No. 6, Movement 4
      Symphony No. 7, Introduction
      Symphony No. 9, Movement 3 (*Adagio cantabile*), Movement 4
        (*Allegro assai*)
    Berlioz: *Romeo and Juliet* (*Allegro fugato*)
      "Fantastic" Symphony, Introduction, Movements 1 and 4
      Overtures: *The Corsair; Francs-Juges; King Lear*
    Boïeldieu: *La Dame blanche* Overture
    Borodin: Symphony No. 2, Movement 3
    Brahms: Overtures: *Academic Festival; Tragic*
      Symphony No. 1, Movement 4
      Symphony No. 2, Movement 2
      Symphony No. 3, Movement 2
    Bruckner: Symphony No. 4, Movement 2; Movement 4, theme 2
      Symphony No. 7, Movement 2
      Symphony No. 9, Movements 1 and 3
    Chausson: Symphony in B Flat, Introduction to Movement 2,
      Movement 3 (*Grave*)
    Copland: "Dance" Symphony, Introduction
    Dvořák: *Carnaval* Overture
      Symphony No. 4, Movement 1
      Symphony No. 5, Movement 2
    Elgar: Symphony No. 1, Introduction to Movement 1, Introduction
        to Movement 4
      Symphony No. 2, Movement 2
    Franck: Symphony in D Minor, Introduction to Movement 1
    Glazunoff: Symphony No. 5, Introduction to Movement 1
    Gluck: Overtures: *Iphigenia in Aulis; Orpheus and Euridice*
    Goldmark: *Rustic Wedding,* Movement 4
    Hanson: Symphony No. 1, Movement 2
      Symphony No. 2, Movements 1 and 2
      Symphony No. 3, Movements 2 and 4
    Harris, Roy: Symphony No. 2, Movement 1
    Haydn: Symphony No. 2 (B. & H. 104), Introduction to Movement 1
      Symphony No. 3 (B. & H. 99), Movement 1
      Symphony No. 5 (B. & H. 93), Movement 2

Symphony No. 7 (B. & H. 97), Movement 2
Symphony No. 8 (B. & H. 98), Introduction
Symphony No. 10 (B. & H. 86), Movement 1, after Introduction
Symphony No. 12 (B. & H. 102), Introduction to Movement 1
Honegger: "Symphony for Orchestra," Movement 2, Movement 3
    (*And. tranquillo*)
Kodaly: "Háry János" Suite, Intermezzo No. 5
Mahler: Symphony No. 2, Movements 1, 4, and 5
   Symphony No. 3, Movements 1, 5, and 6
   Symphony No. 4, Movements 1, 3 (Part 1), and 4
   Symphony No. 5, Movement 4
Mendelssohn: Overtures: *Athalie; Fingal's Cave; Meeresstille; Paulus*
Mozart: Overtures: *Clemency of Tito; Idomeneo; Impresario*
   Symphony No. 1 (K. 16), Movement 1
   Symphony No. 36 (K. 425), "Linz," Movement 1, after Introduction
   Symphony No. 37 (K. 144), Movement 1, after Introduction
   Symphony No. 38 (K. 504), "Without Minuet," Movement 1
   Symphony No. 39 (K. 543), Introduction to Movement 1
   Symphony No. 41, "Jupiter," Movement 1
Mussorgsky: *Khovantschina*
Nicolai: *Merry Wives of Windsor* Overture
Prokofieff: "Classical" Symphony, Movement 3
Rachmaninoff: Symphony No. 2, Introduction to Movement 1,
    Movement 3
Rossini: Overtures: *Il Barbiere di Siviglia; La Gazza Ladra; Tancredi*
Saint-Saëns: Symphony No. 3, Movement 1
Schubert: Symphony No. 4, "Tragic," Movement 1, after
    Introduction
   Symphony No. 7, "Great," Introduction to Movement 1
Schumann: Overtures: *Genoveva; Manfred*
   Symphony No. 1, Introduction to Movement 1
   Symphony No. 3, Movements 3 and 4
   Symphony No. 4, Movement 4
Shostakovitch: Symphony No. 1, Movements 1, 2 (part 1), 3, and
    4 (part 1)
   Symphony No. 5, Movements 1, 3, and 4
Sibelius: Symphony No. 1, Movement 4, final section
   Symphony No. 2, Movement 2, after Introduction
   Symphony No. 3, Movement 1, Movement 4 (*Con energia*)
   Symphony No. 6, Movement 4
Smetana: *Libussa* Overture
Strauss: "Alpine" Symphony, various sections
   Aus Italien, "On the Campagna"
   Ein Heldenleben
Suppé: *Poet and Peasant* Overture
Tchaikovsky: *Romeo and Juliet* Overture
   Symphony No. 3, Movement 1

4/4	Symphony No. 4, Movement 4
(*Cont.*)	Symphony No. 5, Introduction, Movement 2 (*Mod. con anima*), Introduction to Movement 4
	Symphony No. 6, Movement 1

Wagner: Overtures: *Faust; Meistersinger; Rienzi*
  Preludes: *Lohengrin; Parsifal* (6/4, ¢, 6/4, 2/2, 6/4, 2/2)
Weber: Overtures: *Euryanthe; Freischütz; Oberon; Silvana*
Williams, Vaughan: "London" Symphony, Movement 2 (*Lento*), Movement 4 (*Maestoso allegro*)
  "Pastoral" Symphony, Movement 1 (*Molto mod.*)
  Symphony in F Minor, Movement 2

5/4   Barber: *Essay for Orchestra*
       Second Essay for Orchestra
    Bloch: *America*
    Boïeldieu: *La Dame blanche*
    Borodin: *Prince Igor*
       Symphony No. 2, *Finale* (written 3/2:2/4)
    Carpenter: *Sea Drift*
    Copland: *Appalachian Spring*
    Cornelius: *The Barber of Bagdad*
    Debussy: *Fêtes*
       Six épigraphes antiques (arr. Ansermet), No. 2
    Delibes: *Jean de Nivelle* (3/4–2/4 shifting)
       Le Roi l'a dit
    d'Indy: "Istar" Symphonic Variations
       Symphony No. 2
    Glinka: *A Life for the Czar*
    Griffes: *The White Peacock*
    Hanson: Symphony No. 3, Introduction
    Handel: *Orlando*
    Hindemith: *Chamber Music No. 1 for Small Orchestra*
    Holst: *Egdon Heath*
       The Planets
    Koechlin: *Five Chorales in Middle Age Modes*
    Liadoff: *Ballade de l'Apocalypse*
    Liszt: "Dante" Symphony
    Miaskowsky: Symphony No. 8
    Mussorgsky: *Boris Godunov*, Feodor's Tale about the Parrot
       Pictures at an Exhibition, "Promenade"
    Puccini: *La Bohême*
    Rachmaninoff: *Isle of the Dead*
    Ravel: *Daphnis and Chloë*
    Respighi: *The Pines of Rome*
    Rimsky-Korsakoff: *Tsar Saltan*
    Schoenberg: *Pierrot Lunaire*, "Mondestrunken," Part 1 (2/4 and 3/4 in irregular alternation)
    Shostakovitch: Symphony No. 1, Movement 2

Sibelius: *Finlandia* (implied 5/4)
Stravinsky: *Histoire du soldat*
  Le Sacre du Printemps
Strauss: *Don Quixote,* Variation No. 6 (2/4–3/4)
  Macbeth
  Salome
Sullivan: Grand Ballet, *Victoria and Merrie England*
Tchaikovsky: *The Enchantress*
  Mazeppa
  Symphony No. 6, Movement 2
Varese: *Intégrales* ($\frac{2\,1/2}{4}$)
Vassilenko: *George the Beautiful,* Part V
Wagner: *Die Meistersinger* Overture
  Tristan, last act (3 plus 2)

6/4   Beethoven: Symphony No. 9, Movement 4 (*Allegro energico*)
    Borodin: Symphony No. 2, Movement 2 (*Allegretto*)
    Brahms: Symphony No. 3, Movement 1
    Debussy: *Martyrdom of St. Sebastian,* Part 2
      La Mer, Part 1
      Nuages
    Delius: *On Hearing the First Cuckoo in Spring*
      Summer Night on the River
    d'Indy: "Istar" Symphonic Variations
      Symphony No. 2, Movement 2, at start
    Griffes: *The Pleasure Dome of Kubla Khan*
    Holst: *The Planets*
    Kodaly: *Psalmus Hungaricus*
    Mendelssohn: *Märchen von der schönen Melusine* Overture
    Rimsky-Korsakoff: "Le Coq d'or" Suite, Part 2
      Scheherezade, at *Allegro non troppo,* near start
    Saint-Saëns: *Carnival of Animals,* "The Swan"
      Symphony No. 3, Movement 2
    Schumann: Symphony No. 2, Introduction
    Sibelius: Symphony No. 1, Movement 1, after Introduction; Move-
        ment 2, last section
      Symphony No. 2, Introduction to Movement 1, first and last
        sections
      Symphony No. 3, Movement 2
      Symphony No. 7, final pages
    Strauss: *Aus Italien,* "Amid Rome's Ruins"
      Don Quixote, Variation No. 7
    Stravinsky: "Firebird" Suite
      Petrouchka
      Le Sacre du Printemps
    Wagner: *The Flying Dutchman* Overture
    Weber: *Der Beherrschender Geist* Overture
    Williams, Vaughan: Symphony in F Minor, Movement 1, at start

7/4   Barber: *Second Essay for Orchestra*
       Berlioz: *L'Enfance du Christ,* "Incantation Music" (originally 3 + 4)
       Brahms: *Variations on a Hungarian Song* (for pianoforte), Op. 21, No. 2
       d'Indy: "Istar" Symphonic Variations
       Griffes: *The White Peacock*
       Holst: *Egdon Heath*
       Liszt: "Dante" Symphony
       Miaskowsky: Symphony No. 7
       Mussorgsky: *Pictures at an Exhibition*
       Ravel: *Daphnis and Chloë*
       Rimsky-Korsakoff: *Tsar Saltan*
       Schoenberg: *Von Heute auf Morgen*
       Stravinsky: "Firebird" Suite
           Le Sacre du Printemps
       Wagner: *Tristan,* last act (3/4 plus 4/4)

8/4   Gretchaninoff: *Dobrynya Nikititch* (2-3-3)
       Rimsky-Korsakoff: *Mlada* (3-3-2)
       Ruggles: *Men and Mountains*
       Schoenberg: *Von Heute auf Morgen*
       Strauss: *Don Quixote,* Variation No. 7, "The Windmills"
       Whitehorne: *Fata Morgana*

9/4   Brahms: Symphony No. 3, Movement 1
       d'Indy: "Istar" Symphonic Variations
       Hindemith: *Mathis der Maler*
       Holst: *The Planets*
       Krenek: Symphony No. 2
       Massenet: *Le Cid*
       Rimsky-Korsakoff: *Tsar Saltan*
       Sibelius: *Swan of Tuonela*

10/4   Honegger: Sonata for Piano and Violin

11/4   Rimsky-Korsakoff: *Sadko,* Chorus from Act I
           The Snow Maiden
       Stravinsky: *Le Sacre du Printemps*

12/4   d'Indy: "Istar" Symphonic Variations
       Sibelius: *Pelléas and Mélisande,* No. 5
           Symphony No. 2, Movement 3, last section

1/8   Stravinsky: *Le Sacre du Printemps*

2/8   Delius: *A Dance Rhapsody*
       Rimsky-Korsakoff: *Scheherezade*
       Stravinsky: *Histoire du soldat*
           Les Noces
           Petrouchka
           Le Sacre du Printemps

3/8 Beethoven: Symphony No. 1, Movement 2
    Symphony No. 2, Movement 2
    Symphony No. 5, Movement 2
   Berlioz: *Beatrice and Benedict* Overture
    "Fantastic" Symphony, Movement 2
   Borodin: Symphony No. 1
   Brahms: Symphony No. 3, Movement 3
    Variations on a Theme of Haydn's, No. 4
   Chabrier: *España*
   Debussy: *La Mer,* Part 2
   d'Indy: Symphony No. 2, Movement 3
   Dukas: *Sorcerer's Apprentice*
   Dvořák: Symphony No. 4, Movement 3
   Elgar: "Enigma" Variations
    Symphony No. 1, Movement 3
    Variations for Orchestra
   Falla: *The Three-Cornered Hat*
   Franck: *Les Eolides*
   Hanson: Symphony No. 3, Movement 3
   Haydn: Symphony No. 45 (B. & H. 18), "Candle" or "Farewell,"
    Movements 2 and 5
   Ippolitoff-Ivanoff: *Caucasian Sketches*
   Mahler: Symphony No. 2, Movements 2 and 3
    Symphony No. 3, Movement 2, last section
    Symphony No. 4, Movement 1
   Mozart: Symphony No. 1 (K. 16), Movement 3
   Rimsky-Korsakoff: *Scheherezade*
    Spanish Caprice, Variation No. 2
   Schubert: "Unfinished" Symphony, Movement 2
   Schumann: Symphony No. 1, Movement 2
   Sibelius: Symphony No. 2, Movement 2, Introduction
   Strauss: *Aus Italien,* "On the Shores of Sorrento"
    Sinfonia Domestica
   Stravinsky: *Pritbaoutki*

4/8 Dvořák: Symphony No. 5, Movement 1, Introduction
    The Water Fay
   Elgar: Symphony No. 1, Movement 3
   Falla: *El Retablo de Maese Pedro*
   Schoenberg: *Pierrot Lunaire,* "Parodie," Part 1
   Strauss: *Till Eulenspiegel*
   Stravinsky: *Berceuse du chat*
    Histoire du soldat
    Petrouchka
    Pritbaoutki
    Le Sacre du Printemps

5/8   Barber: *Second Essay for Orchestra*
Borodin: Symphony No. 3 (unfinished)
Copland: *Appalachian Spring*
d'Indy: Symphony No. 2, Movement 4
Hanson: Symphony No. 3, Movement 1, final section
Holst: *Egdon Heath*
Rimsky-Korsakoff: *Tsar Saltan*
Rachmaninoff: *Isle of the Dead*
Ravel: Quartet in F
Stravinsky: *Berceuse du chat*
  Chant du rossignol
  Divertimento, "Sinfonia" (2–2–1)
  Histoire du soldat
  Petrouchka
  Pritbaoutki
  Le Sacre du Printemps
Williams, Vaughan: *The Wasps* Overture

6/8   Bax: Symphony No. 3, Movement 1
Beethoven: *The Ruins of Athens* Overture
  Symphony No. 6, Movement 5
  Symphony No. 7, Movement 1 *(Vivace)*
  Symphony No. 9, Movement 4 *(Allegro assai)*
Berlioz: *Harold in Italy* (first *Allegro*)
  "Fantastic" Symphony, "Scenes in the Country," "Dream of a Witch's Sabbath" *(Allegro)*
  Roman Carnival Overture
  Romeo and Juliet (pp. 150–176, Eulenburg Edition)
Brahms: Symphony No. 1, Movement 1
  Symphony No. 4, Movement 2
  Variations on a Theme of Haydn's, Nos. 5, 7
Debussy: *La Mer,* Part 1
Elgar: "Enigma" Variations
Glazunoff: Symphony No. 5, Movement 3
Haydn: "Clock" Symphony (B. & H. 101), Movement 1, after Introduction
  "Drum Roll" Symphony (B. & H. 103), Movement 1, after Introduction
  "London" Symphony No. 5 (B. & H. 95), Movement 2
  "Military" Symphony (B. & H. 100), Movement 4
  "Surprise" Symphony (B. & H. 94), Movement 1, after Introduction
  Symphony No. 8 (B. & H. 98), Movement 4
Honegger: "Symphony for Orchestra," Movement 3
Kodaly: *Psalmus Hungaricus*
Mahler: Symphony No. 3, Movement 3, Section 2
Mendelssohn: *Heimkehr aus der Fremde* Overture
  Symphony No. 3, Movement 1, after Introduction; Movement 4, final section

Mozart: Symphony No. 36, "Linz" (K. 425), Movement 2
    Symphony No. 37 (K. 444), Movement 3
    Symphony No. 38 (K. 504), Movement 2
    Symphony No. 40 (K. 550), Movement 2
Rimsky-Korsakoff: *Scheherezade*
Rossini: *Semiramis* Overture
Saint-Saëns: "Algerian" Suite, Nos. 2 and 3
    Symphony No. 3, Movement 1
Schubert: Symphony No. 5, Movement 2
Sibelius: Symphony No. 2, Movement 3
    Symphony No. 6, Movement 3
Smetana: *The Moldau*
Strauss: "Alpine" Symphony, "On the Mountain Pasture"
    Ein Heldenleben, last section
    Till Eulenspiegel
Tchaikovsky: *Italian Caprice*
    Symphony No. 5, Movement 1, after Introduction
Thomas: *Mignon* Overture
Wagner: *Tristan and Isolde* Prelude
Williams, Vaughan: "London" Symphony, Movement 3
    Symphony in F Minor, Movement 3

7/8   Bartok: *Music for Stringed Instruments, Percussion and Celesta*
    Copland: *Appalachian Spring*
    Falla: *El Amor Brujo*
    Holst: *The Perfect Fool*
    Rimsky-Korsakoff: *Mlada*
    Stravinsky: *Histoire du soldat*
        Les Noces
        Petrouchka
        Le Sacre du Printemps

8/8   Balakireff: Symphony (3–2–3)
    Bartok: *Music for Stringed Instruments, Percussion and Celesta* (3–3–2)
    Copland: "Dance" Symphony
    Holst: *Fugal* Overture (3–2–3)
    Ravel: *Pianoforte Trio* (3–2–3)
    Schoenberg: *Von Heute auf Morgen*
    Stravinsky: *Renard*
    Weiner: *Csongor és Tunde* (4–4)

9/8   Bach: Preludes Nos. 4 and 7, Book II in *The Forty-Eight*
    Barber: *The School for Scandal* Overture
    Beethoven: Pianoforte Sonatas:
        Op. 22 *Adagio con molt' espressione*
        Op. 31, No. 1 *Andante grazioso*
        Op. 79 *Andante*
        Op. 101 *Andante molto cantabile ed espressivo,* Variation 4

9/8   Debussy: *L' Après-midi d'un faune*
(*Cont.*)   *Fêtes*
      Delius: *On Hearing the First Cuckoo in Spring*
      d'Indy: "Istar" Symphonic Variations
      Dukas: *The Sorcerer's Apprentice*
      Falla: *Nights in the Gardens of Spain*
      Hindemith: *Mathis der Maler*
      Saint-Saëns: "Algerian" Suite, Prelude
      Stravinsky: "Firebird" Suite
          Petrouchka
          Le Sacre du Printemps
      Tchaikovsky: Symphony No. 4, Movement 1, after Introduction

10/8   Bartok: *Music for Stringed Instruments, Percussion and Celesta* (3–2–3–2)
      Schoenberg: *Von Heute auf Morgen*

12/8   Bach: Preludes Nos. 9 and 11, Book I in *The Forty-Eight*
          Preludes Nos. 5 and 19, Book II in *The Forty-Eight*
      Beethoven: Pianoforte Sonata, Op. 57 ("Appassionata"), *Allegro Assai*
          Symphony No. 6, Movement 2
          Symphony No. 9, Movement 3
      Brahms: Symphony No. 2, Movement 2 (*L'Istesso tempo*)
      Chopin: "Nocturne in E Flat"
      Debussy: *L'Après-midi d'un faune*
          La Mer, Part 1
          Sirènes
          Six épigraphes antiques (arr. Ansermet), Parts 1 and 3
      Delius: *Appalachia*
          Summer Night on the River
      d'Indy: "Istar" Symphonic Variations
      Dvořák: *The American Flag,* No. 1
      Elgar: Variations for Orchestra, No. 5
          Symphony No. 1, Movement 1
      Handel: *The Messiah,* "Pastoral Symphony" (*Pifferari*)
      Honegger: *King David,* No. 19 (really 6/4 vs. 12/8)
      Liadoff: *The Enchanted Lake*
      Sibelius: Symphony No. 5, at start
      Stravinsky: "Firebird" Suite, at start
          "Pulcinella" Suite
          Le Sacre du Printemps
      Tchaikovsky: *Sleeping Beauty* Ballet
          Symphony No. 5, Movement 2, at start
          Symphony No. 6, Movement 3, at start

15/8   Debussy: *Nocturnes,* No. 2, "Fêtes" (The woods are in 15/8; the strings
          in 5/4.)
          Quartet in G Minor
      d'Indy: "Istar" Symphonic Variations
      Gounod: *Mireille* (9/8–6/8 shifting)

21/8   Holst: *Edgon Heath*

1/16   Stravinsky: *Le Sacre du Printemps*

2/16   Rimsky-Korsakoff: *Russian Easter*
       Stravinsky: *Histoire du soldat*
          Le Sacre du Printemps

3/16   Stravinsky: *Le Sacre du Printemps*

4/16   Stravinsky: *Chant du rossignol*
          Histoire du soldat
          Renard
          Le Sacre du Printemps

5/16   Sessions: Symphony No. 1
       Stravinsky: *Chant du rossignol*
          Histoire du soldat
          Renard
          Le Sacre du Printemps

6/16   Bach: Fugue No. 11 in F Major, Book II in *The Forty-Eight*
       Bizet: *Carmen,* quintet from Act 2
       Falla: *El Retablo de Maese Pedro*
       Rimsky-Korsakoff: *Scheherezade*

7/16   Copland: Symphony No. 1
       Stravinsky: *Chant du rossignol*
          Histoire du soldat
          Renard

8/16   Stravinsky: *Histoire du soldat*

9/16   Beethoven: Pianoforte Sonata, Op. 111, *Arietta* (Donald Francis
         Tovey, in his essay, "Rhythm," in *Musical Articles from the En-
         cyclopædia Britannica* [Oxford University Press, 1944], asserts that
         the second variation in 6/16 should be marked 18/32 and the
         third in 12/32 should be 36/64.)
       Dukas: *The Sorcerer's Apprentice*
       Stravinsky: *Le Sacre du Printemps*

10/16   Copland: Symphony No. 1

12/16   Bach: Prelude No. 13, Book I in *The Forty-Eight*
       Fugue No. 4 and Prelude No. 21, Book II in *The Forty-Eight*
       Beethoven: Pianoforte Sonata, Op. 110, *Adagio, ma non troppo* and
         L'Istesso tempo di Arioso

21/16   Holst: *Egdon Heath*

24/16   Bach: Prelude No. 15, Book I in *The Forty-Eight*
       Sibelius: *Night Ride and Sunrise* (**C**)

The following list of articles, collections of examples of unusual pulsations, and treatises, will serve as explanatory and supplementary material for further study in the field of rhythm. They deserve the student's close study.

Copland, Aaron, "On the Notation of Rhythm," *Modern Music* (May–June 1944). Cf. Marcelle de Manziarle's "On Rhythm, Complex and Simple," *Modern Music* (January–February 1944).

Djoudjeff, Stoyan, *Rhythme et mesure dans la musique populaire bulgare,* with bibliography (Paris: Librarie Ancienne Champion, 1931). This book offers the student a mine of examples of almost every possible combination of odd pulses from the simplest to the most complex. It reveals how these supposedly infrequent pulsations are in reality many centuries old in certain parts of the world.

d'Udine, Jean, *Les Transmutations rythmiques* (Paris: Heugel, 1922).

Möller, Heinrich, *Das Lied der Völker,* 3 vols. (Leipzig: Schott, 1924–29). This includes examples of Balearic, Basque, Bulgarian, Croatian, Hebridean, Irish, Macedonian, Serbian, Slovenian, and Ukranian folk songs with the more usual time-signatures as well as 4/2, 5/4, 7/4, 9/4, 4/8, 5/8, 8/8 (3-2-3), 9/8 (2-2-2-3), 7/16, 9/16, 13/16, and 15/16.

Rimsky-Korsakoff, *100 Chants populaires russes,* 3 vols. (Paris: W. Bessel, 1877).

Sachs, Curt, *Rhythm and Tempo: A Study in Music History* (New York: W. W. Norton, 1953).

Woollett, H., *Pièces d'étude pour piano sur les mesures et les tonalités dites d'exception* (Paris: Alphonse Leduc, 1910).

BIBLIOGRAPHIES

GENERAL REFERENCES

Altmann, Wilhelm, *Kammermusik-Literatur-Verzeichnis* (Leipzig: C. Merseburger, 1931); Supplement by F. Hofmeister (Leipzig: 1936).

——— *Orchester-Literatur-Katalog* (Leipzig: F. E. C. Leuckhart, 1926).

Barlow, H. and S. Morgenstern, *A Dictionary of Musical Themes* [instrumental works], Introduction by John Erskine (New York: Crown Publishers, 1948).

——— *A Dictionary of Vocal Themes* (New York: Crown Publishers, 1950).

Blaukopf, Kurt, *Lexikon der Symphonie* (Teufen, St. Gall, Switzerland: Niggli and Verkauf, 1953).

Burrows, Raymond and Bessie Carroll, *Symphony Themes* (New York: Simon and Schuster, 1950).

——— *Concerto Themes: Music and Bibliographies* (New York: Simon and Schuster, 1951).

[The] Chester Library, Catalogues of *Chamber Music* and *Small Scores* (London: Chester Music Publishing Company).

Clarke, Welford D., *An Illustrated Dictionary of Musical Instruments with a Glossary of Musical Terms* (Chicago, Illinois: Hall and McCreary, 1928).

Cobbett, W. W., *Cyclopedic Survey of Chamber Music,* 2 vols. (London: Oxford, 1929).

Coeuroy, André and Rostand, Claude, *Les Chefs-d'Oeuvre de la Musique de Chambre* (Paris: Editions Le Bon Plaisir, Librarie Plon, 1952).

Cohn, Arthur, *Chamber Music—Past and Present: A Comprehensive Guide* (New York: Farrar, Straus and Young, 1952).

Culshaw, John, *The Concerto* (New York: Chanticleer Press, 1950).

[The] *Edwin A. Fleischer Music Collection in the Free Library of Philadelphia,* 2 vols. (Philadelphia: Private Print, 1933–45). Includes dates of composers, title of each work in its original language with English translation, publisher, instrumentation, length of time for performance, date of composition, information about first performance.

Eulenburgs kleine Partitur-Ausgabe. Thematisches Verzeichnis (Vienna-Leipzig: Ernst Eulenburg).

Grosbayne, Benjamin, "A Perspective of the Literature on Conducting," *Proceedings of the Royal Musical Association* (London: 1941–42).

Helm, Sanford M., compiler, *Catalogue of Chamber Music for Wind Instruments* (Ann Arbor: Music Department, University of Michigan, 1952).

Hill, Ralph, *The Concerto* (London: Penguin Books, 1952).

Jahresverzeichnis der deutschen Musikalien und Musikschriften (Leipzig: Friedrich Hofmeister, 1852 on).

McColvin, L. R. and W. Reeves, *Music Libraries,* 2 vols. (London: Grafton and Company, 1947). See especially Vol. 2.

Müller-Blattau, J., *Taschenlexikon der Fremd-und Fachwörter der Musik* (Berlin: Max Hesse, 1951).

Mueller, John Henry and Kate Hevner, *Trends in Musical Taste* (Bloomington, Indiana: University of Indiana Press, 1942). Discusses trends in programming in some of the major symphony orchestras in the United States.

Müller-Reuter, Theodor, *Lexikon der deutschen Konzert-Literatur—Ein Ratgeber für Dirigenten,* etc., Vol. 1, 1909; Vol. 2, 1921 (Leipzig: C. F. Kahnt). Includes data on German classical and romantic works for orchestra and chamber groups, such as date of composition, instrumentation, publication, first performance, conductors, length of performance, reading lists, etc. Considers Beethoven, Berlioz, Brahms, Bruch, Draeseke, Gernsheim, Haydn, Mendelssohn, Raff, Reinicke, Schubert, Schumann, Richard Strauss, Wagner.

Pazdírek, Franz, *Universal-Handbuch der Musikliteratur aller Zeiten und Völker* (Vienna: Pazdírek and Company, 1904–10).

Reddick, William, *The Standard Musical Repertoire with Accurate Timings* (Garden City, N. Y.: Doubleday and Company, 1947).

Reis, Claire R., *Composers in America* (New York: Macmillan, 1947). Listing of major works by native and foreign-born composers, timings, publishers, recordings, etc.

Saltonstall, C. D. and H. C. Smith, *Catalogue of Music for Small Orchestra,* ed. by Otto E. Albrecht (Washington: Music Library Association, 1947). Order from Secretary, Association Music Division, Library of Congress, Washington, D.C.

Sardá, Antonio, *Léxico technológico musical en varios idiomas, etc.* (Madrid: Unión musical española, 1929). Definitions in French, German, English, Spanish, Catalan, Italian, Portuguese, etc.

Sénéchaud, Marcel, *Concerts symphoniques: symphonies, oratorios, suites, concertos et poèmes symphoniques; guide à l'usage des amateurs de musique* (Lausanne: Marguerat, 1947). Bibliography, instrumentation, date of composition, date of first public performance, timing, and recommended readings.

Seredy, Julius S., compiler, *Analytical Orchestra Guide: A Practical Handbook for the Profession* (New York: Carl Fischer, 1929). Each item is listed according to mood, form, tempo, duration, etc.

Swan, Alfred Julius, *The Music Director's Guide to Musical Literature* (New York: Prentice-Hall, 1941). For voices and instruments; bibliography.

Ulrich, Homer, *Symphonic Music: Its Evolution Since the Renaissance* (New York: Columbia University Press, 1953). Includes major symphonies, concertos, overtures, symphonic poems, ballets, and suites.

Vannes, René, *Essai de terminologie musicale. Dictionnaire universel comprenant plus de 15,000 termes de musique en italien-espagnol-portugais-français-anglais-allemand-latin et grec, disposés en un alphabet unique* (Paris: Editions Max Eschig, 1925). Label on cover bears imprint: M. Eschig, Paris.

Veinus, Abraham, *Victor Book of Concertos* (New York: Simon and Schuster, 1948).

Wotton, Tom S., *A Dictionary of Foreign Musical Terms and Handbook of Orchestral Instruments* (Leipzig: Breitkopf und Härtel, 1907).

York, T. C., compiler, *How Long Does It Play? A Guide for Conductors* (London: Oxford, 1929). Timing of many standard orchestral works.

PROGRAM NOTES

Bagar, Robert C. and Louis Biancolli, *The Concert Companion* (New York: Whittlesey House, 1947).

Biancolli, Louis, *The Analytical Concert Guide* (New York: Doubleday and Company, 1951).

Downes, Olin, *Symphonic Masterpieces* (New York: Dial Press, 1935).

Gilman, Lawrence, *Stories of Symphonic Music* (New York: Harper's, 1928–30).

——— *Orchestral Music: An Armchair Guide,* compiled and edited by Edward Cushing (New York: Oxford University Press, 1951).

Goepp, Philip H., *Great Works of Music,* 3 vols. in 1 (Garden City, New York: Garden City Publishing Company, 1935).

Hale, Philip, *Philip Hale's Boston Symphony Program Notes,* Introduction by Gilman, ed. by Burk (New York: Doubleday, Doran, 1935).

Kretzschmar, Hermann, *Führer durch den Konzertsaal* (6th ed.; Leipzig: Breitkopf, 1921ff; originally published 1878–1880 by A. G. Liebeskind, Leipzig).
  I. Abteilung
    Bänder I/II. *Sinfonie und Suite*
  II. Abteilung
    Band I. *Kirchliche Werke: Passionen—Messen-Hymnen—Psalmen—Motetten —Kantaten*
    Band II. *Oratorien und weltliche Chorwerke*

——— *Führer durch den Konzertsaal: Die Orchestermusik,* begun by Hermann Kretzschmar (Leipzig: Breitkopf, 1932).
    Band I. *Sinfonie und Suite, von Gabrieli bis Schumann* (7th ed.; edited and completed by Friedrich Noack)
    Band II. *Sinfonie und Suite, von Berlioz zur Gegenwart* (7th ed.; edited and completed by Hugo Botstieber)
    Band III. *Das Instrumentalkonzert* (by Hans Engel)

Nef, Karl, *Geschichte der Sinfonie und Suite* (Leipzig: Breitkopf, 1921).

Newmarch, R. H., *The Concert-Goers' Library of Descriptive Notes,* 4 vols. in 1 (London: Oxford, 1936).

O'Connell, Charles, *The Victor Book of Overtures, Tone Poems, and Other Orchestral Works* (New York: Simon and Schuster, 1950).

———— *The Victor Book of Symphonies* (New York: Simon and Schuster, 1948).

Seaman, Julian, ed., *Great Orchestral Music: A Treasury of Program Notes* (New York: Rinehart and Company, 1950).

Sénéchaud, Marcel, *Concerts symphoniques: symphonies, oratorios, suites, concertos et poèmes symphoniques; guide à l'usage des amateurs de musique* (Lausanne: Marguerat, 1947). Bibliography. Instrumentation, date of composition, date of first public performance, timing, and recommended readings.

Spaeth, S. G., *A Guide to Great Orchestral Music* (New York: The Modern Library, 1943).

Upton, G. P., *The Standard Concert Guide: A Handbook of the Standard Symphonies, Oratorios, Cantatas, and Symphonic Poems for the Concert-Goer* (Chicago, Illinois: A. C. McClurg, 1908).

JOHANN SEBASTIAN BACH

Davies, J. H., "A List of Durations and Associated Data on Bach's Works," pages 411–435 in the *Hinrichsen Music Book,* Vol. VII, *Hinrichsen's Musical Year Book* (New York and London: Peters Edition–Hinrichsen Edition, 1952).

Pirro, André, *L'esthétique de Jean-Sébastien Bach* (Paris: Fischbacher, 1907).

Schweitzer, Albert, *J. S. Bach,* English version by Ernest Newman, 2 vols. (London: A. C. Black, 1938).

Spitta, Philipp, *Johann Sebastian Bach,* 2 vols. (New York: Dover Publications, 1951).

Terry, C. D., *Bach's Orchestra* (London: Oxford University Press, 1932).

Vetter, Walther, *Der Kapellmeister Bach-Versuch einer Deutung Bachs auf Grund seines Wirkens als Kapellmeister in Köthen* (Potsdam: Akademische Verlagsgesellschaft Athenaion, 1950).

Volbach, Fritz, "Ueber die Orchester-Besetzung Bach'scher Werke," *Allgemeine musikalische Zeitung,* no. 4 (1913).

LUDWIG VAN BEETHOVEN

Beethoven's Symphonies, arranged for piano, two hands, ed. and annotated by Percy Goetchius (Boston: Oliver Ditson).

Beethoven's Nine Symphonies Fully Described and Analyzed, 2 vols., Edwin Evans, Sr. (London: William Reeves).

Damrosch, Walter, "Hans von Bülow and the Ninth Symphony," *Musical Quarterly* (April 1927). Cf. August Mann's *Dr. Hans von Bülow's Prescriptions for the Cure of Anti-Bülowism;* also, the article in the *Internationale Musikzeitung* concerning August Mann's opposition to Bülow's "misreading" of the trio (Scherzo) in Beethoven's Ninth Symphony adopted by Richter and later conductors.

Grove, Sir George, *Beethoven and His Nine Symphonies* (London: Novello, 1903).

Kolisch, Rudolf, "Tempo and Character in Beethoven's Music," *Musical Quarterly* (New York: April and July 1943).

Scherchen, Hermann, "The Individual Characteristics of Orchestral Instruments, as Exemplified in Beethoven's Symphonies," in *The Nature of Music* (Chicago: Henry Regnery Company, 1951).

Thomas, Theodore and Frederick Stock, *Talks about Beethoven's Symphonies* (Boston and New York: Oliver Ditson, 1930). Analytical essays with diagrams.

Tovey, Sir Donald Francis, *Beethoven* (London: Oxford University Press, 1946).

——— *Essays in Musical Analysis,* Vol. I (London: Oxford University Press, 1935).

Weingartner, Felix, *On the Performance of Beethoven's Symphonies* (New York: E. F. Kalmus, 1939).

JOHANNES BRAHMS

Brown, P. A., *Brahms—The Symphonies* (London: Oxford University Press, 1939).

Evans, Edwin, Sr., *Handbook to the Chamber and Orchestral Music of Brahms,* 2 vols. (London: Reeves, 1933, 1935).

Harrison, Julius, *Brahms and His Four Symphonies* (London: Chapman and Hall, 1939).

STYLE, INTERPRETATION, CRITICISM

Ansermet, Ernest, "Le Geste du chef d'orchestre," in Gea Augsbourg's *Ernest Ansermet et l'orchestre de la Suisse romande* (Lausanne: L'Abbaye du livre, 1943).

Berlioz, Hector, *Evenings in the Orchestra,* tr. Roche (New York: Knopf, 1929).

Blaukopf, Kurt, *Grosse Dirigenten* (Teufen, St. Gall, Switzerland: Niggli and Verkauf, 1953). Bibliography and discography.

Bukofzer, M., "On the Performance of Renaissance Music," *Proceedings of the Music Teachers' National Association* (1941).

Carner, Mosco, "Mahler's Re-Scoring of the Schumann Symphonies," *Of Men and Music* (London: Joseph Williams, 1944). Cf. Felix Weingartner, *Schubert und Schumann,* Vol. 2 in *Ratschläge für Aufführungen klassischer Symphonien* (Leipzig: Breitkopf, 1918).

Deldevez, E. M. E., *Curiosités musicales* (Paris: Firmin Didot, 1873). On doubtful passages in classical compositions and variants in editions.

——— *De l'exécution d'ensemble* (Paris: Firmin Didot, 1888).

Dolmetsch, A., *The Interpretation of the Music of the 17th and 18th Centuries, Revealed by Contemporary Evidence* (London: Novello, 1915).

Dorian, Frederick, *The History of Music in Performance: The Art of Musical Interpretation from the Renaissance to Our Day* (New York: Norton, 1942).

Failoni, Sergio, *Senza Sordina* (Rome: Piccinelli, 1946).

Fuller-Maitland, J. A., *The Consort of Music: A Study of Interpretation and Ensemble* (London: Oxford, 1915).

Furtwängler, Wilhelm, *Gespräche über Musik* (Zurich: Atlantis-Verlage, 1948). English version, L. J. Lawrence's *Concerning Music* (London: Boosey and Hawkes, 1953). Note Chapter V.

Gelatt, Roland, *Music Makers* (New York: Knopf, 1953). Considers, among others, Beecham, Walter, Munch, Mitropoulos, Toscanini.

Gounod, Charles, *Mozart's "Don Giovanni"* (London: Oxford, 1895).

Haas, Robert Maria, *Aufführungspraxis der Musik* (Wildpark-Potsdam: Akademische Verlagsgesellschaft Athenaion, 1928–32). Bibliographies.

Haggin, D. F., *Music in the Nation* (New York: William Sloane Associates, 1949).

Hardy, Rosamond E. M., *On the Origin and History of the Forte and Piano; The Crescendo and Diminuendo in Origins of Musical Time and Expression* (London: Oxford University Press, 1938).

Harrison, Julius, "The Conductor's Role," in *The Musical Companion,* ed. A. L. Bacharach (London: Victor Gollancz, 1934, and New York: Knopf, 1935 and Tudor, 1948).

Henderson, W. J., "Functions of the Conductor," *The Orchestra and Orchestral Music* (New York: Charles Scribner's Sons, 1927).

Herzfeld, Friedrich, *Magie des Taktstocks: Die Welt der groszen Dirigenten, Konzerte und Orchester* (West Berlin: Verlag Ullstein, 1953).

Howes, Frank, "Conductors and Conducting," *Full Orchestra* (London: Martin Secker and Warburg, 1947).

Inghelbrecht, D. E., *Comment on ne doit pas interpréter 'Carmen,' 'Faust' et 'Pelléas'* (Paris: Heugel, 1933).

——— *Diabolus in musica, essai sur la musique et ses interprètes* (Paris: Chiron, n.d.).

——— *Le Chef d'orchestre et son équipe* (Paris: René Julliard, 1949), translated by G. Prerauer and S. Malcolm Kirk, *The Conductor's World* (London: P. Nevill, 1953).

——— *Mouvement contraire. Souvenirs d'un musicien,* I. Vers les Temps Heureux (Domat); II. Vers les Temps Nouveaux (in preparation).

Kling, H., *Der vollkommene Musik-Dirigent* (Hannover: Louis Oertel's Musik-Verlag, 1891). Contains reflections and suggestions concerning the interpretation of older musical works, errors in editions, and reprints of some of Richard Wagner's essays on interpretation. English revised and enlarged version, ed. by Saenger (New York: Carl Fischer, 1902).

Koussevitsky, Serge, "Poetry and Music: Musical Interpretation; and Some Remarks about American Orchestras," *Proceedings of the American Academy of Arts and Sciences,* Vol. 73, no. 1, pp. 1–6, September 1938.

Kufferath, Maurice, *L'Art de diriger, Richard Wagner et la neuvième symphonie. Hans Richter et la symphonie en 'ut' mineur. L'Idylle de Siegfried—Interprétation et tradition* (Paris: Fischbacher, 3rd ed., 1909).

Laloy, Louis, *The Future of Music: Coming Changes Outlined in Regard to Composer, Conductor and Orchestra,* tr. Mrs. Franz Liebich (London: William Reeves, 1914).

Lualdi, Adriano, *L'Arte di Dirigere. Antologia e Guida* (Milan: Ulrico Hoepli, 2nd rev. ed., 1949). The second part of the work contains Italian versions of essays by Berlioz, Schumann, Wagner, Sir Henry Wood, Weingartner, Liszt's letter on conducting, Vittorio Gui's *How to Study an Orchestral Score,* Lazare Saminsky's *The Art of the Orchestral Conductor,* Charles Gounod's *The Interpretation of Mozart,* and Tullio Serafin's *The Orchestral Director.*

Munch, Charles, *Je suis Chef d'Orchestre* (Paris: Editions du Conquistador, 1954), English version, *I Am A Conductor,* tr. Leonard Burkat (New York: Oxford University Press, 1955).

Nietzsche, Friedrich, *Richard Wagner in Bayreuth* (Leipzig: P. Reclams, 1937).

Parry, Sir Hubert, *Style in Musical Art* (London: Macmillan, 1924).

Pochon, Alfred, *Musique d'autrefois: interprétation d'aujourd' hui* (Geneva: Henn, 1943).

Porges, Heinrich, *Die Aufführung von Beethovens 9. Symphonie unter Richard Wagner in Bayreuth, May 22, 1872* (Leipzig: C. F. Kahnt, 1872).

Prager, Sigfrid, *How to Conduct Dvorak's New World Symphony* (New York: E. F. Kalmus, 1940), Brochure.

——— *How to Conduct Franck's Symphony in D Minor* (New York: E. F. Kalmus, 1940), Brochure.

Saint-Saëns, Charles Camille, *Outspoken Essays* (London: Kegan Paul, Trench, Trubner, 1922).

Saminsky, Lazare, "L'Art du chef d'orchestre," *La Revue musicale,* November 1, 1922. Cf. Mr. Saminsky's "The New Art of Conducting," in *Music of Our Day* (New York: Thomas Y. Crowell, 1932) and in Lualdi's *L'Arte di Dirigere.*

Schering, Arnold, *Aufführungspraxis alter Musik* (Leipzig: Quelle and Meyer, 1931).

Schumann, Robert, *On Certain Corrupted Readings of Passages in the Works of Bach, Mozart, Beethoven* in *Essays and Criticisms,* tr. F. R. Ritter, first series (London: William Reeves, 7th ed., 1880). Reprinted in *Robert Schumann, On Music and Musicians* (New York: Pantheon, 1952).

Seidl, Anton, *Ueber das Dirigieren* (Bayreuther Blätter, 1900). The English version appears in the *Memorial Volume to Seidl by His Friends* (New York: Scribner's, 1896–97); and also in *The Music of the Modern World,* ed. by Anton Seidl and others (New York: D. Appleton, 1895).

Shaw, George Bernard, *Music in London 1890–94,* 3 vols. (London: Constable, 1932).

——— *London Music in 1888–89 as Heard by Corno di Bassetto* (New York: Dodd, Mead, 1937).

——— "Shaw on Conductors," interview with Benjamin Grosbayne (*New York Herald Tribune,* Sunday Music Section, May 5, 1939).

Shore, Bernard, *Sixteen Symphonies,* Foreword by Sir Adrian Boult (London: Longmans, Green, 1949, and New York, 1950). Analyses by the first violist of the BBC Orchestra from the point of view of an orchestral player.

——— *The Orchestra Speaks* (New York: Longmans, Green, 1946). A first-hand report on rehearsals under some famous conductors.

Strauss, Richard, *Recollections and Reflections* (London and New York: Boosey and Hawkes, 1953).

Taffanel, Paul, "L'Art de diriger," in the *Encyclopédie de la musique du Conservatoire et dictionnaire du Conservatoire* (Paris: Delagrave, 1925).

Thomson, Virgil, *Music Right and Left* (New York: Henry Holt, 1951).

——— *State of Music* (New York: William Morrow, 1939).

——— *The Art of Judging Music* (New York: Knopf, 1948).

——— *The Musical Scene* (New York: Knopf, 1945).

Tovey, Sir Donald Francis, *A Companion to 'The Art of Fugue, J. S. Bach'* (London: Oxford University Press, 1931).

——— *A Musician Talks,* 2 vols.: *The Integrity of Music,* Vol. 1; *Musical Textures,* Vol. 2 (Oxford, 1941).

——— *Beethoven,* with an editorial preface by Hubert J. Foss (Oxford, 1945).

——— *Essays in Heritage of Music,* "Gluck" in Vol. 1, 1927; "Schubert" in Vol. 2, 1934.

——— *Essays in Musical Analysis:* Vol. 1, *Symphonies,* 1935; Vol. 2, *Symphonies* (2), 1935; Vol. 3, *Concertos,* 1936; Vol. 4, *Illustrative Music,* 1936; Vol. 5, *Vocal Music,* 1937; Vol. 6, *Miscellaneous Notes, Glossary, Index,* 1939; *Chamber Music,* 1944 (Oxford).

——— *Musical Articles from the Encyclopedia Britannica,* 1944.

——— *Musical Form and Matter* (Oxford, 1934).

——— *Some English Symphonists: A Selection from Essays in Musical Analysis* (Oxford, 1941).

——— *The Mainstream of Music and Other Essays,* Introduction by Hubert Foss (Oxford, 1949).

Wagner, Richard, *Sämtliche Schriften und Dichtungen* (Leipzig: Breitkopf, 1912–28).

——— *Prose Works,* tr. by W. A. Ellis (London: Kegan, Paul, Trench, 1892–99). Note various essays: "On the Rendering of Beethoven's Ninth Symphony," "On Founding a Music School in Munich," "Beethoven's Heroic Symphony," "The Overture to Coriolanus," "The Overture to the Flying Dutchman," "The Overture to Tannhäuser," "The Prelude to Lohengrin." See especially Vol. 3, *The Theater* and Vol. 4, *Art and Politics.*

——— *Ueber das Dirigieren* (1869). This classic appears in English in both the Ellis version and in Edward Dannreuther's translation (London: William Reeves, 1885). A fourth edition of the latter version appeared simultaneously in the *Neue Zeitschrift für Musik* and in the *New-Yorker-Musik-Zeitung.* It subsequently became part of the composer's collected works, *Gesammelte Schriften und Dichtungen von Richard Wagner,* 10 vols. (Leipzig: E. W. Fritzch, 1871–1883).

Weingartner, Felix, *Akkorde: Gesammelte Schriften* (Leipzig: Breitkopf, 1912). Includes "Ueber die Art, Liszt zu Dirigieren," "Der Dirigent," "Felix Mottl," and "Brahms, ein Meister der Instrumentationskunst."

——— *Die Symphonie nach Beethoven* (Leipzig: Breitkopf, 4th ed., 1897). English version by Arthur Bles: *The Symphony Writers Since Beethoven,* with a Notice of Weingartner's Symphony No. 5 by D. C. Parker (London: William Reeves, 1924). Cf. Hugues Imbert's *La Symphonie après Beethoven. Réponse à M. Felix Weingartner* (Paris: Fischbacher, 1900), and M. Imbert's "L'Incident Weingartner" in *Le Guide musical* (Brussels), Vol. 47, No. 6, p. 125 (February 10, 1901).

——— *Bayreuth (1876–1896)* (Berlin: S. Fischer, 1st ed., 1897; Leipzig: Breitkopf, 2nd rev. ed., 1904).

——— *Ratschläge für Aufführungen klassischer Symphonien,* Vol. 1 on Beethoven (Leipzig: Breitkopf, 1906), English version by Jessie Crosland as *On the Performance of Beethoven's Symphonies* (Breitkopf, 1907; reissued by E. F. Kalmus, New York, 1939). Vol. 2 on Schubert and Schumann (Breitkopf, 1918). Cf. Mosco Carner, "Mahler's Re-Scoring of the Schumann

Symphonies," in *Of Men and Music* (London: Joseph Williams, 1944). Vol. 3 on Mozart (Breitkopf, 1923). There are no English versions of Vols. 2 and 3.

———— *Ueber das Dirigieren* (Leipzig: Breitkopf, 1895). Reissued many times. English version *On Conducting,* by Ernest Newman (Breitkopf, 1906). Reissued by E. F. Kalmus, New York. French version *Sur l'art de diriger* by Emile Heintz (Breitkopf).

Weissmann, Adolf, *Der Dirigent in XX. Jahrhundert* (Berlin: Propylaen Verlag, 1925).

———— *Der übermächtige Dirigent* in *Die Entgötterung der Musik* (Stuttgart: Deutsche Verlags-Anstalt, 1928).

See also the prose writings of Hector Berlioz, Claude Debussy, Charles Gounod, Rimsky-Korsakoff, Franz Liszt, Romain Rolland, Camille Saint-Saëns, Robert Schumann, Richard Strauss, Peter Tchaikovsky, Richard Wagner, Ralph Vaughan Williams, and Karl Maria von Weber.

TECHNIQUE

Bakaleinikoff, Vladimir, *Elementary Rules for Conducting* (New York: Boosey-Hawkes-Belwin, 1938).

Berlioz, Hector, *The Orchestral Conductor; Theory of His Art.* Various reprints of this classic. Originally the supplement of the composer's *Grand traité d'Instrumentation et d'Orchestration modernes,* 1844. English versions include that issued by Carl Fischer, New York, and the John Broadhouse translation (London: William Reeves, 1936).

Boult, Adrian C., *A Handbook on the Technique of Conducting.* Printed for the Use of the Royal College of Music, Oxford (London: Hall the Printer, 1920 and 1939; 7th rev. ed., London: Oxford Hall, Goodwin and Tabb, 1951).

Braithwaite, Henry Warwick, *The Conductor's Art* (London: Williams and Norgate, 1952).

Cahn-Speyer, Rudolf, *Handbuch des Dirigierens* (Leipzig: Breitkopf, 1919).

Carse, Adam, *Orchestral Conducting* (London: Augener, 1928).

Choisey, Frank, "Faut-il diriger par coeur?" in *La Revue musicale,* Jan. 1, 1906. Letters from Chevillard, Wood, Strauss. Cf. Ferdinand Hiller's "Ueber das Auswendig-Dirigieren" in *Musikalisches und Persönliches* (Leipzig: Breitkopf, 1876).

Clifford, Herbert, *A Comprehensive Manual for Conductors* (London: Boosey, Hawkes, 1939).

Croger, T. R., *Notes on Conductors and Conducting* (London: William Reeves, 1917).

Diestel, Hans, *Ein Orchestermusiker über das Dirigieren,* Foreword by Richard Strauss (Berlin: Adler, 1931).

Dolmetsch, Rudolph, *The Art of Orchestral Conducting,* Illustrated by T. L. Poulton (London: Bosworth, 1942).

Finn, William Joseph, *The Conductor Raises His Baton,* Foreword by Leopold Stokowski (New York: Harper's, 1944).

Goldbeck, Frederick, *The Perfect Conductor: Listening to Music With Your Eye* (New York: Pellegrini and Cudahy, 1951).

Hartmann, Rudolf, *Handbuch des Korrepetierens* (Berlin: Hesse, 1926).

Hoesen, D. Karl van, *Handbook of Conducting* (Rochester, New York: The Eastman School of Music Series; rev. edn., New York: Appleton-Century-Crofts, 1950).

Hutschrenruyter, Wouter, *De Dirigent* (Musica-Bibliothek. Hilversum: J. J. Lispet, 3rd edn., n.d.).

Inghelbrecht, D. E., *Le Chef d'orchestre et son équipe* (Paris: René Julliard, 1949), translated by G. Prerauer and S. Malcolm Kirk, *The Conductor's World* (London: P. Nevill, 1953).

Kempter, Max, *Das Wesen des Dirigierens. Grundlage, System sowie Darstellung der Taktierbewegungen in allen ihren formellen und graduellen Verschiedenheiten im Bilde. 1. Teil. Grundlage-System mit schematischer Darstellung der Taktierbewegungen* (Zurich: E. Kempter-Lott, 1950). No more published.

Klebs, Paul, *Von Rhythmus und von der Technik des Dirigierens* (Cassel: J. G. Oncken, 1924).

Komorn-Rebhan, Maria, *Was wir von Bruno Walter lernten* (Vienna: Wiener Singakademie Veranstaltete Ausgabe, Universal-Edition, 1936–37). A report on Mr. Walter's rehearsals of Handel's *Messiah*, Beethoven's *Missa Solemnis*, Mahler's Eighth Symphony, and the Requiems by Mozart and Verdi.

Lambinon, Nikolas, *Der Orchestermusiker* (Berlin: G. Haas, 1932).

Lewis, Joseph, *Conducting without Fears*, Vol. 1, *Conducting—A General Survey*, 1942; Vol. 2, *Choral and Orchestral Conducting*, 1945 (London: Ascherberg, Hopwood and Crew).

Malko, Nikolai Andreevich, *The Conductor and His Baton, Fundamentals of the Technic of Conducting* (Copenhagen: William Hansen, 1950).

Moore, Gerald, *The Unashamed Accompanist* (New York: Macmillan, 1944).

Müller-Blattau, Joseph, "Die Lehre vom Führen und Folgen in Chor und Orchester (Dirigierlehre)," Parts 21–24 of *Hohe Schule der Musik* (Potsdam: Akad. Verlag. Athenaion, 1936).

Otterstein, Adolph W., *The Baton in Motion* (New York: Carl Fischer, 1940).

Pappoutsakis, Ippocrates, *Diagrams of Basic Movements in Conducting*, Foreword by Francis Findlay (Boston, Mass.: C. C. Birchard, 1943).

Pembauer, Jos., *Ueber das Dirigieren. Die Aufgaben des Dirigenten beleuchtet vom Standpunkte der verschiedenen Disziplinen der Kompositionslehre* (Leipzig: F. E. C. Leuckhart, 1907).

Pfitzner, Hans Erich, *Werk and Wiedergabe*, Vol. 3 in *Gesammelte Schriften* (Augsburg: B. Filser, 1929). Counsel on rehearsal techniques.

Previtali, Fernando, *Guida allo studio della direzione d'orchestra* (Rome: De Santis, 1951).

Recktenwald, Fritz, *Ueber das Dirigieren. Praktische Ratschläge für Kapellmeister, Chormeister und solche die es werden wollen* (Vienna: Ad. Robitschek, 1929).

Royaart, M. C. van de, *De Orkestdirigent* (Hilversum: Harmonie-Uitgave).

Rudolph, Max, *The Grammar of Conducting: A Practical Study of Modern Baton Technique*, Foreword by George Szell (New York: G. Schirmer, 1950).

Scaglia, Carlo, *Guida allo studio della direzione d'orchestra* (Milan: A. and G. Carisch, 1929).

Scherchen, Hermann, *Lehrbuch des Dirigierens* (Leipzig: J. J. Weber, 1929); tr. into English by M. D. Calvoccoressi (Oxford, 6th ed., 1949) as *Handbook of Conducting*. The Spanish ed. appeared in 1933 in Roberto Gerhard's translation as *El Arte de Dirigir la Orquesta* (Barcelona: Editorial Labor).

Schmid, Adolf, *The Language of the Baton* (New York: G. Schirmer, 1937).

Schroeder, Carl, *Handbook of Conducting* (London: Augener, 1889).

Schulweida, Richard, *Vademecum für Kapellmeister. Praktischer Anhang zu den Klavierauszügen der Repertoire-Opern. Eine Zusammenstellung der gebräuchlichsten Aenderungen, Einlagen und Streichungen* (Leipzig: Max Brockhaus, 1901).

Shore, Bernard, *The Orchestra Speaks* (New York and London: Longmans, Green, 1946). A report on rehearsal methods and techniques of over a dozen famous conductors, by the first violist of the BBC Orchestra.

Stoessel, Albert, *The Technic of the Baton,* Preface by Walter Damrosch (New York: Carl Fischer, 1920).

Szendrei, Alfred, *Dirigierkunde* (Leipzig: Breitkopf, 1932).

Thienemann, Alfred, *Die Kunst des Dirigierens* (Potsdam-Leipzig: Selbst-Unterrichts-Briefe. Methode Rustin. Bonnesz und Hachfeld, 3rd edn., 1930).

Thomas, Kurt, *Lehrbuch der Chorleitung,* 3 vols. (Leipzig: Breitkopf, 1948); Vol. 3 considers the orchestra.

———— "Ist der Taktstock notwendig?" in the *Allgemeine Musikzeitung,* No. 32, 68th year.

Wallace, William, "Conductors and Conducting," in the *Musical Times* (London: July 1 through Dec. 1, 1924).

Waltershausen, Hermann Wolfgang, *Die Kunst des Dirigierens* (Berlin: de Gruyter, 1943).

Wilson, Robert Barclay, *The Technique of Orchestral Conducting,* Foreword by Sir Dan Godfrey (London: Stainer and Bell, 1937).

Wood, Sir Henry, *About Conducting,* Foreword by Hubert Foss (London: Sylvan Press, 1945).

ORCHESTRATION AND INSTRUMENTATION

Standard and recent works on instrumentation and orchestration, written at various periods, offer invaluable aid in determining questions of tone balance and style, in determining errors and technical possibilities at any given time, and for related questions. The following list, available in English, should suffice for most students' purposes. It will be noted that there seems to be no agreement among writers concerning the precise meaning of the two words, instrumentation and orchestration. Both have been used to mean a consideration of the technical possibilities of instruments or of the art of combining orchestral tone colors.

Berlioz, Hector, *A Treatise Upon Modern Instrumentation and Orchestration* (French original, 1843; tr. Clarke, London: Novello, 1853; new ed. rev. Bennett, 1904). This classic has been brought up to date with valuable additional examples and comment. Among such revisions and enlargements are Widor's (in French); Weingartner's (in German); Strauss's (in German), issued in Theodore Front's English version in 1948 by E. F. Kalmus, New York; Ettore Panizza's (in Italian), etc.

Carse, Adam, *History of Orchestration* (New York: Dutton, 1925).

——— *The Orchestra from Beethoven to Berlioz* (Cambridge, England: Heffer, 1948).

Casella, Alfredo and Mortari, Virgilio, *La Tecnica dell'Orchestra Contemporanea* (Milan: G. Ricordi, 1950). Publication in New York of English version by Clarence Raybould announced.

Coerne, L. A., *The Evolution of Modern Orchestration* (New York: Macmillan, 1908).

Corder, Frederick, *The Orchestra and How to Write for It* (London and Philadelphia: Curwen, 1902).

Forsyth, Cecil, *Orchestration* (New York: Macmillan, 1935).

Gevaert, F. A., *New Treatise on Instrumentation,* tr. Suddard (Paris: Lemoine, 1909).

Hofmann, Richard, *Practical Instrumentation,* 7 parts, tr. Legge (London: Augener, 1898).

Kennan, Kent Wheeler, *The Technique of Orchestration* and *Orchestration Workbook* (New York: Prentice-Hall, 1952). Bibliography.

Kirby, Percival, *Kettledrums: A Book for Composers, Conductors and Kettledrummers* (London: Oxford University Press, 1930).

Kling, Henri, *Orchestration and Instrumentation,* with Hector Berlioz's *The Orchestral Conductor—Theory of His Art,* rev. and enlarged edn. by Saenger (New York: Carl Fischer, 1902).

Kohs, Ellis B., "An Aural Approach to Orchestration" in *The Musical Mercury* (New York: E. F. Kalmus, March-May double number, 1939).

Malipiero, G. F., *The Orchestra,* tr. Blom (London: Chester, 1920), Brochure.

Piston, Walter, *Orchestration* (New York: W. W. Norton, 1955).

Prout, Ebenezer, *The Orchestra,* 2 vols. (London: Augener, 1897–98).

Read, Gardner, *Thesaurus of Orchestral Devices* (New York and London: Pitman Publishing Corporation, 1953).

Rimsky-Korsakoff, *Principles of Orchestration,* 2 vols., tr. Agate (Edition Russe, Paris, 1914; reissued by E. F. Kalmus, New York, 1932). Digest form by Adolf Schmid (New York: Boosey and Hawkes, 1950).

Widor, Charles, *The Technique of the Modern Orchestra; A Manual of Practical Instrumentation,* tr. Suddard (London: Williams, 1906; New York: Schuberth), rev. and new edn. with an Appendix by Gordon Jacob (London: Joseph Williams, 1946).

SCHOOL ORCHESTRA

Bodegraven, Van and Wilson, Harry Robert, *The School Music Conductor* (Chicago, Illinois: Hall and McCreary, 1942).

Carr, Raymond Norman, *Building the School Orchestra* (New York: G. Schirmer, 1923).

Carse, Adam, *On Conducting School Orchestras* (London: Augener, c. 1928), reprinted from the *Monthly Musical Record.*

——— *The School Orchestra: Organization, Training and Repertoire* (London: Augener, 1925).

Clifford, Hubert, *The School Orchestra: A Comprehensive Manual for Conductors* (London: Boosey and Hawkes, 1939).

Earhart, Will, *The Eloquent Baton* (New York: Witmark, 1931).

Gehrkens, Karl W., *Essentials in Conducting* (Boston: Oliver Ditson, 1919).

——— *Twenty Lessons in Conducting* (Boston: Oliver Ditson, 1919).

Geppert, Hermann, *Praktische Winke für den Leiter eines Schulorchesters* (Markneukirchen: Johannes Adler, n.d.).

Gordon, Philip, *The Availability of Contemporary American Music for Performing Groups in High Schools and Colleges* (New York: Teachers College, 1950).

Hawkes, F. G., *Studies in Time and Tempo; A Handbook for Conductors* (London: The Salvationist Publishing Company, 1936).

Hindsley, M. H., *School Band and Orchestra* (London: Boosey and Hawkes, 1940).

Holmes, Malcolm H., *Conducting an Amateur Orchestra*, Foreword by Archibald T. Davison (Cambridge, Massachusetts: Harvard University Press, 1951).

Howes, Frank, *The Full Orchestra* (London: Martin and Secker, 1947).

Jacob, Archibald, *Musical Handwriting*, Preface by Sir Henry Wood (London: Oxford, 1937), chapters 6 and 7 on "Orchestra Parts and Scores."

Korn, R. H., *How to Organize the Amateur Band and Orchestra* (New York: Carl Fischer, 1928).

Maddy, J. E. and T. P. Giddings, *Instrumental Technique for Orchestra and Band: A Comprehensive Textbook for Organizing and Conducting Amateur Assemblies, with Appendices on Dance Orchestras and Repairing Instruments* (Cincinnati, Ohio: Willis Music Company, 1926).

Mikorey, Franz, *Grundzüge einer Dirigierlehre* (Leipzig: C. F. Kahnt, 1917).

Newton, L. G., and T. Cambell Young, *The Book of the School Orchestra* (London: Oxford University Press, 1936).

Righter, Charles B., *Success in Teaching School Orchestras and Bands* (Minneapolis: Paul A. Schmitt Music Company, 1949).

Scholz, Horst-Günther, *Der Laiendirigent; Anweisungen und Hilfen mit Praktischen Beispielen* (Berlin-Lichterfelde: C. F. Vieweg, 1937).

Waltershausen, Herm. W. von, *Dirigent-Erziehung* (Leipzig: Quelle und Meyer, 1929).

Woods, Glenn H., *School Orchestras and Bands* (Boston: Oliver Ditson, 1920).

Wright, Z. Porter, *The School Band and Orchestra Organizer's Handbook* (Cleveland: H. N. White Company, 1927).

SCORE-READING AND TRANSPOSITION

Johann Sebastian Bach

Incomparable training in the skills of score-reading and transposition is to be found in many of Bach's works. Problems of choice are bewildering; here are a few. Suggested procedure is to study the two-hand arrangements first as written, then transposed to various keys, and then to repeat the procedure with open score arrangements. Where the open score is not easily obtainable, the student may copy it out in this version from the two-hand arrangement.

(1) *371 Four Part Chorales.* Two-hand arrangement (Breitkopf or Kalmus).

(2) *Lieder und Arien für vierstimmigen gemischten Chor,* open score (Breitkopf).

(3) *Chorales,* selected and edited by Charles N. Boyd and Albert Riemenschneider. Both open and close scores, 2 vols. (New York: G. Schirmer, 1939).

(4) *Vierstimmige Kirchengesänge,* open score, eight parts, edited by Woldemar Barghiel (Berlin: Bote and Bock, 1932).

(5) *Two and Three Part Inventions.* Of the many editions, that edited by Bernadus Boekelman (Boston Music Company) stands out. "Printed in Different Colors for Self-Instruction."

(6) Of the various editions of *The Forty-eight,* two stand out in interest, both unfortunately being difficult to obtain at present. (a) *Forty-Eight Fugues for the Wohltemperirte Klavier in Score with Proper Clefs,* students' edition, edited by Charles Vincent, 2 vols. (London: E. Donajowski, 1891). (b) *Joh. Seb. Bach: 16 Fugues with Analytical Expositions in Colors and Appended Harmonic Schemes,* ed. by Bernadus Boekelman, 1895–1912 (New York: Edward Schuberth). Running commentary and analysis. A delight to the eye.

(7) *Kunst der Fuge* (The Art of Fugue), various editions; two hand and open score, some both.

(8) *Das Musikalische Opfer* (The Musical Offering), recent reprint (New York: E. F. Kalmus).

Bernstein, Martin, *Score Reading; a Series of Graded Excerpts* (New York: M. Witmark, 1932).

Daymond, Emily, *Score Reading Exercises* (London: Novello, 1905–08), 2 pts.

Eslava, *Solfège Method,* ed. by Julian Carrillo (New York: G. Schirmer).

Fétis, F. J., *How to Play from Score* (London: William Reeves, 1888).

Gál, Hans, *Directions for Score Reading* (Vienna Philharmonia Edn., 1948).

Gardner, Maurice, *The Orchestrator's Handbook* (Great Neck, New York: Stagg Music Publishing Co., 1948).

Goldbeck, Frederick, *The Perfect Conductor: Listening to Music With Your Eye* (New York: Pellegrini and Cudahy, 1951).

Harding, H. A., *Score Reading Exercises* (London: Weekes, 1912), 2 pts.

Jacob, Gordon, *How to Read Score* (London: Boosey and Hawkes, 1944).

Kling, Henri, *Transposition* (New York: Carl Fischer, 1940).

Kroyer, Theodore, *Der Vollkommene Partiturspieler* (Leipzig: Breitkopf, 1930). Important for historical notes.

Lenz, Donald A., *Transposition by Clef* (Minneapolis: Paul H. Schmitt, 1949).

Lindenburg, Edouard, *Comment lire une partition d'orchestre,* Preface by Arthur Honegger (Paris: Heugel, 1952).

Lovelock, William, *Introduction to Orchestral Score Reading* (London: A. Hammond, 1952). Exercises.

Moore, Earl V. and Glenn McGeogh, *Syllabus for the Introduction to Music Literature* (Ann Arbor, Michigan: Edwards Brothers, 1951). Standard orchestral works analyzed from the point of view of musical form.

Morris and Ferguson, *Preparatory Exercises in Score Reading* (New York: Oxford, 1931).

Nott, F. J., *Score Reading Exercises* (London: Weekes, 1920).

Peppin, A. H., *Elementary Score Reading* (London: Novello, 1909).

Reeves, Aubrey, comp., *Studies in Vocal Score Reading*, 2 vols. (London: Hammond, 1938).

Rice, Eustace B., ed., *Transposition by Clef* (Boston: New England Conservatory of Music, 1900).

Riemann, Hugo, *Introduction to Playing from Score* (London: Augener, 1902).

Rood, Louise, *An Introduction to the Orchestra Score* (New York: Kalmus, 1948).

Schluer, Carl G., *An Introduction to Score Reading* (Bryn Mawr, Pennsylvania: Ditson, Presser, 1950).

Singing Exercises (Solfège des solfèges)—Thirty Four Volumes containing a great number of lessons by Classical and Modern Composers; Selected and Graduated by A. Danhauser and L. Lemoine with Additional Material by Albert Lavignac (Paris: Henry Lemoine, and Philadelphia: Elkan-Vogel, n.d.).

Thienemann, Alfred, *Partiturspiel* (Potsdam-Leipzig: Bonnesz und Hachfeld, n.d.).

Warriner, John, *Transposition (Keyboard and Orchestral)* (London: Novello, 1893).
——— Supplement to above (Novello, 1900?).

Simply studying the excerpts in the various texts on orchestration constitutes in itself a good practical series of graded exercises.

The *Cranz Edition* of many classical and romantic orchestral scores with solo pianoforte reduction at bottom offers the student valuable aid (New York: Southern Music Publishing Company).

One of the most instructive procedures in the study of score-reading is to compare pianoforte arrangements of orchestral works with the orchestral versions. Practically all the standard repertory is available in both forms. Of special interest is a composer's own two versions, e.g., many of Ravel's works, and especially his orchestral version of Mussorgsky's *Pictures at an Exhibition,* with piano two-hand arrangement at bottom of the full score in the Boosey and Hawkes pocket score.

ORGANIZATION

Grant, Margaret and Herman S. Hettinger, *American Symphony Orchestras and How They Are Supported* (New York: W. W. Norton, 1940).

Municipal Auditoriums and *The Movement for Orchestras in American Cities,* two reports compiled by the Construction and Civic Development Department, Chamber of Commerce of the United States (Washington, D.C., n.d.).

Thompson, Helen M., *The Community Symphony Orchestra—How to Organize and Develop It* (Charleston, West Virginia: American Symphony Orchestra League, 1952).

Zanzig, Augustus D., *Starting and Maintaining a Community Orchestra,* Foreword by E. la Prade (New York: National Recreation Association, 1940).

(The numbers in italics indicate pages on which musical excerpts may be found.)

Koechlin, Charles, *Five Chorales in Middle Age Modes,* 116
Kretzschmar, Hermann, 106

Lambinon, Nikolas, 214
Left hand, 75–80, 98–100
Legato, 25, 27, 31, 39, 43, 50, 56, 66, 101–103, 130, 152, 172
Lehar, Franz, 107, 165; "Merry Widow" Waltz, 39
Leoncavallo, Ruggiero, *Pagliacci,* 28
Levi, Hermann, 4, 143
Liadoff, Anatol Constantinovitch: *Ballade de l'Apocalypse,* 116; *Eight Russian Folksongs,* 116; Musical Snuff Box, 146
Liszt, Franz, 159; *Hamlet, 89; Second Hungarian Rhapsody,* 162–165

Mahler, Gustav, 92; Symphony No. 1, 93; Symphony No. 2, *89;* Symphony No. 4, 116
Mascagni, Pietro, *Cavalleria Rusticana,* 28
Massenet, Jules, *Manon,* 187–188
Measure groupings, 151–165, 188, 196, 197
Memorization, 4–5, 37, 115, 116, 152, 197
Mendelssohn, Felix: *Midsummer Night's Dream* Overture, *82;* Songs Without Words, 19; Symphony No. 4, *58*
Mengelberg, Willem, 8, 145
Metronome, 12, 19, 146
Meyerbeer, Giacomo, 109; *L'Africaine, 110*
Miaskovsky, Nicolas, Symphony No. 7, 116
Möller, H., 107
Monteux, Pierre, 132
Mottl, Felix, 143
Mozart, Wolfgang Amadeus, 205, 206; *Don Giovanni,* 134, *135; Magic Flute* Overture, *60,* 61; *Marriage of Figaro* Overture, *23,* 199; Piano Concerto in A Major (K.288), 174–176; Symphony in C, "Linz" (K.425), 51; Symphony in D, "Haffner," *31;* Symphony in G Minor (K.550), 80, 206
Mussorgsky, Modest: *The Feast,* 116; *Pictures at an Exhibition,* 116, 126; *The Ragamuffin,* 116

Nikisch, Artur, 224

O'Connell, Charles, 106

Offenbach, Jacques: *Orpheus in Hades,* 52; *Tales of Hoffmann, 108*
Opera, *see* Vocal music

Percussion section, 9, 65, 222
Phrasing, *see* Measure groupings
Pitch, 8–9, 85–86, 218, 221
Pizzicato, 172, 175, 222
Pochon, Alfred, 143
Poetry, in relation to music, 104
Prerauer, G., 118
Prose rhythms, 104–106, 180

Rachmaninoff, Serge, *Isle of the Dead,* 117
Ravel, Maurice, 143, 144; *Alborado del Gracioso,* 33; *Bolero,* 143, 146; *Daphnis and Chloë, 69,* 117, 122; *Miroirs,* 117; *Mother Goose* Suite, No. 2, 117; *Spanish Rhapsody, 108,* 124, 129, 137, 168–170, *171;* String Quartet, 117
Rebound, 24–25, 30–31, 39, 41, 102, 105, 146–147
Recitative: orchestral, 180–182; vocal, 183–191
Recktenwald, Fritz, 142
Rehearsal, 4, 120–121, 183, 216–226; preparation for, 207–215
Rehearsal hall, 212
Release, *see* Cut-off
Rests, 64–65, 86, 155–158; at end of measure, 184–185
Retards, 28, 47, 77, 148, 173, 202
Rhythm, 104–119, 198; poetry and, 104; prose and, 104–105
Rhythms: combined, 67–74, 120–138; duple, 22, 36–38; shifting, 107–109, 113–117; triple, 30, 36, 38–39
Richter, Hans, 143
Riemann, Hugo, 105
Rimsky-Korsakoff, Nikolai: *Antar,* 168; *Capriccio Espagnol,* 168; "Golden Cockerel" Suite, 126, 168; *Mlada,* 117; *100 chants nationaux russes,* 107; *Russian Easter* Overture, *70,* 117, 126, 167, *168; Sadko,* 182; *Scheherezade,* 25, 27, *59, 82, 90, 121,* 168, 181–182; *Snow Maiden, 70; Tsar Saltan,* 117
Rossini, Gioachino, *Barber of Seville Overture,* 59
Rubato, 159–165

Safonoff, Vassily, 14